TOBACCO CONTROL
POLICY ANALYSIS IN CHINA
Economics and Health

Series on Contemporary China (ISSN: 1793-0847)

Series Editors: Joseph Fewsmith *(Boston University)*
Zheng Yongnian *(University of Nottingham)*

Published

Vol. 1 Legitimacy: Ambiguities of Political Success or Failure in East and Southeast Asia
edited by Lynn White

Vol. 2 China Under Hu Jintao: Opportunities, Dangers, and Dilemmas
edited by Tun-jen Cheng, Jacques deLisle & Deborah Brown

Vol. 3 China's Compliance in Global Affairs: Trade, Arms Control, Environmental Protection, Human Rights
by Gerald Chan

Vol. 4 Political Civilization and Modernization in China: The Political Context of China's Transformation
edited by Yang Zhong and Shiping Hua

Vol. 5 China into the Hu-Wen Era: Policy Initiatives and Challenges
edited by John Wong & Lai Hongyi

Vol. 6 Water and Development in China: The Political Economy of Shanghai Water Policy
by Seungho Lee

Vol. 7 De Facto Federalism in China: Reforms and Dynamics of Central-Local Relations
by Zheng Yongnian

Vol. 8 China's Elite Politics: Political Transition and Power Balancing
by Bo Zhiyue

Vol. 9 Economic Reform and Cross-Strait Relations: Taiwan and China in the WTO
edited by Julian Chang & Steven M Goldstein

Vol. 10 Discontented Miracle: Growth, Conflict, and Institutional Adaptations in China
edited by Dali L Yang

Vol. 11 China's Surging Economy: Adjusting for More Balanced Development
edited by John Wong & Wei Liu

Vol. 12 Tobacco Control Policy Analysis in China: Economics and Health
edited by Teh-Wei Hu

Series on Contemporary China – Vol. 12

TOBACCO CONTROL POLICY ANALYSIS IN CHINA

Economics and Health

Edited by

Teh-wei Hu
University of California, Berkeley, USA

NEW JERSEY · LONDON · SINGAPORE · BEIJING · SHANGHAI · HONG KONG · TAIPEI · CHENNAI

Published by

World Scientific Publishing Co. Pte. Ltd.
5 Toh Tuck Link, Singapore 596224
USA office: 27 Warren Street, Suite 401-402, Hackensack, NJ 07601
UK office: 57 Shelton Street, Covent Garden, London WC2H 9HE

Library of Congress Cataloging-in-Publication Data
Tobacco control policy analysis in China : economics and health / edited by Teh-Wei Hu.
    p. ; cm. -- (Series on contemporary China, ISSN 1793-0847 ; 12)
   Includes bibliographical references and index.
   ISBN-13: 978-981-270-607-2
   ISBN-10: 981-270-607-0
   1. Tobacco use--Government policy--China. I. Hu, Teh-wei. II. Series.
   [DNLM: 1. Tobacco Use Disorder--prevention & control--China. 2. Health
Policy--China. 3. Smoking--economics--China. WM 290 T62814 2007]
   HV5770.C6T628 2007
   362.29'660951--dc22
                                                            2007045603

British Library Cataloguing-in-Publication Data
A catalogue record for this book is available from the British Library.

Copyright © 2008 by World Scientific Publishing Co. Pte. Ltd.

All rights reserved. This book, or parts thereof, may not be reproduced in any form or by any means, electronic or mechanical, including photocopying, recording or any information storage and retrieval system now known or to be invented, without written permission from the Publisher.

For photocopying of material in this volume, please pay a copying fee through the Copyright Clearance Center, Inc., 222 Rosewood Drive, Danvers, MA 01923, USA. In this case permission to photocopy is not required from the publisher.

Typeset by Stallion Press
Email: enquiries@stallionpress.com

Foreword

Tobacco Control Policy Analysis in China: Economics and Health is a timely and important contribution to the tobacco fight in China.

This collection, edited by Professor Teh-wei Hu, brings together a range of experts from diverse fields united in the common understanding that tobacco is a major killer in China. The warning bells are ringing on China's tobacco burden. Nearly 350 million people in China smoke, and 50 percent of those who do not smoke are exposed to harmful second-hand smoke. China is the world's biggest producer of tobacco. China has around one third of the world's smokers, one third of the world's tobacco leaf production and one third of the world's cigarette manufacturing outputs.

Tobacco Control Policy Analysis in China examines how tobacco abuse in China is socially and economically devastating. Smoking contributes heavily to China's burden of disease, costing over $5 billion annually. The tobacco death toll is around 1 million Chinese annually, a figure that is expected to increase to 2.2 million per year by 2020 if smoking rates remain unchanged. Tobacco is a driving force in the rising epidemic of chronic diseases in China and this places increasing pressure on China's health care system.

One of the greatest challenges for China is the fact that tobacco control is both a health and an economic issue. The tobacco industry is a major source of revenue for the Chinese government and there is a state monopoly on tobacco production to generate that revenue. This means that there are opposing views to tobacco control within the Chinese government. Hopefully, this book will help the government to make clearer and stronger pro-health choices. It sets out the evidence in a clear, considered way, taking into account the specific challenges China faces.

Fighting tobacco in China is not an easy task, and some use the loss of revenue as an argument against control. But numerous studies, globally and in China, show that increasing tobacco taxes is actually a win-win situation because the government's revenue rises despite any drop in sales and there is a decrease in smoking-related health costs, diseases and deaths.

The book also looks at how raising tobacco taxes needs to be complemented by other measures that further reduce the demand for tobacco, like banning tobacco advertisement, including strong warnings on labels of tobacco products, and moving towards smoke-free environments. Ultimately, China needs to enact national laws that set the standard for tobacco control for the entire country. At the March 2007 meeting on health care at the Chinese People's Political Consultative Conference, a complete ban on smoking in public places was proposed. Such a law is urgently needed, and it must be clear, strong and enforceable.

The serious health threat posed by passive smoking to adults and children is clearly demonstrated. This book is published at an opportune time as a range of exciting initiatives is bringing a renewed sense of purpose to the tobacco fight in China. The Chinese government has ratified the Framework Convention on Tobacco Control — the international World Health Organization treaty that aims to wage war against smoking and tobacco-related illnesses — declaring itself ready to take on the tobacco fight. The Bloomberg Global Initiative to Reduce Tobacco Use is bringing together a range of cross sectoral partners including government ministries, research institutions, international groups and WHO in a new initiative to reduce tobacco use in China. The upcoming 2008 Olympics is a once-in-a-lifetime opportunity to aid China's tobacco fight. China has committed to a smoke-free Olympics. Delivering on this will send a powerful message and generate momentum for a sustained long-term campaign far beyond the Olympics.

The time for action is now. China needs to introduce comprehensive measures that will affect a sea change in popular attitudes to tobacco. It is vital to shift from an environment where smoking is not just permitted but actively encouraged, to one where the prevailing pressure is not to smoke. Ultimately, it is every person's responsibility to lead by example and contribute to a healthy living environment — as individuals, as parents, as society members and as leaders.

Tobacco Control Policy Analysis in China will further strengthen the momentum of the tobacco fight in China. Timely, thorough and relevant, it forms an important resource that will provide valuable research and recommendations for the ongoing anti-tobacco campaign in China. This book is an important reference for all those involved in fighting tobacco in China.

The World Health Organization commends this collection and looks forward to continuing the fight against tobacco in China.

Henk Bekedam
Director of Health Sector Development
Former China Office Representative
World Health Organization

Preface

In the late 1980s, California became the first state in the United States to use the tobacco tax as a policy instrument to control tobacco use. California also earmarked some of the added tobacco tax revenue for use in tobacco control programs, such as anti-smoking campaigns, health promotion, and research on tobacco-related diseases. I brought the California tobacco control experience to the attention of the late Minister of Health in China, Dr Chen Mingzhang, suggesting that China might adopt a similar policy. He was very enthusiastic about this idea. In the early 1990s, the World Bank team conducted studies on health care reform in China and found a shortage of financial resources to support rural health care insurance. I introduced to the World Bank the idea of using additional revenue from a tobacco tax to finance rural health care. The World Bank adopted this suggestion in its report. The Ministry of Health viewed this policy as a win-win situation. However, as this policy option was introduced to the Chinese Ministry of Finance, the State Tobacco Monopoly Administration, the Ministry of Agriculture, and the State Council, it was found that raising the tobacco tax involved very complex economic issues, such as the long-term sustainability of tobacco tax revenue, the impact on employment in both the cigarette industry and tobacco farming, the potential regressiveness of the tax on low-income smokers, the issue of smuggling, and so forth. All these issues must also be addressed in addition to studying the relationship between the tobacco tax and cigarette consumption.

There is an excellent publication, *Tobacco Control in Developing Countries*, published by the World Bank and the World Health Organization (edited by Pradhat Jha and Frank Chaloupka, Oxford University Press, 2002). The publication covers tobacco control experiences mostly from developed countries but with some findings from developing countries as well. This volume, which follows a similar framework, provides a China-specific system analysis. Using country-specific information for specific policy recommendations leads to more effective policy. Some of the information included in this book has already been presented to the WHO Framework Convention on Tobacco Control (FCTC) Chinese team members and quoted in the document prepared by the Ministry of Health for the Chinese People's Congress in connection with ratifying FCTC legislation. This book is a systematic analysis of the health and economic issues related to tobacco control in China. It is hoped that the information provided herein will be useful not only to Chinese government policy-makers, tobacco control professionals, and researchers, but also to other countries.

During the past 15 years, many organizations have supported the work reported in this book. These include the International Development Research Center/Research Initiative for Tobacco Control, World Bank, Rockefeller Foundation, University of California, Pacific Rim Research Program, and particularly the National Institutes of Health, Fogarty International Center (Grant No. R01-TW05938). The contents are solely the responsibility of the authors and do not necessarily represent the official views of these funding agencies. I am most grateful to many of my colleagues who contributed to this book, especially Professor Zhengzhong Mao at Sichuan University, with whom I have been collaborating for more than 20 years. Thanks to D. Lynne Kaltrieder of The Pennsylvania State University who has provided excellent editing not only of this volume, but also of my writings throughout my professional career. Thanks to Dr Aron Primack at the Fogarty International Center for his leadership and commitment to the tobacco control project. I wish to acknowledge my assistant Amy Penn at the University of California,

Berkeley, for organizing well this volume. I am grateful to Yi Shen Chan for his excellent editorial and production services at World Scientific Publishing Company. Finally, I thank my wife Tien-hwa, for her patient support and understanding, as I was away from home many days for this project during these past years. I am forever grateful.

Teh-wei Hu
Berkeley, California
June 2007

Contents

Foreword   v

Preface   ix

List of Contributors   xvii

1. Introduction   1
   Teh-wei Hu

Section I. Tobacco Use and its Consequences   11

2. Prevalence of Smoking in China   13
   Gonghuan Yang

3. Tobacco Control Programs in China   33
   Anita H. Lee and Yuan Jiang

4. Chinese Physicians: Smoking Behavior, and their Smoking Cessation Knowledge, Attitudes, and Practice   57
   Michael Ong, Yuan Jiang, Elisa Tong, Yan Yang, Quan Gan and Teh-wei Hu

5. Disease Burden from Smoking and Passive Smoking in China   83
   Quan Gan, Kirk R. Smith, S. Katharine Hammond and Teh-wei Hu

6. Economic Burden of Smoking in China   105
   Hai-Yen Sung, Liping Wang, Shuigao Jin, Teh-wei Hu and Yuan Jiang

Section II. Demand for Cigarettes and Household Expenditures Analysis — 127

7. The Demand for Cigarettes in China — 129
   Zhengzhong Mao, Hai-Yen Sung, Teh-wei Hu and Gonghuan Yang

8. Smoking, Standard of Living, and Poverty in China — 159
   Teh-wei Hu, Zhengzhong Mao, Yuanli Liu, Joy de Beyer and Michael Ong

9. Cigarette Smoking and Poverty in China — 173
   Yuanli Liu, Keqin Rao, Teh-wei Hu, Qi Sun and Zhengzhong Mao

Section III. Supply of Tobacco — 187

10. The Role of Government in Tobacco Leaf Production in China: National and Local Interventions — 189
    Teh-wei Hu, Zhengzhong Mao, Hesheng Jiang, Ming Tao and Ayda Yurekli

11. China's Tobacco Industry and the World Trade Organization — 211
    Elisa Tong, Ming Tao, Qiuzhi Xue and Teh-wei Hu

Section IV. Cigarette Taxation — 245

12. Effects of Cigarette Tax on Cigarette Consumption and the Chinese Economy — 247
    Teh-wei Hu and Zhengzhong Mao

13. Cigarette Taxation in China: Lessons from International Experiences — 259
    Teh-wei Hu

14. Earmarked Tobacco Taxes: The US Experience — 277
    Teh-wei Hu, Xiao-peng Xu and Theodore Keeler

Section V. Policy Directions   **303**

15. China at the Crossroads: The Economics of Tobacco   305
    and Health
    Teh-wei Hu, Zhengzhong Mao, Michael Ong,
    Elisa Tong, Ming Tao, Hesheng Jiang,
    S. Katharine Hammond, Kirk R. Smith,
    Joy de Beyer and Ayda Yurekli

Index   **321**

List of Contributors

Teh-wei Hu
School of Public Health
University of California
Berkeley, CA, USA

Joy de Beyer
Tobacco Control Unit
World Bank
Washington, DC, USA

Quan Gan
Center for Tobacco Control Research
 and Education
University of California
San Francisco, CA, USA

S. Katharine Hammond
School of Public Health
University of California
Berkeley, CA, USA

Hesheng Jiang
Sichuan University
Chengdu, Sichuan
China

Yuan Jiang
Tobacco Control Office
China Center for Disease Control
  and Prevention
Beijing, China

Shuigao Jin
China Center for Disease Control
  and Prevention
Beijing, China

Theodore Keeler
University of California
Berkeley, CA, USA

Anita H. Lee
School of Public Health
University of California
Berkeley, CA, USA

Yuanli Liu
Harvard School of Public Health
Harvard University
Cambridge, MA, USA

Zhengzhong Mao
Department of Health Economics
Sichuan University
Chengdu, Sichuan, China

Michael Ong
School of Medicine
University of California
Los Angeles, CA, USA

Keqin Rao
Center for Health Statistics
  of Information
Chinese Ministry of Health
Beijing, China

Kirk R. Smith
School of Public Health
University of California
Berkeley, CA, USA

Qi Sun
Peking University
Beijing, China

Hai-Yen Sung
Institute for Health and Aging
University of California
San Francisco, CA, USA

Ming Tao
School of Management
Fudan University
Shanghai, China

Elisa Tong
Department of General
  Internal Medicine
University of California
Davis, CA, USA

Liping Wang
China Center for Disease
  Control and Prevention
Beijing, China

Xiao-peng Xu
School of Public Health
University of California
Berkeley, CA, USA

Gonghuan Yang
China Center for Disease
　Control and Prevention
Beijing, China

Yan Yang
Tobacco Control Office
China Center for Disease
　Control and Prevention
Beijing, China

Ayda Yurekli
Tobacco Control Unit
World Bank
Washington, DC, USA

Chapter 1

Introduction

Teh-wei Hu

China is the world's largest tobacco consumer, with over 350 million smokers, accounting for nearly one-third of the world's annual tobacco consumption. Smoking is one of the leading causes of preventable premature deaths. An estimated 1 million premature deaths annually are attributable to smoking-related illnesses in China. From a public health standpoint, policy-makers in China should have undertaken active and effective tobacco control interventions to reduce cigarette consumption. These policies include banning cigarette advertisements, banning smoking in public places, prohibiting sales of cigarettes to teenagers, and raising the tobacco tax.

The tobacco industry in China, however, has a unique role in the economy. As a government-owned monopoly, the tobacco industry has provided 8–11 percent of its revenue (profit and tax), over the past decade. During the past 15 years, the tobacco industry has been the top contributor to government revenue among all industries in China. Thus, government policy-makers have been reluctant to initiate tobacco control policies. They have been particularly worried about the negative economic consequence of the most effective tobacco control policy, raising the tobacco tax, fearing that tobacco farmers' income and tobacco industry employment will be adversely affected. Policy-makers also worry about the regressiveness of the tobacco tax, i.e., that low-income smokers would incur a relatively higher financial burden or might switch to a lower price brand with higher nicotine/tar content. In other words, policy-makers are using economic considerations as an argument to avoid these tobacco control policy instruments. Therefore, tobacco control in China is not only a public health issue, but also an economic issue. The purpose of this book is to provide conceptual and empirical evidence on the health burden of smoking and the economics of tobacco control for policy-makers and professionals interested in the Chinese tobacco control issues. This issue of health versus economics is not unique to China, but also exists in other major tobacco-producing countries, such as India, Indonesia, Brazil, and Zimbabwe.

The purposes of policy research are: (1) to inform policy-makers about the consequences of alternative policy options and (2) to provide the essential information upon which to build the specifics of the policy that is adopted. To make research findings policy-relevant, one needs to identify the issues most relevant to policy-makers. In this case, the authors of this book have held numerous meetings and discussions with the Chinese government policy-makers on tobacco control. For policy relevance, one also needs to establish a conceptual model for macrochanges, ranging from epidemiology, health economics, data collection, statistical analysis, and understanding the infrastructure of relevant government agencies. For policy research recommendations to be adopted by policy-makers, information dissemination and knowledge transfer, taking into account political, economic, and scientific considerations, are required. Not all policy research and policy recommendations get implemented. However, even if not implemented, research findings represent an accumulation of knowledge. They make a scholarly contribution to the field, and are available if policy development is needed. Research findings can be used for information dissemination through media or personal contacts more effectively than opinions. Finally, research itself is capacity building for future generations and can arouse the world to increase the pool of research experts.

Research from our tobacco control project in China has been instrumental in China's recent tobacco control policies. The biggest recent policy change has been ratification of the World Health Organization's Framework Convention on Tobacco Control (FCTC). From 2003 to 2005, project researchers annually presented findings to the Chinese FCTC delegation, particularly on the magnitude of economic costs of smoking in China and the health burden of smoking (measured in Disability Adjusted Life Years lost). In addition, project researchers have provided China's Ministry of Health with findings for the People's Congress to help with FCTC ratification activities. Also, project researchers have worked closely with China CDC office to conduct a survey on smoking behaviors among 3,600 physicians in six cities. Findings from this survey prompted China CDC to initiate smoke-free hospitals and medical schools campaign during the 2005 World Smoke-Free day. Finally, research findings on the economic status of Chinese tobacco farmers were highlighted twice in 2004 and 2005 in China's "Health News", the only nationally distributed newspaper related to health care. These findings contradicted the government's belief that farming tobacco leaves could alleviate poverty. This book is a systematic analysis of all these health and economic issues related to tobacco control issues in China.

In 2002, the World Bank and World Health Organization (WHO) jointly published the book *Tobacco Control in Developing Countries* (edited by Prabhat Jha and Frank Chaloupka, Oxford University, 2002). It includes topics ranging from tobacco consumption, demand and supply of tobacco, to policy direction. The World Bank and WHO book covers experiences mostly from developed countries with some findings from developing countries. It is very useful for a general understanding of overall policy issues related to the economics of tobacco control. However, it does not provide a country-specific systematic analysis. Each country has its own economic, political, and social context. For more effective policy input, using country-specific information for specific policy recommendations is most useful. This book addresses the economics of tobacco control in China, while also providing a comprehensive analytical and empirical framework addressing key debated issues of tobacco control in China.

The book is divided into five sections. Section I describes and analyzes tobacco use and its consequences in China. Section II provides the demand for cigarette and household expenditure analyses. Section III addresses the supply of tobacco. Section IV presents cigarette tax issues, and policy directions are discussed in Section V. There are 14 chapters in the book, besides this introductory chapter.

Chapter 2 provides an overview of the prevalence of smoking in China. Citing the 2002 National Smoking Prevalence Survey, China's Ministry of Health published a report entitled "Smoking and Health — 2006 Report" that indicated that 350 million people, or 35.8 percent of China's population above 15 years, are smokers (66 percent of men and 3.1 percent of women). Chinese smokers make up one-third of the world's smoking population. Comparing the figures for 2002 with these of 2006, the number of smokers increased by 30 million, because of China's population growth during that period. The 2002 survey indicated that the smoking prevalence for the 15–24 age group rose, while the age of smoking initiation decreased from 22.4 in the 1980s to 19.7 in 2002.

Given this increase in smoking prevalence over time, it would be useful to review the recent history of tobacco control programs in China. This is provided in Chapter 3. The Chinese government began enacting legislation banning teen smoking and public smoking in 1980. The Ministry of Health in 1984 issued the strongest public statement that smoking harms health. The China Association of Smoking and Health was established in 1990, followed by legislation banning news media cigarette advertisements and smoking in schools. However, there has been a lack of compliance with this legislation. In 2003, the Chinese government signed the World Health Organization's Framework Convention on Tobacco Control, and the China People's Congress ratified the treaty in 2005. China is becoming a visible player on the world stage in addressing tobacco control problems. Chapter 3 examines the achievements and difficulties, and discusses how tobacco control in China can be more effective and support future initiatives.

Since physicians are a role model of health behavior, a special chapter, Chapter 4, reports on the prevalence of smoking among

Chinese physicians. In 2004, China Center for Disease Control conducted a six-city survey of 3,652 physicians' knowledge, attitudes, and practices with respect to smoking. Smoking prevalence was 41 percent for male physicians and 1 percent for female physicians. Only 30 percent reported good implementation of smoke-free workplace policies, and 37 percent of currently smoking physicians reported smoking in front of their patients. Although 95 percent and 89 percent, respectively, know that active and passive smoking causes lung cancer, only 66 percent and 53 percent, respectively, know active or passive smoking causes heart disease. Thus, physician smoking cessation techniques need to be increased among Chinese physicians. These improvements can help reduce the health burden from smoking in China.

Health consequences of smoking can be measured not only by morbidity and mortality, but they can also be translated into two other measurements. One is to estimate the health burden of disease of smoking and passive smoking in terms of Disability Adjusted Life Years (DALY). These are presented in Chapter 5. According to the 2002 WHO report, tobacco smoking was responsible for about 10 million DALYs in China and ranked third in leading risk factors after high blood pressure and alcohol use. Including lung cancer and ischemic heart disease, the effects of secondhand smoking were estimated by the DALY method. In 2002, an additional 450,000 DALYs were lost because of secondhand smoking — around 15 percent of the burden of the same diseases caused by active smoking.

Chapter 6 presents the monetary cost of smoking including both the treatment cost (direct costs) and loss of productivity (indirect costs). The study used the 1998 China National Health Services Survey to estimate the smoking-attributable total costs at US$5.0 billion measured in 2000 value, about $25.43 per smoker ($\geq$ 35 years of age). The share of the economic costs was greater for men than women and greater in rural areas than in urban areas. Of the US$5.0 billion, direct costs were $1.7 billion (34 percent of the total), indirect morbidity costs were 0.4 billion (8 percent), and indirect mortality costs were $2.9 billion (58 percent). The direct costs of smoking accounted for 3.1 percent of China's national wealth expenditures in 2000. To reduce this cost burden in the future, effective tobacco control programs and sustained efforts are needed to curb the tobacco epidemic and economic losses.

Section II contains three chapters. Chapter 7 discusses the demand for cigarettes in China and estimates the quantitative relationship between cigarette price and cigarette consumption, usually measured by price elasticity, and different magnitudes of price elasticities among different income groups in China. This chapter used the 2002 National Smoking Prevalence Survey to estimate an overall price elasticity of −0.16, meaning a 10 percent increase in the price of cigarettes would lead to a 1.6 percent reduction in cigarette consumption. The price effect varies by income level, the highest (in absolute term) at −0.634 for the poor group, and was positive at 0.316 for the high-income groups. The poorest group was most responsive to reducing cigarette consumption because cigarette expenditures comprise a greater percentage of their income than that of the wealthiest smokers. The simulation results indicated that a 10 percent income in cigarette price would lead to an increase of 27 percent in cigarette tax revenue (32 billion yuan, or US$4 billion) inducing 2.1 million smokers to quit, and reducing the annual total cigarette consumption by 1.2 billion packs. As supported by the international literature on tobacco control, increased tobacco tax is often the most effective policy in tobacco control.

One of the major concerns among government policy-makers is the impact of additional tobacco tax on the economic burden to low-income smokers. Both Chapters 8 and 9 address the issue of the effect of smoking on the Chinese household standard of living and its effect on poverty. Chapter 8 reports on interviews and analysis of around 3,400 urban and rural households from 36 townships/districts in Southwest China in 2002. Lower income households with smokers paid less per pack and smoked fewer cigarettes than high-income households with smokers. Poor urban households spent an average of 6.6 percent of their total expenditures on cigarette; poor rural households spent 11.3 percent of their total expenditures on cigarettes. Thus, reducing cigarette expenditures could release household resources to spend on food, housing, and other goods that improve their living standard.

Chapter 9 draws from the 1998 China National Health Services Survey data and estimates the excessive medical spending attributable to smoking may be responsible for the 30.5 million impoverished urban residents and 23.7 million rural residents in China. Smoking-related expenses pushed a significant proportion of low-income families into poverty in China. Therefore, reducing the smoking rate appears to be not only a public health strategy, but also a poverty reduction strategy.

The economics of tobacco production is a major argument that tobacco producing countries use against implementing tobacco control policies. China is the largest tobacco leaf and cigarette producing country in the world. To succeed in tobacco control, it is extremely important to understand and address the tobacco supply issues. Researchers need to develop policy options and predict future outlooks for the tobacco industry under tobacco control programs. Section III contains two chapters. Chapter 10 analyzes the role of government in tobacco leaf production in China. China's tobacco production and cigarette marketing are all under the control of the State Tobacco Monopoly Administration (STMA). The STMA has delegated authority to the China National Tobacco Company (CNTC) for the administration of all aspects of tobacco, from setting tobacco leaf production quotas, procuring tobacco leaf, transporting and storing tobacco leaf, and producing and selling cigarette products. Surveys among more than 1,000 tobacco farmers in southwest China found that compared to other cash crops, tobacco leaf has the lowest economic rate of return. Currently, China has a large surplus of tobacco leaf. One of the factors contributing to this surplus is local governments encouraging farmers to plant tobacco leaves, with the aim of collecting tax revenue from tobacco leaf sales. Thus, to remove the perverse incentive it would be important to remove the local tobacco leaf tax and simultaneously raise the tax on cigarette products at the national level. The central government could redistribute part of the additional tax revenue to subsidize local governments. Crop substitution should be encouraged with technical, financial, and marketing assistance to assist tobacco farmers in this effort.

Chapter 11 provides an analysis of the China tobacco industry and the World Trade Organization. China's state-owned tobacco monopoly has been highly profitable, producing 1.7 trillion cigarettes in 2002 and contributing to 8 percent of the central government revenue — about US$20 billion. In 2001, China joined the World Trade Organization (WTO), which lowered international trade tariffs and opened the market gateway for transnational tobacco companies (TTCS), such as Phillip Morris, British American Tobacco Company, and others. Facing potential international competition within China, CNTC has made steady progress toward consolidation and mergers — from 185 companies in 2000 to 44 companies in 2005. Introduction of TTCs into China's tobacco market may lead the Chinese government to recognize the declining contributions of the tobacco sector and present new opportunities for more tobacco control solutions.

Tobacco tax is the most effective policy instrument in tobacco control. Section IV devotes three chapters on this topic. Chapter 12 examines the effect of cigarette tax on cigarette consumption in the Chinese economy. This chapter analyzes the policy dilemma in China, i.e., on public health versus the tobacco economy. Using published statistics from 1980 through 1997, the chapter estimates the impact of tobacco production and consumption on government revenue and the entire economy. It is estimated that with an additional 10 percent increase in cigarette tax, the central government tax revenue would twice exceed total losses in industry revenue, tobacco farmers' income, and local tax revenue. In addition, between 1.4 to 2.16 million lives would be saved by this tax increase.

Chapter 13 draws upon the international experiences in implementing tobacco taxation to provide lessons the Chinese government can use when considering the feasibility of raising additional taxes on cigarettes. Based on the current international data and Chinese published data, this chapter concludes that there is still leeway to raise existing taxes. The Chinese government should consider conducting some pilot experiments in tobacco tax increases, with some of the new revenues allocated for tobacco control programs as well as for financing health care services among the poor.

The question as to why and how cigarette tax revenue should be allocated for health promotion and anti-smoking programs to complement the goal of tobacco control is the subject of Chapter 14. Although a earmarked tax is not always an ideal tax-expenditure fiscal instrument (since it introduces rigidities and does not permit proper expenditure allocation criteria for general revenue among competing uses), international evidence and experiences have shown that the use of tobacco tax for health promotion and disease prevention may be quite appropriate, in line with the benefit taxation principle. This chapter is drawn from the United States' experience with earmarking tobacco tax for future cigarette tax implementation in China.

Section V, policy directions, is included in Chapter 15, entitled "China at the crossroads: The economics of tobacco and health". It also serves as a concluding chapter to the book. This chapter summarizes the economic aspects of tobacco control policy issues in China by providing arguments for and against the health benefits and costs of tobacco control on the Chinese economy. It indicates that economic gains become less important as the negative health impact of smoking on the population garners more awareness. China stands at a crossroads to implement the economic promises of the World Health Organization's Framework Convention on Tobacco Control and promote the health of its population.

Section I
Tobacco Use and Its Consequences

Chapter 2

Prevalence of Smoking in China

Gonghuan Yang

INTRODUCTION

History of Tobacco in China

Tobacco use was first introduced to China during the 16th and 17th centuries from the West, via the Philippines and Vietnam, to the south of China, and via Korea to the northeast of China.[1]

Tobacco cultivation was started in Taiwan province and extended to Central and Southeast China. From 1931 to 1935, the tobacco-growing area reached 290,000 hectares in 23 provinces, with an annual production of 330,000 metric tons of tobacco. China produced about 100 brands of cigarettes, and many tobacco advertisements featured celebrities. Chinese society accepted smoking as an appealing and glamorous pastime. In this chapter, the focus is on trends in the prevalence of tobacco use over the last 50 years.

---

[1] Wu Y and Zhang ZP, "The History of Tobacco in China", http://xinxiangxian.xx.gov.cn/8848/1/yancao/7.htm (accessed May 2007).

Level and Trends in Tobacco Consumption in China Since 1949

Since 1949, all tobacco companies in China have been state-owned enterprises. Following the Chinese government's publication of a "Draft of regulation on monopoly on cigarettes" in 1951, China established a monopoly business of cigarette manufacture controlled by the state. Tobacco production increased from 154,000 metric tons in 1950 to 2,238,000 metric tons in 1990, 33 percent of world tobacco product.[2] Cigarette production was 852 billion cigarettes in 1980 and then skyrocketed to 1,740 billion cigarettes in 1995. Production then decreased slightly to 1,667.5 billion cigarettes in 2000. About 1,666.8 billion cigarettes were sold in the domestic market; the tax revenue from these sales reached 105 billion yuan,[2] 9 percent of total tax revenue. Since 2000, the production of cigarettes has increased slightly. In 2004, 1,873.35 billion cigarettes were produced, an increase of 4.7 percent since 2003; 1,877.86 billion cigarettes were sold, an increase of 4.5 percent from 2003, and the tax revenue increased 45 billion yuan to 210 billion yuan, 6.8 percent of China's total tax revenue.[3]

China, home of 1.336 billion people and the world's fastest growing economy, is the most sought-after target of transnational companies. Multinational companies are moving quickly to establish themselves in China after a half century during which they withdrew from the China market. In Asia, these companies have had the support of US trade negotiators in forcing open tobacco markets previously closed to foreign companies. Since the mid-1980s, Japan, South Korea, Thailand, and Taiwan have all given into pressure from Washington, DC, and allowed the sale of foreign cigarettes. In Japan, foreign cigarettes now make up nearly 20 percent of the country's cigarette market. RJ Reynolds has manufactured Camel and Winston cigarettes in Chinese factories since the late 1980s. In 2001, Philip Morris (PM) signed an

---

[2] Liu TN and Xiu BL, *Tobacco Economy and Tobacco Control* (Economic Science Press, 2004), 128–129.

[3] State Tobacco Monopoly Administration, China Tobacco Corporation, http://www.tobacco.gov.cn/ycgk.php (accessed May 2007).

agreement with the Chinese government-run tobacco company to manufacture Marlboro and other PM brands in China.[4] At the same time the prevalence of tobacco use has been quickly increasing in China, the hazards of tobacco use also have been garnering awareness.

Trends in the Prevalence of Tobacco Use

No national picture of tobacco-use behavior was available prior to the 1984 National Survey on Smoking. The World Health Organization estimated that the annual per capita consumption of cigarettes per Chinese adult 15 years of age and over was 730 in 1970–1972, 1290 in 1980–1982, and 1900 in 1990–1992.[5]

Since 1984, there have been several national surveys that included tobacco use: 1984 National Survey on Smoking, 1991 National Survey on Hypertension, 1996 National Survey on Prevalence of Smoking Behavior, 2002 National Nutrition State Survey, and 2002 Behavior Risk Factors Survey.

The first national survey on the prevalence of tobacco use in China was carried out in 1984 by the National Patriotic Health Campaign Committee. It covered all 29 provinces, autonomous regions, and municipalities. Stratified random sampling was used to survey 519,600 persons (258,422 males and 261,178 females) aged 15 years and above.

The 1996 National Prevalence Survey on Smoking Behavior was conducted in all urban and rural areas of Mainland China. The total sample size was 130,657 using three-stage probability samples. Of the originally sampled population of 128,766, 120,783 (93.8 percent) persons provided complete data and were included in the final analysis: 63,793 males and 56,020 females (with 485 not identifying gender), two thirds from rural areas and one third from urban areas. The indicators for smoking rates were based on the WHO classification of smoking definitions: *ever smokers* included persons who had

---
[4] CNNMoney.com. Marlboro Man on the Great Wall?, http://money.cnn.com/2005/04/21/news/international/altria_china.dj/ (accessed May 2007).
[5] Corrao M, Guindon G, Sharma N and Shokoohi D, ed. *Tobacco Control Country Profiles* (Atlanta, Georgia: The American Cancer Society, Inc. 2000), 384.

smoked for at least 6 months sometime during their lives; *current smokers* were smoking tobacco products at the time of the survey; *regular smokers* were persons who smoked at least one cigarette daily; and *heavy smokers* smoked at least 20 cigarettes daily at the time of the survey.[6] *Passive smoke exposure* was defined as being exposed to another person while he or she was smoking for at least 15 min daily on more than one day per week.

The 2002 Behavior Risk Factors Survey in 145 DSP points was carried out using multi-step random sampling with questionnaires: 16,407 records were completed; 16,056 records were used in the analysis. The indicators for smoking, current smoking, and average cigarettes and expenditures per day, etc., were calculated by weight-on-age structures from the 2000 census.

Based on these national surveys, we can describe the trends in the prevalence of tobacco use in China. To compare the results from the three surveys, all indicators were calculated with age standardization to the 2000 national census.

In 1984, the average current smoking rate among respondents was 34.45 percent (61.01 percent for males and 7.04 percent for females).[7]

Similar results were obtained from other epidemiological surveys, such as the 1991 National Survey on Prevalence of Hypertension, which reported the current smoking rate.[8]

In the 1996 survey, overall prevalence rates for smokers were 66.9 percent for males and 4.2 percent for females, with an overall prevalence of 37.6 percent among China's population older than 15 years of age. The prevalence of current smokers was 63.04 percent in males, 3.77 percent in females, with the total prevalence of 35.3 percent.

---

[6] World Health Organization, *Guidelines for the Conduct of Tobacco Smoking Surveys for the General Population*. (Geneva: WHO, 1983), Report Number Technical Document No. WHO/SMO/83.4.

[7] Weng XZ, Hong ZG and Cheng DY, "Smoking Prevalence in Chinese Aged and Above," *Chinese Medical Journal* 100, no. 11 (1987): 886–892.

[8] Wu XG, Duan XF, Hao DS, *et al.*, "Prevalence of Hypertension and Trend in China", *Chinese Journal of Hypertension*, Suppl. (1995): 7–13.

In 2002, the ever-smoking rates in males and females aged 15 and over were 66.0 percent and 3.1 percent, respectively; the ever-smoking rate in the whole population dropped 1.8 percent from the 1996 rate, but increased during that period for people aged 15–24. The current smoking rates in males and females aged 15 and over were 57.4 percent and 2.6 percent, respectively, decreases of 5.6 percent and 1.17 percent; the current smoking rate in the whole population was 31.4 percent, less than 3.9 percent in 1996.

Trends in Tobacco Use by Age Group

The 2002 data suggest that the prevalence of smoking had increased in males less than 30 years old and decreased in those older than 45 years compared to the data from 1984 and 1996; the prevalence of tobacco use also increased in people aged 15–24 from 1996 to 2002.

The age of starting to smoke has been drop for both men and women since 1984. In 1996, most smokers reported starting to smoke at the age of 20, three years younger than reported in the 1984 national survey. For men, the average age was about 19 compared to about 22 in 1984. For women, the age of starting to smoke dropped from 28 to 25 during the same period.[9] By 2002, the average age of starting to smoke was about 17 for males and 19 for females.

For the past 20 years, the prevalence of tobacco use among males has remained very high despite some decreases in the rates of current smoking by males over 30. In contrast, the prevalence rate has remained very low among females, despite some increases in rates for women under 25.

According to the 1984 survey, the average number of cigarettes smoked was 13 per day for males and 11 per day for females. Daily per capita consumption in 1996 was 15 cigarettes, two more per day than in 1984. The average number of cigarettes smoked per day by each smoker in 2002 was the same as in the 1996 survey — 15 cigarettes per day per smoker.

---

[9] Yang GH, Fan LX, Samet J, *et al.*, "Smoking in China: Findings of the 1996 National Prevalence Survey", *JAMA* 282, no. 13 (1999): 1247–1253.

Based on the results of the 1996 survey, more than 300 million men and 20 million women are smokers in China, making it the world's largest actual and potential national market for cigarettes.

Based on a one-percent increase in China's population each year, the estimated total number of smokers in 2002 was about 350 million, an increase of more than 30 million smokers since 1996. There were still 300 million current smokers in 2002, although the prevalence of current smokers decreased 3.4 percent from the 1996. The estimated number of current smokers should be close to the actual number since the calculated number of current smokers was 313 million based on the 2002 consumption figure and on an average cigarettes smoked per day by each smoker.

Smoking in Women

For cultural and social reasons, the prevalence of tobacco use by Asian females, generally, is quite low. The prevalence of tobacco use by women in China was about 4 percent in 1996, similar to figures reported by Hong Kong, Singapore, Japan, Thailand, etc. However, the prevalence of tobacco use varies for different generations of women: the prevalence rate of ever smoked by women born between 1915 and 1935 (i.e., women aged 50 and over in the 1984 survey and aged 60 and over in the 1996 survey) was 10–15 percent,[10] consistent with the tobacco industry's marketing strategy from 1930 to 1940 (reference 1984 and 1996 survey). Meanwhile, the prevalence of tobacco use was higher (10.2 percent) among the Northeast women than in other areas according to both the 1996 and 2002 surveys. However, the prevalence level of tobacco use has been increasing among younger women in the south of China, such as Guangdong province.

---

[10] Chinese Academy of Preventive Medicine, Chinese Association of Smoking or Health, Ministry of Health and National Patriotic Health Campaign, *1996 National Prevalence Survey on Smoking Pattern* (Beijing: Scientific and Technologic Press of China, 1997).

Smoking in Adolescence

In recent years, more than 10 studies on smoking prevalence and smoking-related knowledge, attitudes, and behaviors have been conducted among adolescents in China. These studies include the Global Youth Tobacco Survey (GYTS)[11–13] and a 1998 survey that covered 12 urban areas and 12 rural areas in 16 provinces. The GYTS included over 10,000 students aged 13–15 from four cities. The 1998 survey focused primarily on middle-school students, but also included nonstudents of middle-school age in the 12 rural areas. The survey results present a picture of adolescence nonsmokers and smokers.

- Overall, the reported prevalence rates of experimenting with cigarettes were 47.8 percent for boys and 12.8 percent for girls aged 12–18; the corresponding figures for ever-smoking were 9.4 percent for boys and 0.6 percent for girls.[14] The China GYTS also indicated that 32.5 percent of the male students and 13 percent of the female students aged 12–15 had tried smoking; the average age of smoking initiation was 10.7 years of age.[15] A slight increase in the prevalence among middle-school students was seen in the later survey compared with earlier surveys; the smoking rate among male students was still significantly higher than that of female students, but the smoking rate among female students in the big cities of China is increasing.

---

[11] Wang SQ, Yu JJ, Zhu BP, Liu M and He GQ, "Cigarette Smoking and its Risk Factors Among Senior High School Students in Beijing, China, 1988", *Tobacco Control* 3, no. 2 (1994): 107–114.

[12] Li X, Fang X and Stanton B, "Cigarette Smoking Among School Boys in Beijing, China", *Journal of Adolescence* 22, no. 5 (1999): 621–625.

[13] Warren CW, Riley L, Asma S, Erikson MP, Green L, Blanton C, Loom C, Batchelor S and Yach D, "Tobacco Use by Youth: A Surveillance Report from the Global Youth Tobacco Survey Project", *Bulletin of the World Health Organization* 78, no. 7 (2000): 868–876.

[14] Yang GH, Ma JM, Samet J, *et al.*, "Smoking in Adolescents in China", *The British Medicine Journal* (in press).

[15] Warren CW, Riley L, Asma S, Erikson MP, Green L, Blanton C, Loom C, Batchelor S and Yach D. "Tobacco Use by Youth: A Surveillance Report from the Global Youth Tobacco Survey Project", *Bulletin of the World Health Organization* 78, no. 7 (2000): 868–876.

- The prevalence of experimenting with cigarettes increased sharply with age for boys; the majority of 15–16 year-old males had experimented. While the prevalence of experimenting among girls also increased with age, less than 20 percent of 15–16 year-old girls had experimented.
- By region, the prevalence rates of experimenting for boys were similar in the urban and rural locations (48.1 percent versus 47.4 percent, respectively). For girls, the prevalence rates for experimenting were twice as high in the urban areas (15.6 percent) as in the rural areas (7.6 percent).
- With regard to the age of initiation, about 6 percent of boys and 2 percent of girls took their first puffs by age 10; 3 percent of boys and 0.3 percent of girls were smoking by age 15.
- The source of the first cigarette smoked was most commonly peers (44.0 percent); 18.5 percent obtained the cigarette themselves, and only 4.6 percent obtained the cigarette from a family member.
- The major reasons for initiation of smoking were: (1) curiosity, (2) peer pressure, and (3) the need for social interaction.
- The China GYTS indicated that 92 percent of the students surveyed believed that smoking is harmful to people's health, and 81 percent believed that passive smoking is harmful. About 85 percent of the students said that their parents had advised them not to smoke.[16] But no association was found between knowledge and behavior with respect to tobacco use.
- From 1988 to 2000, several studies also focused on the risk factors related to smoking among adolescents. A variety of risk factors may push young people to begin smoking, while other protective factors may steer them away from smoking. Weak performance in school was a relevant personal factor associated with experimenting. Peer smoking and school performance were even stronger determinants for becoming a smoker than

---

[16] *Ibid.*

for experimenting.[17-19] Outside environmental factors, such as cigarette advertising, were related to attitudes on smoking among adolescents.[20] And socioeconomic, cultural, and other environmental factors, such as the social norms on smoking, also related to smoking behavior among adolescents.[21]

Tobacco Use by Education

The smoking rate by educational level was the same in China as in other countries — lowest among those with at least a college education, the highest among those with only primary school education. However, there was no decline in tobacco use by males with a high educational level, except those elders who are illiterate: the rates of current smoking among males with at least a college education were about 45 percent, 48 percent, and 45 percent in the 1984, 1996, and 2002 surveys.

Tobacco Use by Occupation

The current smoking rate among male health workers was 42.5 percent according to the 2002 survey. Although the rate in China is still higher than among the health workers in other countries, the

---

[17] Zhu BP, Liu M, Wang SQ, et al., "Cigarette Smoking Among Junior High School Students in Beijing, China, 1988", *International Journal of Epidemiology*. Vol. 5 (1992): 854–861.
[18] Crowe JW, Torabi MR and Nakornkhet N, "Cross-Cultural Study of Samples of Adolescents' Attitudes, Knowledge, and Behaviors Related to Smoking", *Psychology Report* 75, no. (3 Pt 1) (1994): 1155–1161.
[19] Osaki Y, Minowa M and Mei J. A Comparison of Correlates of Cigarette Smoking Behavior Between Jiangxi Province, China and Japanese High School Students", *Journal of Epidemiology* 9, no. 4 (1999): 254–260.
[20] Lam TH, Chung SF, Betson CL, et al., "Tobacco Advertisements: One of the Strongest Risk Factors for Smoking in Hong Kong Students", *American Journal of Preventive Medicine* 14, no. 3 (1998): 217–223.
[21] Sun WY and Ling T, "Smoking Behavior Among Adolescents in the City, Suburbs, and Rural Areas of Shanghai", *American Journal of Health Promotion* 11, no. 5 (1997): 331–336.

decline in this group was the largest among all occupational groups. The current-smoker rate in male teachers did not decline as much as among the health workers.

Tobacco Use in Different Areas

In 1996, the ever-smoker rates in urban and rural areas were 34.5 percent and 39.2 percent, and the current-smoker rates were 31.8 percent and 36.9 percent, respectively. In 2002, the ever-smoker rates between urban and rural areas were 29.5 percent and 37.8 percent, and the current-smoker rates were 25.0 percent and 33.0 percent, respectively. Although the prevalence level of tobacco use declined in both urban and rural areas, it is very obvious that the decline in the tobacco use rate was greater in urban than in rural areas.

There were no obvious geographic differences in tobacco use among male smokers, but great differences among females, with higher smoking rates in the northeast and north areas.

SMOKING ADDICTION AND CESSATION

Cessation of smoking can prevent some tobacco-related deaths and reduce the harmful effects on health caused by tobacco use, but cessation is not easy. And the picture of cessation among Chinese smokers was quite different from that of Western countries.

Cessation of smoking is a dynamic cyclical process. Over time, many people alternate between smoking and nonsmoking. Thus, smoking cessation is not a discrete action, but rather a complex, multi-stage process. The trans-theoretical model uses stages of changing to integrate processes and principles of change on people's behavior. This model conceives of behavioral change as a process involving progress through five stages: pre-contemplation, contemplation, preparation, action, and maintenance.[22] Pre-contemplation

---

[22] Prochaska OS, Redding CA and Evens KE, "The Trans-theoretical Model and Stage of Change", in *Health Behavior and Education,* eds. Karen G, Frances ML and Barbara KR (San Francisco: Jossey-Bass Publishers 1997).

(stage 1) is defined as a stage in which current smokers have no intention of giving up smoking within the next six months. During contemplation (stage 2), current smokers intend to give up smoking within the next six months. Current smokers in the preparation stage (stage 3) are seriously preparing to give up smoking within the next 30 days and are taking some steps in this direction, such as reading relevant materials. The fourth stage, the action stage, is defined as the first six months after smokers stop smoking. Finally, the maintenance stage (stage 5) continues from six months after stopping smoking until the person reaches a confirmed nonsmoker stage without relapse.

To develop a profile of cessation, current smokers were asked in both the 1996 and 2002 surveys whether they had ever quit and if they intended to give up smoking. Whether current smokers answered that they intended or did not intend to quit, so long as they responded that they had quit before and had relapsed at the time of the survey, they were classified as relapsed smokers. Based on the response to this question, the ever-smokers were divided into two groups: quitters (former smokers) and current smokers. Current smokers were re-divided into three groups: never quit and not intending to quit; never quit and intending to quit; and relapsed quitters. Relapsed quitters were not asked about their intent to quit again. We asked former smokers how long they had successfully quit (less than six months, less than one year, less than two years, two years and over, and do not know). We further classified quitters as taking action (quitting period of less than one month), maintenance (quitting period of more than one month and less than two years), and success (two years and longer).

Systematic large-scale research on cessation is not very plentiful, but the 1996 and 2002 surveys did provide exact data to outline the cessation process among Chinese smokers.[23,24]

---

[23] Yang GH, Ma JM and Samet MJ, "Smoking Cessation in China: Findings from the 1996 National Prevalence Survey", *Tobacco Control* 10 (2001): 170–174.
[24] Yang GH, Fan LX, Samet J, *et al*., "Smoking in China: Findings of the 1996 National Prevalence Survey", *JAMA* 282, no. 13 (1999): 1247–1253.

Most Smokers do not Try to Quit; 80 Million Smokers have Relapsed

In the 1996 survey, 64.9 percent of ever-smokers said that they did not intend to quit; the proportion decreased in 2002, when 43.9 percent of current smokers said "No, I am not planning to quit". The proportion of relapses increased from 10.5 percent in the 1996 survey to 33 percent in the 2002 survey, meaning that about 80 million smokers tried to quit and relapsed. However, compared with the 1996 data, although unsuccessful, more smokers attempted to quit. In addition, 32.5 percent of ever-smokers had relapses, and about 63 percent of ever-smokers had quit for very short periods, less than six months, even less than one month. These data suggest that the quitters need to be assisted and guided in their cessation attempts with psychological and medical assistance.

Quitters Increased by 10 Million

In 1996, the proportion of those who had quit was 9.5 percent of ever-smokers; in the 2002 survey, the figure had increased to 12 percent. Although the proportion increased by only 2 percent, the change represents an increase of 10 million quitters. Moreover, the proportion of quitters who had stopped smoking for more than two years doubled compared to 3.5 percent of ever-smokers in 1996.

The numbers of those willing to quit, trying to quit, and successfully quitting increased with age and varied greatly by educational level and occupation.

The most common reason for quitting was illness, which explains why the rate of quitting was higher in older people.

EXPOSURE TO SECONDHAND SMOKE

Nonsmokers inhale secondhand smoke (SHS), a combination of side-stream smoke that is related to the cigarette's burning, and mainstream smoke exhaled by active smokers. Passive or secondhand smoking exposure has been causally linked to respiratory tract diseases and other adverse health effects in children and to cancer and heart disease in adults.

Exposure to SHS is difficult to measure accurately since it is not a direct consequence of actions by the exposed subject. Indicators of exposure to SHS range from surrogate indicators to direct measurements of exposure and biomarkers. One useful index is the husband's smoking status as an estimate of Environmental Tobacco Smoke (ETS) exposure for wives, but this is far from accurate since smoking by other family members may be important sources of SHS; the husband may smoke outside the home and information about exposure before marriage is not captured.[11] Indirect measures include self-reported exposure and description of the source of SHS in relevant microenvironments, most often the home and workplace, collected using questionnaires.

Various methods were used to determine the prevalence of environmental tobacco smoke exposure in China. They range from simple questionnaire reports to measurements of tobacco combustion products in the air of indoor environments and of biomarkers of tobacco smoke in human fluids and tissues. Studies comparing questionnaire indexes of SHS exposure to levels of biomarkers have shown that these different indicators are correlated, although their results are not perfectly concordant. The term passive smoking is used in this paper to describe SHS exposure as measured by questionnaire. *Secondhand smoke* was defined in the 1996 and 2002 surveys as being exposed to another person while he or she is smoking for at least 15 minutes daily on more than one day per week. In the 1984 survey, *passive smoke exposure* was defined only as being exposed to another person while he or she is smoking on more than one day per week. Thus, the results from the 1984 survey are probably underestimates.

SHS Exposure

There is no obvious decline in SHS exposure, but some laudable progress has been made.

In the 1984 national survey in China, 39 percent of 343,563 current nonsmokers reported exposure to secondhand smoke more than one day a week. In the 1996 national survey, 53.5 percent (53.2 percent to 53.8 percent) of 84,912 current nonsmokers reported exposure to SHS, defined as being in the presence of passive smoke at least 15 minutes per day on more than one day a week. The prevalence rate of SHS exposure in females (57.0 percent) was higher than in males (45.5 percent). The 2002 survey revealed that 52.9 percent (51.9 percent to 53.9 percent) of 10,203 nonsmokers were exposed to SHS based on the definition, sampling frame, and sampling methods in the 1996 survey.[25] The prevalence rate of SHS exposure in females (54.6 percent) was higher than in males (49.2 percent).[26] Thus, the total exposure to SHS showed no obvious change between 1984 and 1996. However, we found some laudable progress in the prevention of SHS. According to the 1996 survey, the highest prevalence of exposure to SHS (60 percent) was in women in the reproductive age range, with higher exposure in younger groups than in older age groups. The prevalence of exposure to SHS in women in the reproductive age range had obviously declined by 2002, although exposure to SHS in males had increased.

Meanwhile, exposure to SHS in urban areas decreased from 55.4 percent to 49.7 percent between 1996 and 2002, but there was an increase in rural areas — from 52.38 percent in 1996 to 54.0 percent in 2002.

Due to colder climates in North China, people are more conditioned to close windows and doors, so exposure to SHS is more serious; the levels generally reached 60 percent and higher.

Children's Exposure to SHS

The vast majority of children exposed to tobacco smoke do not choose to be exposed. Children's exposure is involuntary, arising from smoking, mainly by adults, in places where children live, work, and play. Unfortunately, a few reports are available on ETS exposure

---

[25] Yang GH, Ma JM, Liu N, *et al.*, "Smoking and Passive Smoking, 2002 (in Chinese)", *Chinese Journal of Epidemiology* 26, no. 2 (2005): 77–83.
[26] *Ibid.*

among Chinese children. A survey on distribution, frequency, and intensity of asthma was carried out among 71,867 subjects in six areas of Guangdong province. The overall prevalence rate was 0.94 percent. The group with the highest prevalence of asthma comprised children less than seven years old. More than half (54.7 percent) of the patients with asthma reported frequent exposure to side-stream smoke.[27] A cross-sectional survey of 1,449 pregnant women, who have never smoked and made their first prenatal visit to the Women and Children's Hospital of Guangzhou, China, during 1996–1997, found that 60.2 percent (95 percent Confidence Interval 57.7 percent to 62.7 percent) of the never-smoking pregnant women had a husband who currently smoked. Women with smoking husbands ($n = 872$) were more exposed to ETS than those with nonsmoking husbands ($n = 577$) at home (71 percent versus 33 percent), in public places (77 percent versus 66 percent), and at work (60 percent versus 50 percent of working women), and they took less action against passive smoking in public places.[28] In general, passive smoking is an important public health problem in China, especially for women and children.

Places of Exposure to SHS

Home, public places, and indoor work places are the main places for exposure to SHS.

According to the 1996 survey, the majority of passive smokers were exposed to SHS every day, with 71.2 percent reporting SHS exposure at home, 25.0 percent in their work environments, and 32.5 percent in public places (multiple choices offered).[29] These levels are

---

[27] Tang T and Ding Y, "Zhen Epidemiological Survey and Analysis on Bronchial Asthma in Guangdong Province", *Journal of Zhonghua Jie He He Hu Xi Za Zhi* 23, no. 12 (2000): 730–733.

[28] Loke AY, Lam TH, Pan SC, Li SY, Gao XJ and Song YY, "Exposure to and Actions Against Passive Smoking in Non-Smoking Pregnant Women in Guangzhou, China", *Acta Obstetricia of Gynecologica Scandinaviau* 79, no. 11 (2000): 947–952.

[29] Chinese Academy of Preventive Medicine, Ministry of Health, *et al.*, *1996 National Survey on Prevalence of Smoking in China* (China Science and Technology press, August 1997).

higher than those of other countries. For example, in the United States, 37 percent of men and women over 18 years old in 1993, and 31 percent in 1997 reported exposure to SHS.[30]

The 2002 survey revealed increases in the frequencies of SHS exposure at home (82 percent), public places (66.8 percent), and indoor work places (36.7 percent) (multiple choices offered).[31]

SHS exposure varied greatly by sex, age, and regions. For men, exposure was reported with approximately equal frequency as taking place at home (65.3 percent) and in public places (78.8 percent), and a little less frequently in indoor work places (49.2 percent). For women, the home (88.2 percent) was the dominant locus with far less common exposure rates at work (31.5 percent) and in public places (61.8 percent), especially for the rural women, where 91.6 percent of secondhand smokers were exposed to SHS at home.

IMPACT OF TOBACCO CONTROL IN CHINA

The Framework Convention on Tobacco Control (FCTC) has been in effect since February 27, 2005. If tobacco control is successful, the forecast of a world tobacco epidemic in the 21st century would be reversed. FCTC provides a comprehensive tobacco control strategy that includes: (1) education and information, (2) legislative measures, (3) litigation, (4) economic measures, (5) cessation efforts, (6) crop substitution and diversification, (7) advocacy, and (8) administration and management. Most essential is a strong political commitment at the national level that is reinforced by supportive international agencies. Compared with other countries in the past 20 years, China has not done very well, but we can evaluate the impact of tobacco control for China from data on knowledge about tobacco use and health, attitudes on tobacco control policies, and implementation of intervention strategies.

---

[30] Yang GH, Fan LX, Samet J, et al., "Smoking in China: Findings of the 1996 National Prevalence Survey", *JAMA* 282, no. 13 (1999): 1247–1253.

[31] Yang GH, *Death and Their Risk Factors Among Chinese Population* (China: Peking Union University of Medical Sciences Press, China, 2005), 249.

Knowledge About the Harmful Effects of Tobacco Use on Health

To measure knowledge about how tobacco use harms health, we compared the results from the 1996 and 2002 surveys because the questions were the same in both surveys. Three groups of questions were chosen: (1) Do you think that smoke or SHS is harmful to your health? (four choices: no harm, a little, serious, and unknown); (2) Do you think that smoking in pregnancy is harmful to the fetus? (three choices: yes, no, and unknown); (3) Do you know that tobacco use is the cause or an important risk factor of lung cancer, respiratory disease, and coronary heart diseases? (three choices for each disease: yes, no, and unknown). For the first group of questions, we compared the proportion of respondents who chose serious harm in their answers. For groups 2 and 3, we compared the proportion who chose "yes".

In 2002, more people knew that tobacco use is very harmful than in 1996; however, more than half the population still did not know in 2002 that smoking and SHS are harmful to their health. In particular, only 43.82 percent people knew that smoking in pregnancy is harmful to the fetus, and only 22.2 percent of people knew smoking is an important risk factor to coronary heart disease. Since only 6.93 percent had this knowledge in 1996, the progress is quite good. But it is still important that health education spread the knowledge on the risks of tobacco use in China.

In addition, while knowledge about the adverse relationship between smoking and good health has been improving greatly in China, it is still poor in the rural and Western areas, and among people with lower education levels, and farmers. For example, only 36 percent of people in Tibet knew that smoking can lead to lung cancer.

Attitudes About Tobacco Control

To measure the change in people's attitudes about tobacco control, we compared the results from the 1996 and 2002 surveys as the questions were the same in both surveys: (1) Do you agree with banning smoking in main public places, such as hospitals, schools, stations, airports, government buildings, and so on? (2) Do you agree with a comprehensive ban on cigarette advertisements?

Attitudes on tobacco control did not improve; in fact, the attitudes of respondents on these two questions became more negative: 61.1 percent of respondents supported banning smoking in public places in 2002, down from 74 percent who did in 1996; 45 percent of respondents supported banning all cigarettes ads in 2002, down from 63.9 percent in 1996.

Responses differed by education, occupation, urban and rural, and geographic areas. In particular, a lower proportion of people supported both policies in southwest areas of China.

Implementation of Tobacco Control Policies

To measure the implementation of tobacco control policies, we used three questions: (1) Is there any policy to restrict smoking in your work place? (2) Is there any policy to restrict smoking in your home? (3) In the past one year, have you gotten any advice to quit smoking cigarettes from any medical staff? Because these questions that related to implementation of tobacco control policies were not asked in the 1996 survey, we cannot examine changes on this issue.

Banning Smoking in Public Places

Two-thirds of respondents were employed; of these, 31.8 percent reported some policy on banning smoke in their work places; extrapolating from these answers, 41.2 percent of hospitals, 36.2 percent of schools, and 25 percent of government buildings in China have a policy banning smoking in their work places.

Restrictions on Smoking at Home

According to the responses, 11.5 percent reported limiting smoking indoors; 38.1 percent limited smoking in at least partial areas, such as the bedroom; 54.4 percent reported not limiting smoking in their homes; in rural areas, that proportion reached 58.3 percent.

Advice to Quit by Health Workers

We used the question "In the past one year, have you gotten any advice to quit cigarettes from any medical staff?" to measure indirectly the role of medical workers in tobacco control.

The results show that in the 2002 survey, 30.3 percent of smokers (36.2 percent in urban areas, 28.9 percent in rural areas) received advice on quitting cigarettes.

SUMMARY

At present, tobacco use is still an important public health problem in China. In contrast to declines in the prevalence of tobacco use in most other countries; the high consumption of tobacco use in the Chinese population appears very serious. From 1984 to 1996, the prevalence of smoking among men rose rapidly, reaching a peak between 50 percent and 80 percent. On the other hand, compared with the historic situation in China, progress looks pretty good. From 1996 to 2002, the current smoking rate in males declined from 63 percent to 57 percent, although the ever-smoking rate remained constant at about 66 percent. Sixty-five percent of current smokers did not want to quit.

Among young men and women in China under 25 years old, the prevalence of tobacco use increased. Based on the experience of other countries, the rates of tobacco use in women will increase when international tobacco companies come into China. This is a great challenge for China's public health, its government, and its future.

Exciting progress in tobacco control has been made in the past decade. Although the prevalence level of tobacco use in Chinese males is still very high, it decreased 6 percent — from 63.0 percent in 1996 to 57.4 percent in 2002; during the same years, tobacco use by male health workers decreased 13 percent — from 55.4 percent to 42.5 percent. Although quitting rates are not high, 10 million smokers are trying to quit. The rates of SHS are not declining, but the exposure to SHS among women of childbearing age has declined. Although some progress has been made in the past decade, China still faces a long path to true tobacco control.

Chapter 3

Tobacco Control Programs in China

Anita H. Lee and Yuan Jiang

BACKGROUND

A report by China's Ministry of Health in May 2006 entitled "Smoking and Health — 2006 Report" published alarming numbers, which many in the field of public health and tobacco control have already known. Citing the 2002 National Smoking Prevalence Survey, the report stated that 350 million people, or 35.8 percent of China's population above age 15, are smokers (66 percent of men and 3.1 percent of women). Chinese smokers make up one-third of the world's smokers. Comparing these figures with the corresponding numbers from the 1996 National Smoking Prevalence Survey, the report noted that smoking prevalence was down 1.8 percent (3.1 percent for men and 1 percent for women). The number of smokers, however, increased by 30 million because of the growth of the population. The report pointed out that smoking prevalence for the 15–24 age group rose, and the age of smoking initiation decreased from 22.4 in the 1980s to 19.7 in 2002.[1]

---

[1] Chinese Ministry of Health, *China "Smoking and Health" Report* (Beijing: Ministry of Health, 2006).

China has a number of dubious distinctions with respect to tobacco. China is the largest producer and consumer of tobacco in the world. It grows a third of the world's tobacco crop, and produces and consumes one-third of the world's cigarettes. It has the highest number of smokers: one-third of the world's smokers live in China.[2] It is the country with the highest number of smoking attributable deaths: one million deaths annually.[3] This is one in four such deaths in the world. Smoking attributable deaths in China are estimated to rise to 2 million by the year 2020.[4]

Because of the immense health and social costs of smoking, political awareness of the scale and burden of this public health crisis is rising. The Chinese government has joined the rest of the world in tobacco control. In 2003, China became a signatory to the World Health Organization's Framework Convention on Tobacco Control, the first international treaty to address the tobacco problem. As a signatory, China is legally committed to undertaking a multitude of anti-tobacco measures. The National People's Congress, the highest law making body in the country, ratified the treaty in 2005.

China is becoming an increasingly visible player on the world stage among the developed nations and is committed to playing an active part in the global effort to address the tobacco problem. Public statements from senior Chinese officials have indicated that the Chinese Government is increasingly aware of the health risks of the high prevalence of smoking and is ready to do something to address the mounting health crisis. At a WHO tobacco control conference in Geneva in February 2006, the Chinese Ambassador to the United Nations announced that as part of the effort to reduce consumption, China will not approve any new cigarette factories, including joint ventures with foreign companies and will put existing

---

[2] World Health Organization, *Tobacco Control Country Profile* (2003).
[3] Liu BQ, Peto R, Chen ZM *et al.*, "Emerging Tobacco Hazards in China: 1. Retrospective Proportional Mortality Study of One Million Deaths", *British Medical Journal* 317, no. 7170 (1998): 1411–1422.
[4] Niu SR *et al.*, "Emerging Tobacco Hazards in China: 2. Early Mortality Results From a Prospective Study", *British Medical Journal* 317, no. 7170 (1998): 1423–1424.

tobacco production under strict control through taxes and industry reorganization.[5] Beijing is also poised to organize a Smoke-Free Olympic Games in 2008.

Tremendous difficulties and challenges lie ahead, however, because tobacco is a significant source of revenue for the central government and many provincial governments, and is the source of livelihood for tens of millions of people in China. Tobacco leaf growing is a major source of income for farmers in many poor regions.[6] It is estimated that the tobacco tax and profit contribute 7.38 percent of total government revenue.[7] The conflict between public health concerns and economic considerations weighs heavily in policy considerations.

The purpose of this chapter is to review what has been done with respect to tobacco control in China, examine the achievements and difficulties, discuss how tobacco control efforts can be more effective, and suggest future policy directions.

THE GOVERNMENT'S LEADERSHIP ROLE IN TOBACCO CONTROL

China's tobacco control efforts began in 1979. The State Council approved the issue by the Ministry of Health, Ministry of Finance, Ministry of Agriculture, and Ministry of Light Industry of a notice entitled "On the Hazards of Smoking and Tobacco Control Advocacy Notice". During the 1980s, health information campaigns were initiated. The strongest official public statement that smoking was harmful to health was made in 1984 by the then Minister of Health.[8] The establishment of the National Institute of Health

---

[5] Chinanews.com, China proposes ban on new cigarette factories, http://www.chinanews.cn//news/2005/2006-02-09/18550.html (accessed May 2007).
[6] Hu TW and Mao Z, "Economic Analysis of Tobacco and Options for Tobacco Control: China Case Study", in *HNP Discussion Paper Economics of Tobacco Control Paper Number 3* (Washington, DC: World Bank, 2002).
[7] Hu TW et al., "China at the Crossroads: The Economics of Tobacco and Health", *Tobacco Control* (2006).
[8] Mackay J, "China's Tobacco Wars", *Multinational Monitor* 14, nos. 1–2 (1992).

Education in that year provided central coordination for national health education on tobacco. The Chinese Academies of Preventive Medicine and Medical Sciences and the National Institute of Health Education were the main movers of tobacco control activities in the 1980s. China held its first "No Smoking Day" in Shanghai in 1987, and since then has conducted "National No Tobacco Day" activities in conjunction with the World Health Organization's "World No Tobacco Day" activities.

In 1990, health advocates and volunteers established the Chinese Association on Smoking and Health. Formed under government auspices and composed of volunteers, the association has been responsible for organizing anti-tobacco education and activities since then, including campaigns for "Smoke-Free Schools", "Smoke-Free Hospitals", "Smoke-Free Institutions", and "Smoke-Free Families" as well as activities for creating tobacco-advertising-free cities. In 2004, the association was renamed the Chinese Association on Tobacco Control (CATC). CATC is "guided, supervised and administrated by the Ministry of Health and Ministry of Civil Affairs in carrying out its professional activities".[9]

Within the government, the National Tobacco Control Office coordinates tobacco control work. The office was established in the Chinese Center for Disease Control and Prevention (CDC) under the Ministry of Health. As the focal point of the country's tobacco control initiatives, the office has wide-ranging responsibilities in research, training, coordination, and spearheading, of tobacco control programs. These responsibilities include providing the scientific evidence for anti-tobacco legislation; planning and promotion of anti-tobacco programs; training and coordination of public health professionals in tobacco control, and so forth. The National Tobacco Control Office provides the leadership role to the tobacco control work throughout the country and is also the focal point for participation in international anti-tobacco activities. The resources devoted to this office, however, are very limited.

---

[9] Chinese Association on Tobacco Control, Brief Introduction on Chinese Association on Tobacco Control, Beijing (2006).

Since its establishment, there have been four professionals in this office on a permanent basis, and in 2006, 12 contract staff were employed.

Legislative Framework of Tobacco Control

The first anti-tobacco legislation in China was passed in 1991 and took effect in 1992. The People's Republic of China Tobacco Monopoly Law mandates scientific research and technological development of tobacco monopoly commodities to improve the quality of tobacco products and reduce the content of tar and other hazardous materials in these products. The law also bans or restricts smoking on public transport and in public places and bans smoking by students. It requires the printing of tar levels and health warnings on local and imported cigarette packets. The law also bans tobacco advertising on TV and radio, and in newspapers and magazines. And it mandates improved education about the health effects of smoking, with particular emphasis on young people.[8]

Since this landmark legislation, other legislations such as laws on the protection of minors, on advertisements, and on prevention of juvenile delinquency have all included tobacco control in their provisions. To date, 23 pieces of legislations, regulations, and notices have been promulgated for tobacco control.[10] The following paragraphs give an overview.

The Law on the Protection of Minors, also passed in 1991, makes it illegal for anyone to smoke in any areas within a primary school, secondary school, kindergarten, or nursery. The aim is to prevent youths from smoking. The law also clearly regulates that no one can sell cigarettes or any tobacco products to minors in any commercial location.

The 10th session of the National People's Congress in 1994 passed the People's Republic of China Advertisement Law, which clearly forbids the use of radio broadcasts, movies, television,

---

[10] Li Y and Jiang Y, "Overview of Tobacco Control Legislation Banning Smoking in Public Places", *Journal of Environment and Health* (in Chinese) 4, no. 24 (2007): 221–223.

newspapers, and magazines to publicize cigarettes. It also forbids advertisements of cigarettes and tobacco products in movie theatres, waiting rooms, meeting halls, and sports stadiums. Cigarette advertisements in other venues must include the notice that "smoking is hazardous to health". Similar provisions were included in the Tobacco Monopoly Law, but this 1994 legislation took precedence over the earlier legislation.

The Prevention of Juvenile Delinquency Act in 1999 stipulates that parents and guardians of minors must educate young people not to smoke and not to abuse alcohol. Such regulations are aimed at educating young people to lead a healthy lifestyle and to have high moral standards. This legislation further emphasizes that no one can sell cigarettes to minors in any commercial locations.

In addition to national legislation, there are also regulations, legislations, and administrative guidelines at different governmental levels on the control of tobacco advertisements. An example of provincial level legislation is the Legislation on the Implementation of People's Republic of China Advertisement Law of the Hunan Province. It stipulates that "tobacco advertisements need to adhere to strict regulations, and must get the approval from the Administration of Industry and Commerce at the provincial level".

An example of administrative guidelines to give effect to legislation is the Interim Measures on Tobacco Advertising issued by the State Administration for Industry and Commerce in December 1995. There are also administrative measures at the local level, such as Beijing's Outdoor Advertising Regulations passed in 1998, which stipulates no outdoor advertisements of cigarettes.

In addition, agencies at different levels that monitor and regulate advertisements have also issued guidelines and regulations. In 1999, the State Administration for Industry and Commerce issued a response on whether advertisements should be regarded as cigarette advertisements when they advertise the cigarette company but not the cigarettes. The guidelines clarify that advertisements by cigarette manufacturers and sellers, in which the design, slogans, and/or visuals are similar to those of its cigarettes, and which indirectly promote the brand name, image, logo, and the packaging of the cigarette, will be deemed cigarette advertisements even if cigarettes are not included in the advertisements.

Since the 1980s, the government has issued regulations to restrict smoking in public places to protect nonsmokers from secondhand smoke. An example is the Health Regulations in Public Places promulgated by the State Council in 1987. In 1991, the Ministry of Health issued implementation details for these regulations, which banned smoking in the following public venues: (1) sports stadiums, (2) libraries, museums, and art museums, (3) shopping malls, shops, and bookstores, (4) waiting rooms of public transportation, and (5) trains, ferries, and passenger planes. In 1997, the Ban on Smoking in Public Transport and Waiting Rooms and Civilian Airport and Civilian Aircraft in the No Smoking Regulations was passed.

As noted, 23 laws, regulations, and notices dealing with tobacco control exist at the national level. In addition, many local governments have passed their own laws and regulations. By the end of 2006, 154 cities, 45.7 percent of the 337 prefectures of city level and above, had passed their own ban on smoking in public areas.[10]

Effectiveness of the Legislative Framework

Such a legislative framework is definitely an achievement and is due in no small measure to the tireless work and advocacy of tobacco control and health professionals in China. Legislation and regulations, however, are only a first step. The critical factor for success is effective implementation and strong enforcement of the legislation and regulations. Without monitoring compliance, they have no teeth at all.

There has been no official report or published research on the implementation and enforcement of these regulations. However, a visitor to China can easily see with his own eyes that enforcement is not strong. Smoking can be seen everywhere. Even where direct advertisement of cigarettes is banned, indirect advertising is not uncommon. Luggage carts at a major airport show the logo of a prominent cigarette brand, the manufacturer of which is a company with the same name as the brand and just happens to be a conglomerate with many business interests. At major tourist locations, signposts and other visual materials often display the name of the sponsor as the manufacturer of a famous cigarette brand. In Formula One Grand Prix racing in Shanghai, tobacco advertisements are prevalent on racecars and drivers' uniforms, even though tobacco billboards are no longer allowed. Commercial interests and multi-million dollar sponsorship deals appear to take precedence over health interests.[11] Smokers' convenience also appears to trump the right of nonsmokers to smoke-free air. In public areas with clear "No Smoking" signs, it is not uncommon to see smokers puffing away with little regard for other people. The social norm in China is for nonsmokers to suffer secondhand smoke in silence and acquiescence.

Facts and Figures Tell the Story

Apart from these impressionistic observations, the results of the 2002 National Prevalence Survey also bear evidence that the smoking epidemic in China is widespread, and if left unchecked, will lead to dire consequences.

The 2002 National Prevalence Survey found that smoking rates in males and females aged 15 and above were 66.0 percent and 3.1 percent, respectively. Compared with the 1996 National Prevalence Survey, the smoking rate had dropped by 1.8 percent in the whole population, but increased among people aged 15–24. The number of total smokers was about 350 million, 30 million more than that in 1996. The rate of quitting smoking was increasing, from 9.42 percent in 1996 to 11.5 percent in 2002. However, the rate of no intention to quit among smokers was at a high of 74 percent. The average cigarette consumption per person per day (14.8 cigarettes) remained the same as in 1996. The picture of passive smoking in nonsmokers did not show any improvement over 1996, with no change in the overall prevalence of passive smoking for either men or women. Knowledge about smoking and health conditions in the population had improved, especially among those with a higher level of education,

---

[11] Agence France Presse (AFP), "Shanghai Skirts Ban to Allow F1 Tobacco Ads", *The Straits Times*, Singapore (2004).

but was still poor in the western areas. The prevalence of smoking in Chinese males had reached its peak and leveled off. Communication on harm from smoking remained weak since people did not understand or support the tobacco control strategies, especially in the western areas. The survey concluded that the prevalence of tobacco use would not decrease in the short term and that the disease burden caused by tobacco use would still be heavy in the next 30–50 years.[12]

With 350 million smokers, a number still increasing in spite of the leveling off of the smoking prevalence rate, and half of nonsmokers, or about 500 million people, exposed to secondhand smoke, the disease burden from tobacco is immense. The economic cost of smoking in China was calculated at US$5 billion in 2000, with $1.7 billion in direct costs, $0.4 billion in indirect morbidity costs, and $2.9 billion in indirect mortality costs.[13]

The authoritative report on smoking and lung cancer published by the Ministry of Health in May 2006 entitled *"Smoking and Health — 2006 Report"* and referred to earlier in this chapter describes the tobacco problem as being "of epidemic proportions". It seeks to reinforce the knowledge that smoking leads to many diseases. It emphasizes that smoking is not only harmful to the 350 million active smokers, but also harmful to the women and children and other nonsmokers who inhale secondhand smoke. The report describes smoking as the number one killer, with one million people in China dying from smoking attributable diseases each year. The report also notes the rapid increase in the mortality rate from lung cancer and the lower age of lung cancer patients, and the fact that lung cancer has taken over stomach cancer as the number one killer cancer in China. It points out the experience of many other countries that have seen the impact of smoking on health after 20–30 years. In China, the increase in consumption of tobacco started in the 1980s, reaching a peak in the middle of the

---

[12] Yang GH *et al.*, "Smoking and Passive Smoking in Chinese, 2002", (in Chinese), *Zhonghua Liu Xing Bing Xue Za Zhi* 26, no. 2 (2005): 77–83.
[13] Sung HY *et al.*, "Economic Burden of Smoking in China, 2000", *Tobacco Control*, June, 15(Suppl 1) (2006): i5–i11.

1990s. Therefore, the health impact of tobacco consumption is only beginning to be felt in China. The report warns that the next 10 years will see the serious consequences of the increase in tobacco consumption in the 1980s and 1990s.[1]

Dilemma in the Government's Position

At the very heart of China's tobacco problem is the oft-cited policy dilemma of economics versus health. China is the largest producer of tobacco in the world. A government monopoly, the China National Tobacco Company (CNTC), produces 1.6 trillion cigarettes a year, roughly one-third of the world's total, and equal to the total cigarette production of the next seven biggest cigarette-producing countries.[1] A news story in the *Shanghai Daily* on December 21, 2006 entitled "China Leads the World in Cigarette Consumption" noted that " tobacco contributed more than 240 billion yuan in tax last year. Of each packet of cigarettes, retailers take eight to 10 percent, producers 10 percent, monopoly administration 40 percent and 40 percent is tax". The contribution of the tobacco tax and profit to central government revenue was calculated at 160 billion yuan in 2003, representing 7.38 percent of total government revenue. Although this percentage is lower than the high of 11.2 percent in 1996, the absolute amount increased twofold from 83 billion yuan in 1996 to 160 billion yuan in 2003.[7] In some provinces, such as Henan and Yunnan, where tobacco leaf farming and cigarette manufacturing are major economic activities, the contribution of tobacco to the provincial revenue is over 50 percent.[14]

It is interesting to note that the tobacco industry has a very special place in the policy and politics arena in China. The state monopoly CNTC sees itself as the organizer and manager of a state industry. Therefore, it does not have the "apologist" posture of commercial tobacco companies in the western world.[8] The CNTC acknowledges

---

[14] Hu TW *et al.*, "The Role of Government in Tobacco Leaf Production in China: National and Local Interventions, *International Journal of Public Policy* 2, nos. 3–4 (2007): 235–248.

that smoking is harmful to health and is working to reduce the tar and nicotine content in cigarettes. It cooperates with the Ministry of Health on health warnings on cigarette packets, and it participates in government anti-smoking educational activities. The CNTC was also a participant in the negotiating team when China participated in several rounds of international tobacco control negotiations leading to the FCTC.[15,16] Unlike the multinational tobacco companies in the western world, which have been demonized by lawsuits, movies, and an active anti-tobacco campaign, the CNTC is able to maintain a relatively secure position. Its activities are comprehensive and multifaceted. It provided health education and education on laws and regulations, academic conferences, human resource development, and sharing of scientific and technological information and management expertise. There are also discussion forums, essay competitions, social services, and so forth. The CNTC, and consequently the state tobacco industry, enjoys a certain respectability and status throughout the country. Over four million households rely on tobacco for their livelihood as tobacco leaf farmers, workers in tobacco manufacturing, or retailers.[15] In China, as in many other countries, means of livelihood is inextricably linked with social stability, which is of paramount importance to the country.

It is ironic that the health versus economics argument may not be all that it is hyped up to be. A senior tobacco control expert has calculated that even if smoking prevalence in China decreases 1 percent every year, as has occurred in industrialized nations that have been more successful in addressing the tobacco problem, the number of smokers in China will not decrease in the next 30 years because the increase in the size of the population is also projected to be 1 percent per year during this period. The argument of the tobacco lobby that tobacco control measures are detrimental to the economic well-being and social stability of the country cannot be borne out in fact. With all the anti-tobacco legislations in place so far, the

---

[15] Liu T and Xiong B, *Tobacco Economy & Tobacco Control (in Chinese)*. (Beijing: Economic Science Press, 2004).
[16] World Health Organization, The WHO FCTC: A Global Health Treaty.

smoking prevalence rate in China has only gone down a total of 1.8 percent in the six years from 1996 to 2002. With no tobacco control measures, however, even if the smoking prevalence rate remains the same, the number of smokers will increase to 430 million by the next 20 years. The need for urgent action is critical.

Economic considerations appear to weigh heavily in the government's policy considerations. Despite all the public statements on the need for tobacco control, there is as yet no national plan, miniscule resources are devoted to tobacco control and helping smokers quit, and no clearly articulated message from senior government leaders exhorts smokers to *"quit"*, preferring instead to urge smokers *"to lead a healthy lifestyle"*. The authoritative document *"Smoking and Health — 2006 Report"* of the Ministry of Health packaged the anti-smoking message with lung cancer prevention. A clear-cut message exhorting people to "Quit Smoking" has so far not been forthcoming from any political champion or government leadership.

Even though some headway has been made in China's tobacco control efforts, it is only the beginning of a very long process. Government determination and political will are the most critical factors for success. Without the investment of significant resources by the government, tobacco control will languish in empty words. Vigorously enforced legislation and coordination among the various ministries and departments at all levels will not happen without strong leadership by the government.

WHO'S FRAMEWORK CONVENTION ON TOBACCO CONTROL

Despite this dilemma in official policy, China emerged as a responsible player in the global stage with its participation in the first international public health treaty spearheaded by the World Health Organization. The Framework Convention on Tobacco Control (FCTC) represents the first coordinated global effort to reduce tobacco use. The Chinese government has been an active participant in the negotiations and talks during the drafting stage of this treaty. With the approval of the State Council, a 12-member interdepartmental negotiating team including representatives from the National Development Reform Commission, the Ministry of Health, and the Ministry of Foreign Affairs took part in the drafting of the FCTC. China became a signatory to the Convention in November 2003, and it was ratified by the 17th session of the Standing Committee of the 10th National People's Congress in August 2005. In October of the same year, a ceremony was held to mark the official implementation of the Convention in China, and it took effect in January 2006.

With the ratification of the treaty, China signified to the international community the importance it attaches to tobacco control and its readiness to cooperate with the international community to address this public health crisis and to protect the health of the community. Such a commitment is a landmark in China's tobacco control work, and hopefully it will give impetus to tobacco control efforts.

Strategic Directions for Implementing FCTC

A publication prepared by the China CDC and presented to delegates at the Fourth Plenary Session of the 10th National People's Congress held in March 2006 in Beijing listed the following recommendations as the steps for implementing the Convention.

(1) Legislate smoking bans in public areas as soon as possible to protect the health of the community, and strengthen the enforcement of such bans in order to develop more smoke-free environments. Priority areas are government buildings and hospitals.
(2) Promote the habit of not smoking, not offering cigarettes as a courtesy, and smoking cessation among government employees of all levels, health care workers, teachers, and other occupational groups as an example to the community.
(3) Strengthen the effort to promote the harms of cigarette smoking on personal health and social well-being by using media channels and the Internet. Organize seminars, competitions, and other activities to develop a supportive social environment for tobacco control.

(4) Build and sustain capacity for tobacco control by developing interagency cooperation to do policy analysis, develop policy, and build up and sustain the capacity of the national tobacco control network.
(5) Increase the provision of smoking cessation services. Regulate the market for smoking cessation products by incorporating one to two low cost and effective products into the national formulary.
(6) Strengthen anti-smoking educational and promotional efforts among young people by developing "smoke-free schools" and "health promotion schools". Incorporate information on the harmful effects of smoking into school curricula. Increase community participation to develop "smoke-free family" and "smoke-free streets" around school areas, etc. to build a social norm supportive of tobacco control.

Research into the papers of this session showed that tobacco control was not on the agenda, and it was unclear from official documents what if any action or discussion resulted from such a publication. In the report on the work of the government delivered by Premier Wen Jiabao, no mention was made of the tobacco problem, while AIDS and avian flu got mentioned as warranting "intensified efforts to prevent and treat", according to the official translation of the report.

Main Focus Areas in Implementation of FCTC

Notwithstanding its lack of prominence on the national political stage, the FCTC, and the commitment to its implementation is a platform on which tobacco control work in China can be built. With the approval of the State Council, the National Development and Reform Commission set up an Interagency Committee on the FCTC, comprising 12 ministries and departments, with the Vice Minister of Health as the focal person for tobacco control and the development and implementation of a National Plan for Action. The effectiveness and speed with which such an agency can spearhead the nation's tobacco control program remains to be seen.

The FCTC represents a paradigm shift in developing a regulatory strategy, focusing on both demand and supply reduction strategies.[16] China is thus legally committed to undertaking a multitude of measures to reduce the demand as well as the supply of tobacco. In the short period since the ratification of the FCTC, attention has been focused in the following areas:

(1) Strengthening and developing necessary legislation. To implement the FCTC, existing tobacco control legislation and research on specific policies must be strengthened. The provisions on the banning of smoking in public areas in the Regulations on the Management of Public Health need to be strengthened and submitted to the State Council for consideration. Priority will be given to tobacco control legislation that pertains to educational institutions, health institutions, and institutions that provide services to young people.

With regard to tobacco advertisements, the Interim Measures on Tobacco Advertisement stipulates clearly that tobacco advertisements are banned in four venues (waiting rooms, cinemas, conference halls, and sports stadiums) and five media channels (broadcasting, movies, television, newspapers, and magazines). But cigarette advertisements are not banned in other venues and media channels. In accordance with the intent of the FCTC, the State Administration on Industry and Commerce is liaising with relevant departments to draw up the amendments to the regulations. In the amendment process, special consideration will be given to differences in economic, cultural, and social requirements at the local and national levels. There will also be a need to clearly define a cigarette advertisement as well as define the concepts of cigarette advertising and corporate advertising campaigns of cigarette companies.

(2) Capacity building. To strengthen the capacity of provinces to implement the FCTC, the Central Government has since 2005 given special resources to 24 poorer provinces and regions in the middle and western part of China to develop a team of public health professionals with expertise in tobacco control and to conduct educational programs.[17]

---

[17] Speech by Vice Minister of Health Jiang Zuojun reported in *Ministry of Health Affairs Bulletin,* Issue 38 (in Chinese) (2007).

The focus will be on increasing knowledge and awareness of the FCTC and conducting anti-tobacco programs such as Smoke-Free Schools, Smoke-Free Hospitals, Smoke-Free Government Offices, and Smoke-Free Public Places. The emphasis is on young people, health workers, and managers, and efforts will be made to increase their awareness of the harms of smoking, lowering smoking prevalence, and building a positive environment for the implementation of the FCTC. Meanwhile, the participation and organization of conferences and international tobacco control activities continue, building the capacity of public health professionals at the national as well as local levels.

(3) "Smoking and Health" monitoring mechanism. As part of the monitoring mechanism under FCTC, the Ministry of Health established a serial report on Smoking and Health, starting in 2006. There will be a theme for each year; in 2006, the theme was tobacco control and lung cancer prevention. As noted, the authoritative report on smoking and lung cancer was published in May 2006, entitled "*Smoking and Health — 2006 Report*". The objective of the report was to increase the community's awareness of the correlation between smoking prevalence and the high prevalence of lung cancer and the increasing mortality rate from lung cancer. In the report, the community is urged to be aware of the harms of smoking and to lead a healthy lifestyle.

INTERNATIONAL TOBACCO CONTROL INTERVENTION PROGRAMS IN CHINA

Recognizing that one in three cigarettes in the world is smoked in China, the international public health community has played an active role in conducting tobacco control programs in China and in building up the capacity of Chinese public health professionals. Since the 1990s, organizations such as the World Health Organization and the World Bank have conducted tobacco control programs in China with varying degrees of success. A WHO Country Profile on Tobacco or Health describes China as the "ultimate test case for global tobacco control" and states that "to a large extent, the success of tobacco control in the world hinges on success in China".[18]

To their credit, health professionals in China have responded enthusiastically to and participated actively in these international projects. China also played host in 1997 to 1,800 delegates from all over the world who attended the 10th World Conference on Tobacco or Health in Beijing. The opening of the conference by President Jiang Zemin underscored the enormity of the public health crisis of smoking in China.[19] Since the mid-1990s, China has participated in international programs such as the International Quit and Win competitions, a program that provides an incentive to encourage smokers to quit, and has also organized annual National World No Tobacco Day events in response to the WHO's World No Tobacco Day initiatives each year on 31 May.

A notable example of an international project in China that is of long term is the World Bank's Health VII project. This project was started in 1996 with the goals of increasing the capacity of the health sector in China to carry out health promotion, and also preventing and controlling vaccine preventable diseases. The main focus of the health promotion component was tobacco control. There was active Chinese participation, and valuable lessons were learned.

Tobacco Control in Seven Cities in China: Health VII (1996–2004)

The health promotion component of the project, focusing on tobacco, was designed as a pilot project in seven cities: Beijing, Tianjin, Shanghai, Chengdu, Luoyang, Liuzhou, and Weihai. Intervention programs included city-wide strategies and specific strategies for neighborhoods, schools, hospitals. and workplaces. At the city level, city

---

[18] World Health Organization, "Tobacco-Free Initiative", *Country Profiles Tobacco or Health 2000*.
[19] Mackay J, "Beyond the Clouds — Tobacco Smoking in China", *Journal of the American Medical Association* 278, no. 18 (1997): 1531–1532.

departments were required to put tobacco control on their agenda and to meet specific goals. The law of no smoking in public places was vigorously enforced. Mass media channels were used to publicize knowledge on the harms of smoking and to advocate a smoke-free lifestyle. Participating cities were organized to take part in National World No Tobacco Day activities and in the Quit and Win Competition.

Specific strategies were built on the Smoke-Free Family and Smoke-Free Workplace programs of these cities, and efforts were made to encourage smokers to quit. With the Smoke-Free School program and banning the sale of cigarettes to young people, efforts were made to decrease the chance that young people would come into contact with cigarettes. Teachers who smoked were encouraged to quit and to act as role models for young people. For students, the emphasis was on refusing the first cigarette. Tobacco control messages were included in the school curriculum. Similarly, doctors were encouraged to quit smoking and to serve as role models. Smoking by medical workers in front of patients was banned.

In an attempt to evaluate the impact of these interventions, a Behavioral Risk Factor Survey has been conducted each year since 1996 among the general population of these seven cities. The surveys were conducted through face-to-face interviews with a random sample of at least 2,400 in each city. All seven cities conducted the survey yearly, until 2002 when one city discontinued its participation.

Results of the Behavioral Risk Factor Survey in the intervention cities show that the public's knowledge of the harms of tobacco use has increased. After eight years, the smoking prevalence of the male population in these cities decreased from 69.6 percent to 55 percent. The quit rate increased from 15.3 percent to 22.2 percent. Exposure to passive smoke decreased from 52.2 percent to 43.5 percent.[20] However, since there were no data from nonintervention cities, it cannot be established that the decreases were attributable to the Health VII project.

---

[20] World Bank, World Bank Loan for the Disease Prevention Program in China: Health Promotion Project (in Chinese), http://www.chinacdc.net.cn/n272442/n27253 0/n294176/n340510/appendix/040531.pdf (accessed May 2007).

The project also included training at the city and county levels, and thousands of people have been trained in health promotion techniques. Policies and regulations were also enacted in the cities. According to a report prepared for the World Bank, "Tobacco Control in Seven Cities in China: Health VII" in 2002, each of the seven cities enacted a regulation forbidding smoking in public places, and most cities banned outdoor tobacco advertising and sale of cigarettes to minors. The report cited the following changes in selected indicators between 1996 and 2000 according to the Behavioral Risk Factors Survey, although no claim is made that these changes were due to the program[21]:

- Knowledge of the danger of smoking for pregnant women increased from 56 percent to 64.5 percent;
- Knowledge of the risk of lung cancer from smoking increased from 81.7 percent to 87.2 percent;
- Knowledge of the risk of heart disease from smoking increased from 20.4 percent to 23.8 percent;
- Smoking prevalence among men decreased from 64.2 percent to 57.7 percent;
- Smoking prevalence among women decreased from 5.5 percent to 3.7 percent; and
- Smoking prevalence among male youth aged 15–20 decreased from 18.6 percent to 9.8 percent.

Lessons Learned from the Health VII Project

As a multi-year, multi-million dollar project, the need for evaluation was keenly felt. However, evaluation efforts were hindered by a lack of baseline data. The emphasis of the project was on the execution of the intervention, and there was no planning for pre- and post-tests or for control groups. It was thus impossible to attribute the perceived improvement in any tobacco control indicator to the

---

[21] Wiesen E, *Tobacco Control in Seven Cities in China: Health VII What Do We Know About the Program and Its Impact?* A report prepared for the Office of Tobacco Control, World Bank (2002).

project or to measure the impact and effectiveness of the program. Evaluations of some intervention programs were conducted, albeit inconsistently. Overall, the experience pointed to the need for clearly planned and vigorous evaluation procedures to determine the impact of the program.

INTERNATIONAL EXPERIENCE IN SUCCESSFUL TOBACCO CONTROL PROGRAMS

In a sense, the road to effective tobacco control is very well documented and proven. The experience in many countries in the last quarter of a century can show the way. In a study of tobacco control programs in six countries, the editors De Beyer and Brigden listed several factors for success in tobacco control.[22] It will be illuminating to measure China's progress against these yardsticks.

The success factors listed include strong and comprehensive legislation (China is building up its legislation); strong implementation and enforcement of legislation (sadly lacking in China); an organizational home and sufficient resources for tobacco control work (China CDC's National Tobacco Control Office has only meager resources); strong political support and political champions (political support in ratifying FCTC, but since then no high level "champion" or substantive support); key role by non-government organizations and charismatic individuals (nonexistent; the national organization China Association on Tobacco Control has yet to prove its leadership, and no charismatic leaders have emerged); coalition of individuals and broad-based groups, such as consumer rights groups, women's rights activists (nonexistent in China); effective advocacy (a small group of advocates does exist); transformation of social norms (social norm in China is acceptance and acquiescence of smokers); solid information base and widely publicized (Ministry of Health's annual report on Smoking and Health is a step in this direction); and a tax increase (at the core of China's policy dilemma in tobacco control).

---

[22] De Beyer J and Brigden LW, *Tobacco Control Policy: Strategies, Successes and Setbacks*, (Washington, DC: World Bank, 2003).

In the Chinese context, the government's role is crucial to many of the critical success factors gleaned from international experience. In marked contrast to the way another health issue such as AIDS has been tackled, political leaders and health officials are approaching the tobacco issue with caution rather than speed. It is interesting to note that in the government initiative to address the AIDS problem since 2003, there is already in place a national plan, relevant legislation, an AIDS office, and a high-powered committee headed by Vice Premier Wu Yi, with the Minister of Health as vice chair. Government resources devoted to the issue are significant, with 830 million yuan from the central government devoted to AIDS work in 2005 alone.[23] Highly visible educational billboards are seen in public places. Whether a political champion will emerge to kick the tobacco control program in China into a high gear and enable it to gather momentum in the next few years is an unfolding story.

ECONOMIC INTERVENTIONS

Apart from public health interventions, one of the most important weapons that a government can use in the war against tobacco is economic interventions. Worldwide experience has shown that raising the tax on the sale of cigarettes is very effective in reducing consumption.[24] The FCTC requires that signatory countries recognize the effectiveness of price and tax measures in reducing consumption of cigarettes and are committed to implementing such price and tax policies.

Yet, raising the tobacco tax is not on the political agenda in China. In all the discussions and policy initiatives on the implementation of FCTC, there is as yet no mention of increasing taxation on

---

[23] Health News, "China will invest 830 million yuan in Aids prevention next year" (in Chinese), http://news.xinhuanet.com/mrdx/2005-10/28/content_36950 72.htm (accessed May 2007).
[24] The World Bank, *Curbing the Epidemic: Governments and the Economics of Tobacco Control* (Washington, DC: The World Bank, 1998).

cigarettes. The focus is concentrating instead on nonprice tobacco control measures. This is unfortunate, as there is good reason for China to make use of this taxation tool. A study published in 2002 showed that by introducing a 10 percent increase in the cigarette tax per pack in China, the increase in the government's revenue would be more than double the loss sustained by the industry and farmers. Furthermore, between 1.44 and 2.16 million lives would be saved.[25] The current tax rate on tobacco in China is 67 percent at the producer level, which translates to an effective tax rate of 38 percent at the retail level.[7] This is low compared to the world median of 60 percent. The World Bank proposes that taxes should account for two-thirds to four-fifths of the retail price of cigarettes.[26] Thus, China definitely has room for an increase in the tobacco tax as a measure to control tobacco use.

However, concern among policy leaders about the possible negative economic impact of such a tax increase seems overriding. As discussed earlier in this chapter, the tobacco tax is a significant component in government revenue, both at the national level as well as in those provinces where the tobacco industry is a significant economic activity. A proposal in the Health VII project by Shanghai to raise the tobacco tax was vetoed by the central government. More recently, in response to a call for stronger tobacco control by a member at the March 2007 meeting of the National Committee of the Chinese People's Political Consultative Conference, an official from the China National State Monopoly rebutted the notion, stating that tobacco control will adversely affect the country's stability and, therefore, the pace cannot be too fast.[27]

---

[25] Hu TW and Mao Z, "Effects of Cigarette Tax on Cigarette Consumption and the Chinese Economy". *Tobacco Control* 11, no. 2 (2002): 105–108.

[26] Mackay J, Eriksen M and Shafey O, *The Tobacco Atlas*, 2nd ed. (Atlanta, Georgia: American Cancer Society, 2006).

[27] Anhui News, "Deputy director general of State Tobacco Monopoly Administration: Tobacco Control will affect Social Stability" (in Chinese). http://news.anhuinews.com/system/2007/03/08/001685409.shtml (accessed May 2007).

It remains a huge challenge to persuade government officials to adopt this public policy of increasing the tobacco tax or even to begin a policy debate on this strategy, which worldwide evidence has shown is effective in reducing the demand for cigarettes. The following chapters in this book will look further into the supposed negative economic impact of this policy and will examine the policy itself in further detail.

Chapter

4

Chinese Physicians: Smoking Behavior, and their Smoking Cessation Knowledge, Attitudes, and Practice

Michael Ong, Yuan Jiang, Elisa Tong, Yan Yang, Quan Gan and Teh-wei Hu

INTRODUCTION

China consumes more cigarettes than any other country in the world and is home to 350 million current smokers.[1] Its smoking prevalence rate is 31 percent; 57 percent of men and 3 percent of women smoke.[1] Additionally, 52 percent of nonsmokers in China are exposed to secondhand smoke either at home or at work.[1] Smoking in China has tremendous health consequences, with 514,000 premature deaths

---

[1] Yang GH, Ma JM, Liu N and Zhou LN, "Smoking and Passive Smoking, 2002 (in Chinese)", *Zhonghua Liu Xing Bing Xue Za Zhi* 26, no. 2 (2005): 77–83.

due to smoking-related illnesses in 1998[2] and accounting for over 7 percent of all deaths.[3] These mortality numbers are underestimates because they do not account for secondhand smoke-related deaths.

Physicians can play a key role in smoking cessation.[4–7] Simple interventions, such as advising a smoker to quit, and more intensive interventions, such as counseling or pharmacologic therapy, increase the odds of a smoker quitting.[4,5] Physicians can also serve as role models for healthy behaviors by not smoking. Smoke-free hospitals are important for the health of patients and health care workers and can help with smoking cessation.[8]

Little is known about Chinese physicians' smoking behavior and their smoking cessation attitudes and practices.[9] One study of 500 physicians in the city of Wuhan showed a smoking prevalence of 61 percent for men and 12 percent for women.[10] This study also found

---

[2] Liu BQ, Peto R, Chen ZM et al., "Emerging Tobacco Hazards in China: 1. Retrospective Proportional Mortality Study of One Million Deaths", *BMJ* 317, no. 7170 (1998): 1411–1422.

[3] He J, Gu D, Wu X et al. "Major Causes of Death Among Men and Women in China", *New England Journal of Medicine* 353, no. 11 (2005): 1124–1134.

[4] The Tobacco Use and Dependence Clinical Practice Guideline Panel, Staff, and Consortium Representatives, "A Clinical Practice Guideline for Treating Tobacco Use and Dependence: A US Public Health Service Report", *JAMA* 283, no. 24 (2000): 3244–3254.

[5] Schroeder SA, "What to Do with a Patient Who Smokes", *JAMA* 294, no. 4 (2005): 482–487.

[6] Coleman T, "ABC of Smoking Cessation. Use of Simple Advice and Behavioural Support", *BMJ* 328, no. 7436 (2004): 397–399.

[7] Lancaster T and Stead L, "Physician Advice for Smoking Cessation", *Cochrane Database of Systematic Reviews* no. 4 (2004): CD000165.

[8] Stillman FA, Becker DM, Swank RT et al., "Ending Smoking at the Johns Hopkins Medical Institutions. An Evaluation of Smoking Prevalence and Indoor Air Pollution", *JAMA* 264, no. 12 (1990): 1565–1569.

[9] de Beyer J, Kollars N, Edwards N and Cheung H, *Research on Tobacco in China: An Annotated Bibliography of Research on Tobacco Use, Health Effects, Policies, Farming, and Industry* (Washington, DC: The World Bank, 2004).

[10] Li H, Fish D and Zhou X, "Increase in Cigarette Smoking and Decline of Anti-Smoking Counselling Among Chinese Physicians: 1987–1996", *Health Promotion International* 14, no. 2 (1999): 123–131.

that 58 percent of physicians usually advise smokers to quit, and that 85 percent thought that physicians should be nonsmoking examples and should help smokers quit.[10] A second study of 361 physicians working in a rural teaching hospital in Hebei province demonstrated a smoking prevalence of 31.9 percent for males only. Among all physicians in the study, those aged 50–54 years (31.6 percent) had the highest smoking prevalence.[11]

This chapter is a report on the first geographically diverse survey of physicians from six different cities throughout China regarding their smoking behavior and their smoking cessation knowledge, attitudes, and practices.

POPULATION AND METHODS

Population

The survey was conducted between July 2004 and October 2004 on physicians from six cities: Chengdu, Guangzhou, Haerbin, Lanzhou, Tianjin, and Wuhan (Fig. 1). These cities were selected as representative of different regions throughout China. In each city, hospitals were stratified by catchment size into provincial, city, and district-level hospitals. Non-hospital-based physicians were included by considering two community health centers as the equivalent of one district-level hospital. In each stratification category, five hospitals were randomly selected for survey inclusion. Within each hospital, at least two departments were randomly selected for survey inclusion. All physicians from selected departments were contacted by telephone and asked to participate in the survey. To ensure that the survey sample comprised at least 35 percent men, an additional department was randomly drawn for survey inclusion if the initial departments selected consisted of less than 35 percent men. The initial power calculation determined a necessary sample size estimate of 450 physicians in each city,

---

[11] Smith DR, Wei N, Zhang YJ and Wang RS, "Tobacco Smoking Habits Among a Cross-section of Rural Physicians in China", *Australian Journal of Rural Health* 14, no. 2 (2006): 66–71.

Fig 1: Surveyed Cities

based on an expected 25 percent smoking prevalence and a SD of 4 percent from previous unpublished data on physicians[12] and 95 percent confidence intervals. The sample sizes were increased to 600 physicians in each city to account for nonresponders and missing data. The overall refusal rate for all sites was 6.2 percent. A total of 3,652 physicians completed the survey.

Design and Procedures

The survey was a modified form of the Global Health Professional Survey[13] and was conducted in Chinese. The survey and study were approved by the institutional review boards of the Chinese Center for Disease Control and Prevention and the University of California,

---

[12] Yang G, Fan L, Tan J et al., "Smoking in China: Findings of the 1996 National Prevalence Survey", *JAMA* 282, no. 13 (1999): 1247–1253.

[13] Tobacco Use and Cessation Counseling — Global Health Professionals Survey Pilot Study, 10 Countries, 2005. *MMWR Morb Mortal Wkly Rep* 54, no. 20 (2005): 505–509.

Berkeley. Consenting physicians were surveyed with a combined in-person interview and self-administered questionnaire. The in-person interview asked questions about smoking cessation practices and personal smoking behavior. It was followed by the self-administered questionnaire that asked questions about smoking cessation knowledge, smoking cessation beliefs, and personal characteristics. Consenting physicians were given an option to complete the entire survey via self-administered questionnaire, but none chose this option. Interviews were conducted by Chinese Center for Disease Control and Prevention staff. A quality control team in each city examined 10 percent of the questionnaires every day to ensure consistency across interviewers and among different days.

Respondents were classified as current, former, or never smokers according to World Health Organization classifications.[14] Current smokers were defined as individuals who had smoked at least 6 months during their lifetime and were smoking tobacco products at the time of the survey. Former smokers were defined as individuals who had smoked at least 6 months during their lifetime but no longer currently smoked. Never smokers were defined as those individuals who had never smoked or had smoked less than 6 months during their lifetime. Heavy daily smokers were defined as current daily smokers who smoked on average at least one pack of cigarettes a day.

Statistical Analyses

All statistical analyses were performed using SAS version 9.1 (SAS Institute, Inc.; Cary, NC; 2003) in 2005 and 2006. Chi-square tests and 95 percent confidence intervals were calculated using PROC SURVEYFREQ and PROC SURVEYMEANS with stratification at the city level and clustering at the hospital level. The two-tailed significance level was set at 5 percent ($p < 0.05$). Instances of missing data were

---

[14] WHO, *Guidelines for the Conduct of Tobacco Smoking Surveys for the General Population* (Geneva, Switzerland: World Health Organization, 1983), Document WHO/SMO/83.4.

dealt with by logical imputation. Logical imputations could not be performed for 100 individuals with missing data in the analyzed variables, and further complex imputations were not performed *a priori* for the small group of individuals (< 3 percent sample); these individuals were eliminated from the final analysis, leaving 3,552 physicians in the final sample.

Bivariate and multivariate analyses were conducted for two outcomes: (1) if physicians usually asked about smoking status, and (2) if they usually advised smokers to quit. Variables were selected *a priori* for analysis based on hypothesized relationships with smoking cessation activity and included sociodemographic variables, smoking status, medical training, beliefs regarding smoking cessation, and knowledge of health harm. Analyses were performed using SAS 9.1 for Windows (Cary, NC) (PROC SURVEYLOGISTIC) with stratification at the city level and clustering at the hospital level. Multivariate models were constructed using forward stepwise automated methods and manual entry of variables statistically associated with our outcomes in bivariate analyses. Variables were retained based on their statistical association with the outcome of interest or to retain face validity. The multivariate analysis presented here focuses on two key variables: (1) knowledge about the relationship between ischemic heart disease and passive smoking, and (2) knowledge about the relationship between ischemic heart disease and active smoking. We focus on ischemic heart disease knowledge because it appears to represent more sophisticated knowledge of smoking harm; univariate analyses showed relatively few physicians were aware of its relationship to smoking despite its being a common cause of death in China.[3] Other predictor variables in this multivariate analysis included age, gender, smoking status, specialty, and all belief questions on smoking cessation (Should physicians offer to help smokers quit? Does counseling on the health harm of smoking help with smoking cessation? Does counseling on secondhand smoke health harms help with smoking cessation?). Odds ratios were calculated with 95 percent confidence intervals, and two-tailed $p < 0.05$ was considered statistically significant in all analyses.

RESULTS

Table 1 describes the physician sample. Over half of respondents were male, and subjects were evenly distributed throughout the cities. Over 60 percent of all surveyed physicians were under the age of 40, while less than 3 percent were over the age of 60

Table 1: Characteristics of Participants in the Present Study

	Physicians	
	Men ($n = 1958$)	Women ($n = 1594$)
Number of physicians	55.1	44.9
Age		
<30	30.1	27.0
30–39	31.8	32.5
40–49	20.9	25.4
50–59	13.7	13.1
≥60	3.5	2.0
Regions		
Chengdu	15.9	17.2
Guangzhou	17.2	14.9
Haerbin	13.1	21.1
Lanzhou	19.6	14.2
Tianjin	18.2	15.1
Wuhan	16.0	17.5
Specialties		
Internal medicine	21.8	33.1
Surgery	41.0	7.7
Gynecology	1.6	19.5
Pediatrics	2.5	6.2
Orthodontics	4.8	7.3
Emergency medicine	3.0	2.0
Traditional Chinese medicine	7.1	6.4
Other specialty	18.2	17.8

(state-mandated retirement age). Most physicians were in internal medicine, surgical, or gynecologic specialties.

Smoking Prevalence of Physicians

Table 2 shows that 22.9 percent (95 percent CI 19.3 percent to 26.6 percent) of surveyed physicians were current smokers, and most smoked less than a pack of cigarettes a day. Figure 2 shows smoking status by age. There were few former smokers in the survey (2.7 percent), although prevalence increased generally with age. Current and heavy daily smoking prevalence increased with age except in physicians over the age of 60. Male physicians had a much higher smoking prevalence than female physicians (40.7 percent versus. 1.0 percent, respectively; Table 2).

Table 2: Smoking Prevalence Among Chinese Physicians and General Population

	Physicians, %	General Population, %[12]
Men (n = 1,958)		
Current smokers	40.7	
	(35.5–45.9)	63.0
Heavy smokers	7.0	
	(5.4–8.7)	7.5
Former smokers	4.7	
	(3.7–5.8)	3.9
Never smokers	54.6	
	(48.9–60.2)	33.1
Women (n = 1,594)		
Current smokers	1.0	
	(0.6–1.4)	3.8
Heavy smokers	0.2	
	(< 0.1–0.4)	0.2
Former smokers	0.3	
	(98.1–99.4)	0.4
Never smokers	98.7	
	(< 0.1–0.6)	95.8

95 percent confidence intervals are reported in parentheses.

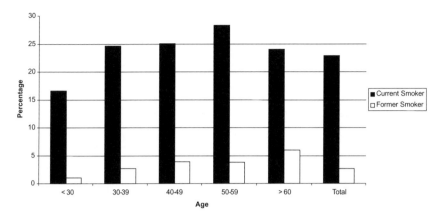

Fig. 2: Breakdown of Surveyed Physicians by Current and Former Smokers by Age

Physician Smoking Behavior, Attitudes, and Practices

Table 3 shows that most physicians believed that physicians should be nonsmoking role models and that hospitals should be completely smoke-free. Current smokers were significantly more likely to disagree with these attitudes than never smokers. More than one third of current smokers had smoked in front of their patients, and nearly all had smoked during their work shift. Less than one third of physicians reported good implementation of a smoke-free policy at their hospital, and current smokers were significantly less likely to report such implementation than never smokers.

Physician Attitudes and Practices Towards Patients Who Smoke

Table 4 shows that only two third of all physicians believed that they should offer to help smokers quit, with no significant difference between the current and the never smokers. Less than one third of all physicians believed smokers would follow their cessation advice. While nearly two thirds of all physicians believed that counseling about the harmful effects of smoking helps with smoking cessation, only half believed that counseling about the health harm to family

Table 3: Chinese Physicians' Attitudes and Practices Regarding Physician Smoking (percentage)

	All (n = 3,552)	Female (n = 1,594)	Male (n = 1,958)	Current Smoker (n = 813)	Former Smoker (n = 97)	Never Smoker (n = 2,642)
Attitudes						
Physicians should set a nonsmoking example*†	86.4 (83.7–89.1)	90.8 (87.8–93.8)	82.9 (80.2–85.6)	75.2 (72.2–78.1)	91.8 (86.7–96.9)	89.7 (86.7–92.7)
Hospitals should be completely smoke-free*†	86.3 (83.5–89.2)	91.5 (89.2–93.7)	82.2 (79.0–85.4)	72.3 (68.3–76.4)	95.9 (92.3–99.5)	90.3 (87.6–93.1)
Practices						
Have smoked in front of patients*	8.5 (6.4–10.7)	0.3 (0.1–0.5)	15.2 (12.2–18.3)	36.9 (32.1–41.7)	3.1 (<0.1–0.7)	0
Have smoked during shift*	21.0 (17.6–24.4)	0.6 (0.2–1.0)	37.6 (32.7–42.5)	90.5 (88.9–92.1)	10.3 (1.5–19.1)	0
Good implementation of smoke-free hospital† policy	29.7 (26.7–32.6)	31.6 (28.3–34.9)	28.1 (24.2–31.9)	25.8 (20.9–30.8)	33.0 (26.5–39.5)	30.7 (27.8–33.6)

*Significant ($p < 0.05$) difference between male and female physicians. †Significant ($p < 0.05$) difference between all three subgroups, and between male current smokers and male never smokers. 95 percent confidence intervals are reported in parentheses.

Table 4: Chinese Physicians' Attitudes and Practices Regarding Patient Smoking Cessation (percentage)

	All (n = 3,552)	Female (n = 1,594)	Male (n = 1,958)	Current Smoker (n = 813)	Former Smoker (n = 97)	Never Smoker (n = 2,642)
Attitudes						
Physicians should offer to help smokers quit*	66.0 (61.5–70.4)	69.4 (64.2–74.5)	63.2 (58.4–68.0)	63.3 (58.5–68.2)	66.0 (53.5–78.4)	66.8 (61.8–71.7)
Most smokers will follow my smoking cessation advice*†	29.3 (26.7–32.0)	33.0 (29.8–36.2)	26.4 (23.7–29.1)	25.0 (19.4–30.5)	22.7 (12.3–33.1)	31.0 (27.9–34.0)
Counseling on health harm from smoking usually helps with smoking cessation†	65.7 (61.7–69.6)	67.3 (61.9–72.6)	64.4 (60.7–68.0)	55.8 (51.5–60.2)	66.0 (54.5–77.4)	68.7 (64.3–73.0)
Counseling on health harm to family members from secondhand smoke usually helps with smoking cessation*†	53.6 (49.4–57.8)	58.2 (52.7–63.6)	49.9 (45.6–54.2)	41.1 (35.6–46.5)	45.4 (29.3–61.4)	57.8 (53.8–61.8)

(Continued)

Table 4: *(Continued)*

	All (n = 3,552)	Female (n = 1,594)	Male (n = 1,958)	Current Smoker (n = 813)	Former Smoker (n = 97)	Never Smoker (n = 2,642)
Practices						
Usually ask patients if they smoke[†]	47.8 (41.2–54.3)	45.9 (39.1–52.8)	49.2 (42.4–56.1)	44.3 (37.0–51.5)	43.3 (32.9–53.7)	49.0 (42.3–55.6)
Usually advise smokers to quit[†]	64.4 (60.7–68.0)	66.5 (61.3–71.7)	62.6 (58.8–66.4)	53.1 (47.5–58.7)	67.0 (54.6–79.4)	67.7 (63.3–72.1)
Usually provide positive encouragement when advising smokers to quit[*†]	41.4 (37.9–44.9)	45.7 (40.9–50.6)	37.9 (34.3–41.5)	30.5 (25.2–35.8)	47.4 (31.9–62.9)	44.5 (41.1–48.0)
Usually set a quit date when advising smokers to quit[†]	6.1 (4.8–7.3)	6.2 (4.8–7.6)	5.9 (4.3–7.6)	4.6 (2.9–6.2)	6.2 (1.3–11.0)	6.5 (5.2–7.8)
Have used Chinese herbs or acupuncture when helping smokers quit[†]	16.4 (13.9–19.0)	16.3 (13.6–19.0)	16.5 (12.7–20.4)	12.5 (9.1–16.0)	16.5 (7.4–25.6)	17.6 (15.2–20.0)
Have used nicotine replacement therapy when helping smokers quit	6.6 (4.3–9.0)	6.5 (4.1–8.8)	6.8 (3.9–9.7)	5.9 (2.7–9.1)	13.4 (0.6–26.2)	6.6 (4.3–8.9)
Have used bupropion when helping smokers quit	4.5 (3.2–5.8)	3.8 (2.4–5.2)	5.1 (3.1–7.1)	4.9 (2.6–7.2)	5.2 (0.0–10.3)	4.4 (3.1–5.7)

*Significant ($p < 0.05$) difference between male and female physicians. [†]Significant ($p < 0.05$) difference between all three subgroups, and between male current smokers and male never smokers. 95 percent confidence intervals are reported in parentheses.

members from secondhand smoke would help. Never smokers were significantly more likely than current smokers to hold these three beliefs.

Less than half of all physicians usually asked their patients if they smoke (Table 4). However, two thirds of all physicians reported that they usually advise smokers to quit. Less than half usually provided positive encouragement when advising smokers to quit. Few set quit dates or used pharmacotherapy (i.e., nicotine replacement therapy or bupropion) when helping smokers to quit. Chinese herbs and acupuncture were used more frequently than pharmacotherapy, but their overall use was still low (16 percent). Never smokers were more likely than current smokers to ask about smoking status, advise smokers to quit, provide positive encouragement, set quit dates, or use Chinese herbs or acupuncture to assist with quitting.

Physician Smoking Knowledge

Nearly all (95 percent) physicians believed active smoking causes lung cancer as shown in Table 5. Most physicians also believed that passive smoking causes lung cancer (89 percent), asthma in adults (84 percent), and in children (82 percent), and that active smoking causes chronic obstructive pulmonary disease (89 percent). Current smokers were significantly less likely ($p < 0.05$) to hold these smoking knowledge beliefs compared to never smokers.

In contrast, only two thirds (67 percent) of physicians believed that active smoking causes ischemic heart disease. Even fewer (53 percent) believed that passive smoking causes ischemic heart disease. Only one-fifth (21 percent) of physicians believed that passive smoking causes sudden infant death syndrome. Current and never smokers did not differ significantly ($p < 0.05$) on these smoking knowledge beliefs.

Gender Differences

Tables 3–5 also show that as with smoking prevalence, significant gender differences exist on smoking behavior, knowledge, attitudes, and practices. Female physicians were significantly less likely than

Table 5: Chinese Physicians' Knowledge of Harm (percentage)

	All (n = 3,552)	Female (n = 1,594)	Male (n = 1,958)	Current Smoker (n = 813)	Former Smoker (n = 97)	Never Smoker (n = 2,642)
Active smoking and lung cancer[†]	95.3 (94.2–96.4)	96.1 (94.8–97.6)	94.6 (93.1–96.1)	92.6 (90.6–94.6)	97.9 (95.4–1.00)	96.1 (95.1–97.0)
Passive smoking and lung cancer*[†]	89.4 (87.2–91.7)	91.2 (88.7–93.9)	87.9 (85.6–90.2)	83.8 (80.1–87.4)	92.8 (86.8–98.8)	91.0 (88.7–93.3)
Active smoking in chronic obstructive pulmonary disease[†]	88.7 (86.3–91.0)	89.5 (86.3–92.5)	88.0 (85.7–90.3)	85.6 (82.0–89.2)	92.8 (87.8–97.7)	89.4 (87.1–91.7)
Passive smoking and asthma in adults*[†]	83.5 (80.4–86.6)	85.8 (82.8–88.8)	81.6 (78.0–85.3)	79.1 (73.8–84.4)	90.7 (82.5–98.9)	84.6 (82.0–87.1)
Passive smoking and asthma in children*[†]	81.6 (78.6–84.6)	85.8 (82.4–89.1)	78.2 (75.1–81.3)	75.3 (71.3–79.2)	85.6 (76.1–95.1)	83.4 (80.2–86.6)
Active smoking and ischemic heart disease*	66.8 (62.5–71.0)	64.6 (60.9–68.4)	68.5 (63.6–73.4)	67.3 (61.2–73.4)	76.3 (65.9–86.7)	66.2 (62.1–70.4)
Passive smoking and ischemic heart disease*	52.6 (48.4–56.9)	49.6 (45.0–54.2)	55.1 (50.6–59.5)	53.8 (47.2–60.3)	63.9 (51.4–76.4)	51.9 (47.5–56.2)
Passive smoking and sudden infant death syndrome	20.7 (18.6–22.9)	21.0 (18.6–23.4)	20.5 (17.6–23.3)	19.1 (13.0–25.1)	18.6 (9.1–28.0)	21.3 (19.6–23.0)

*Significant ($p < 0.05$) difference between male and female physicians. [†]Significant ($p < 0.05$) difference between all three subgroups, and between male current smokers and male never smokers. 95 percent confidence intervals are reported in parentheses.

male physicians to smoke in front of patients or during a shift. Female physicians also were significantly more likely than male physicians to agree with all smoking attitude questions, except for the belief that counseling on the health harm of smoking helps with smoking cessation. The only significant gender difference regarding smoking cessation practices was that female physicians were more likely to provide positive reinforcement when advising smokers to quit. Female physicians were significantly more likely than male physicians to know that passive smoking causes lung diseases, such as lung cancer, childhood asthma, and adult asthma. However, female physicians were significantly less likely than male physicians to know that smoking, either passive or active, causes heart disease.

Among never smokers, gender differences were fewer. Female physicians were significantly more likely than males to believe that physicians should be nonsmoking models, that hospitals should be smoke-free, that physicians should help smokers quit, and that smokers would usually follow their smoking advice. However, male never smoking physicians were significantly more likely than their female counterparts to ask about smoking status.

Predictors of Asking About Smoking Status or Advising Smokers to Quit

Multivariate analyses showed that physicians were more likely to ask about smoking status or advise smokers to quit if they held beliefs that most smokers would follow their smoking cessation advice, and that counseling on the health harm of direct or passive smoking usually helps with smoking cessation (Table 6). In addition, internal medicine physicians were more likely than surgeons and other specialists to advise smokers to quit.

Other significant predictors of asking about smoking status included being younger than 30 years of age, knowledge of the relationship between passive smoking and ischemic heart disease, and believing physicians should offer to help smokers quit. In addition, current smokers were significantly less likely than never smokers to advise smokers to quit.

Table 6: Predictors of Asking About Smoking Status and Advising Smokers to Quit

Characteristic	Usually Asks if a Patient Smokes		Usually Advises Smokers to Quit	
	Bivariate	Multivariate	Bivariate	Multivariate
Attitudes				
(Always or usually compared to sometimes, usually not, or never)				
Physicians should offer to help smokers quit*	1.31 (1.12–1.53)	1.17 (1.01–1.35)	1.53 (1.24–1.89)	1.21 (0.92–1.60)
Most smokers will follow my smoking cessation advice*†	2.25 (1.98–2.53)	1.58 (1.41–1.78)	3.85 (2.94–5.04)	2.05 (1.68–2.50)
Counseling on direct health harm from smoking usually helps with smoking cessation*†	6.46 (5.30–7.89)	4.35 (3.49–5.42)	19.36 (14.61–25.65)	9.89 (7.43–13.17)
Counseling on passive smoking health harm usually helps with smoking cessation*†	3.40 (2.75–4.20)	1.30 (1.04–1.64)	8.87 (6.84–11.51)	2.00 (1.59–2.51)
Knowledge				
(Definite relationship compared to possible or no relationship)				

(Continued)

Table 6: *(Continued)*

Characteristic	Usually Asks if a Patient Smokes Bivariate	Usually Asks if a Patient Smokes Multivariate	Usually Advises Smokers to Quit Bivariate	Usually Advises Smokers to Quit Multivariate
Active smoking and ischemic heart disease	1.75 (1.49–2.07)	1.12 (0.92–1.35)	1.62 (1.40–1.89)	1.04 (0.96–1.13)
Passive smoking and ischemic heart disease*	1.84 (1.44–2.35)	1.36 (1.03–1.79)	1.58 (1.31–1.89)	1.06 (0.89–1.26)
Age (compared to less than 30)				
30–39*	0.62 (0.51–0.74)	0.63 (0.53–0.74)	0.81 (0.67–0.97)	0.94 (0.81–1.09)
40–49*	0.42 (0.36–0.50)	0.44 (0.37–0.53)	0.67 (0.56–0.81)	0.82 (0.63–1.06)
50–59*	0.44 (0.37–0.53)	0.42 (0.35–0.51)	0.68 (0.54–0.85)	0.73 (0.52–1.01)
60+*	0.43 (0.26–0.73)	0.41 (0.23–0.72)	0.86 (0.56–1.32)	1.14 (0.71–1.84)

(Continued)

Table 6: *(Continued)*

Characteristic	Usually Asks if a Patient Smokes		Usually Advises Smokers to Quit	
	Bivariate	Multivariate	Bivariate	Multivariate
Smoking status (compared to never smoker)				
Current smoker[†]	0.83	0.98	0.54	0.66
	(0.72–0.95)	(0.85–1.14)	(0.42–0.71)	(0.45–0.96)
Former smoker	0.80	0.88	0.97	1.19
	(0.53–1.20)	(0.55–1.41)	(0.54–1.75)	(0.59–2.40)
Male gender (compared to female)	1.14	1.09	0.84	1.02
	(0.96–1.36)	(0.90–1.32)	(0.69–1.03)	(0.81–1.29)
Physician specialty (compared to internal medicine)				
Surgery[†]	0.65	0.86	0.47	0.68
	(0.50–0.85)	(0.67–1.10)	(0.34–0.64)	(0.49–0.93)
Other*[†]	0.29	0.38	0.34	0.45
	(0.22–0.38)	(0.28–0.50)	(0.27–0.42)	(0.35–0.59)

Reported values are odds ratios and 95 percent confidence intervals are reported in parentheses. Knowledge questions compare definite relationship to possible or no relationship. *$p < 0.05$ for multivariate analysis of asking patients about smoking status.
[†]$p < 0.05$ for multivariate analysis of advising smokers to quit.

DISCUSSION

This is the first geographically diverse survey of Chinese physicians' smoking behavior and their smoking cessation attitudes and practices. Smoking prevalence is high with few former smokers among male physicians, in contrast to the low smoking prevalence among female physicians. This pattern is reflective of China's general population, although overall prevalence among physicians is lower. Table 7 compares Chinese physicians to counterparts in the US, UK, and Japan. Chinese physicians have a substantially higher smoking prevalence than physicians in the US (3.3 percent)[15] or UK (6.8 percent),[16] although these countries also have lower general population smoking prevalence (US, 20.9 percent[17]; UK, 20.9 percent[18]). Japan's smoking prevalence rate (33.8 percent)[19] is similar to China's.

Table 7: Current Smoking Rates Among Physicians and General Population by Country and Year of Survey

Country	Physicians (percentage)	Population (percentage)
China	22.9 (2004)*	34.1 (1996)[1]
Japan	20.2 (2000)[19]	33.8 (2000)[19]
United Kingdom	6.8 (2000)[16]	26.0 (2002)[18]
United States	3.3 (1991)[15]	20.9 (2005)[17]

* Results from present study.

---

[15] Nelson DE, Giovino GA, Emont SL et al., "Trends in Cigarette Smoking Among US Physicians and Nurses", *JAMA* 271, no. 16 (1994): 1273–1275.

[16] WHO, WHO Health Professionals and Tobacco Control. A Briefing File for the WHO European Region, www.euro.who.int/document/Tob/TOB_Factsheet.pdf. (accessed January 2, 2007).

[17] Tobacco Use Among Adults — United States, 2005, *Morbility and Mortality Weekly Report* 55, no. 42 (2006): 1145–1148.

[18] WHO, European Health for All Database, June, http://data.euro.who.int/hfadb (accessed September 12, 2005).

[19] Ohida T, Sakurai H, Mochizuki Y et al., "Smoking Prevalence and Attitudes Toward Smoking Among Japanese Physicians", *JAMA* 285, no. 20 (2001): 2643–2648.

Chinese physicians have a slightly higher smoking prevalence than Japanese physicians (20.2 percent), but Japanese physicians have a smaller gender discrepancy in smoking prevalence (27 percent males and 7 percent females)[19] than their Chinese counterparts. A recent survey of Hong Kong physicians found that only 4.3 percent smoke, although the response rate was low (19 percent).[20] However, this low smoking prevalence is not surprising given the historically close ties between the Hong Kong and the UK medical training systems.[21] Male Chinese physicians' smoking prevalence is similar to those of US and UK physicians prior to the first Surgeon General's report detailing the health consequences of smoking.[22–24] In both the US and UK, where smoking prevalence has greatly declined in the general population, physicians have taken the lead in substantially reducing their cigarette consumption.[23,24] This decline underscores the need for targeted efforts aimed at smoking cessation among Chinese physicians since physicians can act as role models for healthy behavior and can guide smokers through the various stages[25,26] of the smoking cessation process.

---

[20] Abdullah AS, Rahman AS, Suen CW *et al.*, "Investigation of Hong Kong Doctors' Current Knowledge, Beliefs, Attitudes, Confidence and Practices: Implications for the Treatment of Tobacco Dependency", *Journal of the Chinese Medical Association* 69, no. 10 (2006): 461–471.

[21] What Medical Future for Hong Kong? *Lancet* 344, no. 8931 (1994): 1169–1170.

[22] Garfinkel L, "Cigarette Smoking Among Physicians and Other Health Professionals, 1959–1972", CA-A *Cancer Journal for Clinicians* 26, no. 6 (1976): 373–375.

[23] Pierce J and Gilpin E, Trends in physicians' smoking behavior and patterns of advice to quit. *Tobacco and The Clinician: Interventions for Medical and Dental Practice*. Vol 94-3693 (Bethesda, MD: National Institutes of Health, 1994).

[24] Doll R and Peto R, "Mortality in Relation to Smoking: 20 Years' Observations on Male British Doctors", *BMJ* 2, no. 6051 (1976): 1525–1536.

[25] Prochaska JO and DiClemente CC, "Stages and Processes of Self-Change of Smoking: Toward an Integrative Model of Change", *Journal of Consulting and Clinical Psychology* 51, no. 3 (1983): 390–395.

[26] Prochaska JO, DiClemente CC and Norcross JC, "In Search of How People Change. Applications to Addictive Behaviors", *American Psychologist* 47, no. 9 (1992): 1102–1114.

Reducing smoking prevalence among Chinese physicians is an important tobacco control measure since physicians who currently smoke are significantly less likely to advise smokers to quit. Such a reduction requires both uptake prevention and cessation among physicians. Because physicians under the age of 30 have a lower smoking prevalence, smoke fewer cigarettes than their older colleagues, and ask patients about smoking status more frequently, there is hope that smoking prevalence may decline and smoking cessation practices may improve in the future. Maintenance of the low smoking rate among Chinese female physicians will be critical in reducing overall physician and general population smoking rates. Increased smoking behavior by Chinese female physicians could encourage similar behavior among Chinese women in general; a 1 percent increase in smoking prevalence by Chinese women would result in over 6 million additional smokers. In addition, our findings suggest that physicians who are never smokers are more likely than current smokers to advise their patients to quit smoking.

Smoke-free hospitals protect the health of patients and nonsmoking health care workers from secondhand smoke. While Chinese physicians generally agree that they should serve as nonsmoking role models and that hospitals should be smoke-free, their actions are less reflective of their beliefs. Behaviors such as smoking in front of patients or during a work shift were more common than expected. Chinese hospitals are already nominally smoke-free, but our findings suggest that enforcement is lax and requires improvement. Strengthening smoke-free hospital policy implementation could help reduce smoking[8,27] while protecting the health of patients and nonsmoking health care workers from secondhand smoke.

Physician education is important, particularly on counseling smokers about the harm of active and passive smoking, as physicians who believe such counseling is effective are significantly more likely to ask about smoking status and to advise smokers to quit. Physicians also need more education on the ischemic heart disease

---

[27] Fichtenberg CM and Glantz SA, "Effect of Smoke-Free Workplaces on Smoking Behaviour: Systematic Review", *BMJ* 325, no. 7357 (2002): 188.

risks of active and passive smoking, as heart disease is the leading cause of death in China.[3] While both male and female physicians need more education on ischemic heart disease risks, female physicians seem less aware of these risks and should be particularly targeted. In addition, knowledge about ischemic heart disease risks from passive smoking is associated with an increased likelihood of a physician usually asking about smoking status. Furthermore, physician education about sudden infant death syndrome risks from passive smoking may be useful in a society that has a "one-child" policy. Current medical school curriculum has been shown to alter smoking behavior in young adults.[28] Incorporating and adapting smoking cessation best practices[4] into the medical school curriculum may help educate and prevent new physician smokers. Such curricula are critical for surgeons and other non-internists, as their rates of asking and advising smokers to quit are much lower than internists.

The high self-report rate of Chinese physicians advising smokers to quit is offset by lower responses of asking about smoking status and providing substantive assistance. In contrast, physicians in the US ask about smoking status at two thirds of all visits, but only recommend quitting at 20 percent of visits (although they report higher rates).[29] Hong Kong physicians are more like US physicians: 77 percent report usually asking about smoking status, and 29 percent report usually advising smokers to quit.[20] The low rate of asking about smoking status suggests that many smokers are unidentified and thus cannot be advised to quit. Chinese physicians need more education about offering assistance to smoking patients. Standard smoking cessation practices, such as setting quit dates or using pharmacotherapy like NRT and bupropion,[4] are rarely used. Even if these strategies were culturally inappropriate or unsuitable for the Chinese

---

[28] Zhu T, Feng B, Wong S, Choi W and Zhu SH, "A Comparison of Smoking Behaviors Among Medical and Other College Students in China", *Health Promotion International* 19, no. 2 (2004): 189–196.

[29] Thorndike AN, Rigotti NA, Stafford RS and Singer DE, "National Patterns in the Treatment of Smokers by Physicians", *JAMA* 279, no. 8 (1998): 604–608.

context (e.g., low availability of pharmacotherapy),[30] use of Chinese herbal preparations or acupuncture[31] for smoking cessation assistance is also low. Similarly, Hong Kong physicians rarely use pharmacotherapy (7 percent).[20] Educating physicians about effective advising techniques is critical, particularly since physicians who believe their patients who smoke will follow their smoking cessation advice are more likely to ask about smoking status and advise smokers to quit.

Developing a comprehensive approach to smoking cessation in China's medical care system is important. Nurses and psychologists can also provide effective smoking cessation interventions.[32] A comparison of our findings with a recent study of Chinese nurses shows that Chinese nurses ask about smoking status (26.3 percent) and advise smokers to quit (53.6 percent) less frequently than physicians.[33] Nurse education on smoking cessation is also limited;[34,35] a concerted approach towards improving smoking cessation education for both physicians and nurses would be beneficial. In addition, counseling resources can be pooled using telephone-based smoking cessation quitlines.[5,36]

---

[30] Fitzpatrick L, Can Asia Kick the Habit? *Time Asia* (2005).

[31] White AR, Rampes H and Campbell JL, "Acupuncture and Related Interventions for Smoking Cessation", *Cochrane Database of Systematic Reviews* no. 1 (2006): CD000009.

[32] Mojica WA, Suttorp MJ, Sherman SE *et al.*, "Smoking-Cessation Interventions by Type of Provider: A Meta-Analysis", *American Journal of Preventive Medicine* 26, no. 5 (2004): 391–401.

[33] Chan SS, Sarna L, Wong DC and Lam TH, "Nurses' Tobacco-Related Knowledge, Attitudes, and Practice in Four Major Cities in China", *Journal of Nursing Scholarship, First Quarter* 39, no. 1 (2007): 46–53.

[34] Chan SS, Sarna L and Danao LL, "Are Nurses Prepared to Curb the Tobacco Epidemic in China? A Questionnaire Survey of Schools of Nursing", *International Journal of Nursing Studies* (2007).

[35] Sarna L, Danao LL, Chan SS *et al.*, "Tobacco Control Curricula Content in Baccalaureate Nursing Programs in Four Asian Nations", *Nursing Outlook* 54, no. 6 (2006): 334–344.

[36] Zhu SH, Anderson CM, Tedeschi GJ *et al.*, "Evidence of Real-World Effectiveness of a Telephone Quitline for Smokers", *New England Journal of Medicine* 347, no. 14 (2002): 1087–1093.

This study did not survey physicians in rural areas, where 60 percent of the population resides. Rural smoking rates are lower in part due to income differences[37,38] but may be underestimated due to unmeasured nondaily smoking behavior. Improvements in the Chinese economy may increase rural smoking rates. This study relied on self-reported smoking behavior, which may underestimate smoking compared to cotinine measurements[39] and may overestimate smoking cessation practices.[29] This study had few elderly smokers, in part because the mandatory retirement age for physicians in China is 60.

China is a key battleground in the fight against the global tobacco epidemic. Educating and engaging Chinese physicians is a necessary first step to reduce the burden of tobacco in China. This effort may be supported by China's ratification of the World Health Organization's Framework Convention on Tobacco Control,[40] which recommends cigarette tax increases,[41,42] enforcement of smoke-free environments, advertising restrictions and countermarketing, and provision of cessation aids.[5,43,44] As a result of this survey, the China Centers for Disease Control has begun a nationwide nonsmoking campaign for physicians and medical students, and a smoke-free

---

[37] Hu TW and Tsai YW, "Cigarette Consumption in Rural China: Survey Results from 3 Provinces", *American Journal of Public Health* 90, no. 11 (2000): 1785–1787.

[38] Wu J, Wen W, Yuan H, and Deng Z, "Survey of Smoking and Human Health in Guangdong Province", *Wei Sheng Yan Jiu* 26, no. 3 (1997): 192–195.

[39] Perez-Stable EJ, Benowitz NL, and Marin G, "Is Serum Cotinine a Better Measure of Cigarette Smoking than Self-Report?," *Preventive Medicine* 24, no. 2 (1995): 171–179.

[40] Roemer R, Taylor A, and Lariviere J, "Origins of the WHO Framework Convention on Tobacco Control", *American Journal of Public Health* 95, no. 6 (2005): 936–938.

[41] Hu TW, "Cigarette Taxation in China: Lessons From International Experiences", *Tobacco Control* 6, no. 2 (1997): 136–140.

[42] Hu TW and Mao Z, "Effects of Cigarette Tax on Cigarette Consumption and the Chinese Economy", *Tobacco Control* 11, no. 2 (2002): 105–108.

[43] *Tobacco Control in Developing Countries* (New York: Oxford University Press 2000).

[44] Schroeder SA, "Tobacco Control in the Wake of the 1998 Master Settlement Agreement", *New England Journal of Medicine* 350, no. 3 (2004): 293–301.

hospital campaign; however, this is only a first step. Further interventions can target physician smokers, monitor smoke-free hospitals, and educate about effective smoking cessation practices. Experiences from countries where physicians smoke less and more effectively carry out smoking cessation practices need to be shared with Chinese physicians.

ACKNOWLEDGMENT

This study was supported by a grant from the United States National Institutes of Health Fogarty International Center (Grant No. R01 TW05938-01).

Chapter 5

Disease Burden from Smoking and Passive Smoking in China

Quan Gan, Kirk R. Smith, S. Katharine Hammond and Teh-wei Hu

BACKGROUND

China is the largest producer and consumer of cigarettes in the world. According to the 1984 and the 1996 national smoking surveys, more than 70 percent of men above age 30 were smokers[1-3] (Table 1), and the total smoking population exceeds 350 million. As a result, China's health burden from tobacco smoking is the greatest among all countries.

The number of passive tobacco smokers in China is more than the number of active smokers. According to the 1996 national smoking

---

[1] CAPM, *1996 National Prevalence Survey of Smoking Pattern*: Chinese Academy of Preventive Medicine, 1997: 403.
[2] Weng XZ, Hong ZG and Chen DY, "Smoking Prevalence in Chinese Aged 15 and Above". *Chinese Medical Journal* 100, no.11 (1987): 886–892.
[3] Yang G, Fan L, Tan J, Qi G, Zhang Y and Samet JM, "Smoking in China: Findings of the 1996 National Prevalence Survey. *Journal of the American Medical Asociation* 282, no. 13 (1999): 1247–1253.

Table 1: Age and Gender-Specific Active Smoking and Passive Smoking Rates in China Based on Results from Two National Smoking Surveys

		Male					Female			
		30–44 (Percent)	45–59 (Percent)	60–69 (Percent)	70+ (Percent)	Total (Percent)	30–44 (Percent)	45–59 (Percent)	60–69 (Percent)	70+ (Percent)	Total (Percent)
Smoking rate	1984[a]	74.1	75.4	71.2	59.7	73.4	5.5	15.6	18.9	16.6	11.2
	1996[b]	73.4	72.6	68.6	61.4	71.6	2.4	6.7	12.7	6.6	5.4
Passive smoking rate	1996[c]	45.6	45.3	37.2	34.3	43.4	61.8	56.0	44.3	49.4	56.8

[a] Smoking rates in 1984[2]; [b] Smoking rates in 1996[1]; [c] Passive smoking rates in 1996[1].

survey, 53.5 percent of all nonsmokers above age 30 reported exposure to secondhand tobacco smoke (SHS) for more than 15 minutes a day for at least one day per week[1,3] (Table 1) as did 49 percent of teenage nonsmokers between ages 15 and 19 (49.4 percent among teenage males and 48.5 percent among teenage females). The total number of passive smokers is as many as 400 million. Despite the high exposure rate, the public's awareness of the harmful effects of smoking is very low, suggesting a need for a much greater health education effort. According to the 1996 national smoking survey[1] (Table 2), over two-thirds of smokers (69 percent) thought smoking did little or no harm to health, compared to 55 percent of nonsmokers, while two-thirds (67.2 percent) of smokers thought passive smoking caused little or no harm compared to 57.1 percent of nonsmokers. Only 40 percent of the respondents knew smoking could cause lung cancer, and only about 4 percent knew smoking could cause heart disease. Respondents were not asked whether lung cancer and heart disease could be caused by passive smoking; had these questions been asked, one might have expected even lower percentages of correct answers.

To illustrate the magnitude of tobacco-related health costs to the Chinese population, this chapter discusses the disease burden attributable to active and passive tobacco smoking in China around the year 2000, based on the best available evidence. Several studies have documented the disease burden caused by active smoking in China.[4-6] Findings from these studies were used in this chapter to estimate the burden caused by active smoking. While no prior study examined the disease burden from passive smoking in China, the results from the authors' recent study on this topic are presented in this chapter. The disease burden caused by passive smoking was

---

[4] Liu BQ, Peto R, Chen ZM, Boreham J, Wu YP and Li JY, "Emerging tobacco hazards in China: 1. Retrospective proportional mortality study of one million deaths", *British Medical Journal* 317, no. 7170 (1998): 1411–1422.

[5] Ezzati M and Lopez AD, "Regional, disease specific patterns of smoking-attributable mortality in 2000", *Tobacco Control* 13, no. 4 (2004): 388–395.

[6] WHO, *The World Health Report*, (Geneva: The World Health Organization, 2002).

Table 2: Awareness of the Harm Caused by Smoking and Passive Smoking in China

	Smoking Does Harm to One's Health				Passive Smoking Does Harm to One's Health				Smoking Can Cause		
	Serious Harm (Percent)	Little Harm (Percent)	No Harm (percent)	Do not Know (percent)	Serious Harm (Percent)	Little Harm (Percent)	No Harm (Percent)	Do not Know (Percent)	Lung Cancer (Percent)	Heart Disease (Percent)
Smokers	23.3	61.1	7.5	8.1	17.6	56.4	10.8	15.3	36.0	3.8
Nonsmokers	36.6	52.6	2.0	9.1	28.8	52.7	4.4	14.7	42.1	4.2

Based on results from the 1996 National Prevalence Survey of Smoking Pattern.[1]

estimated for just two major diseases — lung cancer and ischemic heart disease (IHD) — although a number of other diseases have also been found in studies in other countries.

The Disease Burden Approach

The disease burden is estimated in terms of both premature mortality and Disability-Adjusted Life Years (DALYs). Mortality reflects the number of premature deaths caused by a specific risk factor, while DALYs is a health gap measure (Health Adjusted Life Years — HALYs) that extends the idea of potential years of life lost due to premature death, to also include equivalent years of "healthy" life lost to illness or injury (together termed "disability").[7-9] DALYs is the sum of two measures: the years of life lost from mortality (YLLs), and the years of life lost from living with disability (YLDs):

$$DALYs = YLLs + YLDs, \qquad (1)$$

where YLLs is the number of years of life lost from death due to a specific disease, while YLDs is the number of years living with a disease, adjusted by a factor that accounts for the severity of the disease.

DISEASE BURDEN CAUSED BY ACTIVE SMOKING IN CHINA

In this chapter, active smoking attributable mortality for each disease in 2000 was estimated by applying the proportion of the total active smoking attributable mortality for each disease[4] to the projected

---

[7] Murray CJ and Lopez AD, *The Global Burden of Disease: A Comprehensive Assessment of Mortality and Disability from Diseases, Injuries, and the Risk Factors in 1990 and Projected to 2020*, (Geneva, Switzerland: World Health Organization, 1996).
[8] Gold MR, Stevenson D and Fryback DG, "HALYS and QALYS and DALYS, Oh My: Similarities and Differences in Summary Measures of Population Health", *Annual Review Public Health* 23 (2002): 115–34. Epub October 25, 2001.
[9] Steenland K and Armstrong B, "An Overview of Methods for Calculating the Burden of Disease Due to Specific Risk Factors", *Epidemiology* 17, no. 5 (2006): 512–519.

total active smoking attributable mortality in 2000 by Liu *et al*.[4] The disease burden (DALYs) for each disease was estimated similarly by applying the total active smoking attributable mortality for each disease[4] to the estimated total active smoking attributable DALYs in 2000 by WHO.[6] We also updated the lung cancer and IHD burden estimates based on the results from our recent study.[10]

Many studies have documented the risk of lung cancer from active smoking in China.[4,11–16] In a meta-analysis Yu and Zhao[16] found an odds ratio (OR) of 3.01 (95 percent CI: 2.64–3.46) for smoking men and 2.32 (95 percent CI: 2.02–2.66) for smoking women compared to nonsmokers. Liu *et al*.,[4] in a large proportional mortality study, reported similar findings [RR = 2.72 (95 percent CI: 2.62–2.82) for men and 2.64 (95 percent CI: 2.48–2.80) for women]. The lung cancer risks in China are lower compared to what is known in western countries, where the RR of lung cancer from smoking is as high as 10–15. The much lower risk observed in China is likely due to two reasons. First, on average smokers smoked 13 cigarettes per day in 1984 and 15 per day in 1996 in China, much lower than the consumption level in countries with more mature smoking patterns

---

[10] Gan Q, Smith KR, Hammond S and Hu TW. Disease Burden of Adult Lung Cancer and Ischemic Heart Disease from Passive Tobacco Smoking in China. (submitted, 2007).

[11] Fu WZ and Luo DY. "A Case-control Study of 103 Lung Cancer Patients in Chengdu (in Chinese)", *Journal of the Environment and Health* 1, no. 3 (1984): 11–13.

[12] Chen BY and Chen PP. "The Environmental Epidemiological Analysis of the Risk Factors of Lung Cancer (in Chinese)". *Journal of the Environment and Health* 10, no. 3 (1993): 130–131.

[13] Cui L, Yuan JC, Yang Y, Qin XB and Gu GM, "A Case-Control Study of Lung Cancer Risk Factors among Males in Jiangyan (in Chinese)", *Henan Journal of Tumors* 14, no. 4 (2001): 251–253.

[14] Dai Q, Ji BT, Xu M and Gao YT, "An Analysis of the Attributable Risks of Smoking on Cancers in Shanghai (in Chinese)", *Tumor* 14, no. 4 (1994): 208–211.

[15] Deng J, Gao YT, Wang ZX, Liao ML, Zhao JJ and Ruan ZX, "The Relationship between Smoking, Air Pollution and Lung Cancer — A Prospective Study of 210,000 Adults in Shanghai (in Chinese)", *Tumor* 12, no. 6 (1992): 258–260.

[16] Yu SZ and Zhao N, "Combined Analysis of Case-Control Studies of Smoking and Lung Cancer in China", *Lung Cancer* 14, Suppl. 1 (1996): S161–170.

(e.g. the daily consumption rate for smokers was around 30 in the US in 1970). Second, elevated lung cancer risks from burning coal and biomass fuel have been documented by many studies.[17,18] Since coal and biomass have been commonly used as sources of heating and cooking fuel in the latter half of the last century in China, this increased background lung cancer rate among nonsmokers could lead to lower relative risk of lung cancer from smoking. Lung cancer accounted for 14 percent and 9 percent of active smoking-attributable mortality among men and women, respectively, resulting in 115,000 male deaths and 15,000 female deaths in China in 2000 (Table 3). Besides lung cancer, many other types of cancer have also been linked to smoking in China, including esophageal cancer, stomach cancer and liver cancer. Overall, all cancers caused 36 percent of the smoking attributable mortality among males and 15 percent among females.

The two main respiratory diseases caused by active smoking are Chronic obstructive pulmonary diseases (COPD) and tuberculosis (TB). The relative risk for smokers to develop COPD (1.4–1.7) is lower than the risk for lung cancer; however, among all smoking-related diseases, COPD claimed the most deaths due to the high prevalence rate in the entire population. COPD accounted for 363,000 deaths in 2000 (Table 3), approximately 39 percent of all smoking-caused mortality. Another important smoking-related disease is TB.[4-19] an estimated 40,000 deaths from TB in 2000 were attributable to active smoking (Table 3).

The third category of diseases caused by active smoking is cardiovascular diseases, which mainly include stroke and IHD. The mortality caused by IHD and stroke together in China is as high as 230,000, only

---

[17] Luo RX, Wu B, Yi YN, Huang ZW and Lin RT, "Indoor Burning Coal Air Pollution and Lung Cancer — A Case-Control Study in Fuzhou, China", *Lung Cancer* 14, Suppl. 1 (1996): S113–119.

[18] Lan Q and He X, "Molecular Epidemiological Studies on the Relationship between Indoor Coal Burning and Lung Cancer in Xuan Wei, China", *Toxicology* 198, no. 1–3 (2004): 301–5.

[19] Bates MN, Khalakdina A, Pai M, Chang L, Lessa F and Smith KR, "Risk of Tuberculosis From Exposure to Tobacco Smoke: A Systematic Review and Meta-analysis", *Archives Internal Medicine* 167, no. 4 (2007): 335–342.

Table 3: Active Smoking Attributable Mortality and DALYs in China in 2000

Disease Type	Attributable Mortality (in thousands)			Attributable DALYs (in thousands)		
	Male	Female	Total	Male	Female	Total
Neoplastic	271	26	297	3,487	252	3,739
Lung	115	15	130	1,054	107	1,161
Esophagus	41	3	44	549	32	581
Stomach	42	3	45	711	39	750
Liver	53	3	56	906	40	946
Five minor sites	20	3	23	267	34	301
Chronic obstructive pulmonary disease, etc.	273	90	363	1,644	577	2,221
Pulmonary tuberculosis	34	5	40	600	91	691
Stroke	60	0	60	1,215	0	1,215
Ischemic heart disease	119	51	170	1,037	358	1,395
Total	758	172	930	7,983	1,278	9,261

(Estimates based on WHO[6], Liu et al.[4] and Gan et al.[10])

next to COPD and cancers. In 2000, around 170,000 deaths from IHD and 60,000 deaths from stroke could be attributable to active smoking (Table 3). The two together accounted for about one quarter of the total active smoking attributable mortality.

On average, nine years of life were lost for each male death from active smoking in 2000, and seven years of life for each female death from active smoking.[6] Years of life lost from mortality (YLL) accounted for around 70 percent of the total DALYs caused by smoking.[6] While COPD claimed the most deaths from smoking, at 3.8 million DALYs, cancers were responsible for the most life years lost (~40 percent), mostly (~86 percent) in men (Table 3).

Overall, active smoking caused nearly one million deaths in 2000 in China (Table 3). The active smoking-caused mortality accounted for about 14 percent of the total adult male mortality, compared to 3 percent among adult women. In terms of DALYs, active smoking was responsible for the loss of over 9 million years of life, 4.4 percent of the total DALYs lost in that year in the entire Chinese population (211 million).

According to *The World Health Report 2002*,[6] active smoking is the second leading cause of premature mortality in China only after high blood pressure (Table 4). Likewise, the number years of life lost (DALYs) from active smoking is third after that from high blood pressure and alcohol use (Table 5). Worldwide, an estimated 4.9 million deaths in 2000[6] (nearly 20 percent of them in China) were caused by tobacco. To put tobacco smoking into context with other major risk factors, the number of lives lost caused by active smoking in China is almost three times the number caused by urban air pollution, 2.4 times the number caused by unsafe water, almost eight times the number caused by illicit drug use, and nine times the number of lives lost from all road traffic accidents.

DISEASE BURDEN CAUSED BY PASSIVE SMOKING IN CHINA

Previously, the disease burden of passive smoking has not been included in evaluation of the burden. In the calculations here, epidemiologic and exposure information from China were used wherever possible. To maintain consistency with the WHO Global Burden of

Table 4: Top Ten Risk Factors for Mortality in China in 2000

Risk Factors	Number of Deaths (in thousands)		
	Male	Female	Total
Blood pressure	604	644	1,249
Active smoking	758	172	930
Alcohol	395	56	451
Indoor smoke from solid fuels	116	311	428
Low fruit and vegetable intake	229	197	426
Cholesterol	189	225	414
Urban air pollution	150	152	302
Overweight	139	156	295
Physical inactivity	112	114	226
Occupational risks	193	27	220

(Estimates based on WHO[6])

Table 5: Top Ten Risk Factors for Loss of Healthy Life (DALYs) in China

Risk factors	Years of Healthy Life Lost (in thousands)		
	Male	Female	Total
Alcohol	12,020	1,941	13,961
Blood pressure	6,783	6,044	12,827
Active smoking	7,983	1,278	9,261
Underweight	4,048	3,972	8,020
Occupational risks	5,720	1,010	6,730
Indoor smoke from solid fuels	2,569	3,528	6,097
Overweight	2,430	2,804	5,234
Low fruit and vegetable intake	2,718	2,042	4,760
Cholesterol	2,376	2,195	4,571
Iron deficiency	1,876	2,462	4,338

(Estimates based on WHO[6])

Disease and the Comparative Risk Assessment Projects,[20] however, data on population and background disease rates were used from these databases. These are derived in a consistent and coherent manner across all countries, which requires some adjustment in each of the 14 regions covered. By population, China makes up ~85 percent of WPRO-B (Western Pacific Regional Office — countries with low child and adult mortality rates)[6]; thus, this factor is applied to data from that WHO subregion. As a result, in some cases there are some minor differences from official Chinese national statistics, but the overall impact on the burden of disease comparisons is small. This analysis was restricted to adults above 30 years of age because the few deaths from lung cancer under 30 were mostly among young children, and few were attributable to active or passive smoking.[4] It was also assumed that the relative risk was constant for both sexes above this age.

To be consistent with the databases used in the Comparative Risk Assessment Project for 2000[5] and the 2002 Global Burden of Disease database,[20] DALYs discounted at 3 percent were used with age-weighting applied.

---

[20] GBD, http://www3.who.int/whosis/menu.cfm?path=evidence,burden,burden_estimates,burden_estimates_2002N&language=english: Global Burden of Disease Project, World Health Organization, 2005.

As is common in such calculations,[21,22] the burden of disease from passive smoking was determined here by multiplying the population attributable fraction of disease due to the risk factor, SHS, by the background disease rate. As active smoking is such an important cause of lung cancer in all parts of the world, the average lung cancer rate is greatly affected by smoking rates. As the impact of SHS on smokers (smokers breathing second-hand tobacco smoke from both their own and other people's smoking) is not distinguishable from the effect of active smoking, conducting the analysis with the lung cancer rate in nonsmokers is more conservative, i.e., it results in lower but more certain estimates. Since no mortality statistics are available specifically for nonsmokers in China, the number of lung cancer deaths among Chinese nonsmokers was estimated by first calculating the active smoking attributable lung cancer mortality among smokers and essentially removing it from the total.

The passive smoking attributable burden estimation was started by first calculating the burden among all nonsmokers; such information is not directly available from the national health surveys. As noted, the RRs reported by Liu et al.,[4] were used to estimate the active smoking attributable burden of lung cancer. This estimate was taken out of the lung cancer burden in the entire Chinese population to estimate the burden among nonsmokers:

$$D_{nons} = (D_{total} - D_{smka})*(1 - P_s), \qquad (2)$$

where within a specific age/sex group,

D_{nons}: Disease burden from lung cancer among all nonsmokers;
D_{total}: Disease burden from lung cancer among both smokers and nonsmokers;
D_{smka}: Active smoking attributable disease burden from lung cancer;
P_s: Prevalence of active smoking.

---

[21] Neubauer S, Welte R, Beiche A, Koenig HH, Buesch K and Leidl R, "Mortality, Morbidity and Costs Attributable to Smoking in Germany: Update and a 10-year Comparison", *Tobacco Control* 15, no. 6 (2006): 464–471.

[22] McGhee SM, Ho LM, Lapsley HM, Chau J, Cheung WL and Ho SY, "Cost of Tobacco-Related Diseases, including Passive Smoking, in Hong Kong", *Tobacco Control* 15, no. 2 (2006): 125–130.

A similar approach was applied to estimate the IHD burden among nonsmokers, where the IHD risk estimate from He and Lam[23] was used. A meta-analysis of 25 Chinese epidemiologic studies on IHD and active smoking was conducted by He and Lam[23]; it was estimated that smoking men and women were 1.72 (95 percent CI: 1.61–1.83) and 2.69 (95 percent CI: 1.82–3.98) times respectively more likely, to die from IHD.

Then, the passive smoking attributable disease burden was estimated by applying the RRs of lung cancer and IHD to the disease burden among nonsmokers. In a meta-analysis Gan et al.[24] pooled 19 published Chinese case-control studies on passive smoking and lung cancer. Gan et al.[24] found that non-smoking women who were exposed to SHS regularly in a lifetime face a 63 percent (OR = 1.63, 95 percent CI: 1.12–2.37) increased risk of lung cancer compared to nonexposed women. Smoking by husband was also associated with an OR of 1.28 (1.03–1.59). Only one study with lifetime risk from SHS exposure among males was identified by Gan et al.[24] The study found no increased risk from such exposure. Given the limited evidence of studies on males, the same relative risks among females were applied to males in the current study.

Compared to the evidence of the effects of smoking on heart disease, the evidence of passive smoking in China is limited, and the findings are mixed.[25–27] The disease burden from IHD caused by

---

[23] He Y and Lam TH, "A Review on Studies of Smoking and Coronary Heart Disease in China and Hong Kong," *Chinese Medical Journal* 112, no. 1 (1999): 3–8.

[24] Gan Q, Hammond S, Colford Jr J and Hu TW, "Exposure to Secondhand Smoke and the Risk of Lung Cancer in China: A Systematic Review and Meta-analysis", (submitted 2007).

[25] He Y, "Women's Passive Smoking and Coronary Heart Disease (in Chinese)", *Chinese Journal of Preventive Medicine* 23, no. 1 (1989): 19–22.

[26] He Y, Lam TH, Li LS, Du RY, Jia GL and Huang JY, Passive Smoking at Work as a Risk Factor for Coronary Heart Disease in Chinese Women Who Have Never Smoked", *British Medical Journal* 308, no. 6925 (1994): 380–384.

[27] Wen WQ, Shu XO, Gao YT, Yang G, Li Q and Li HL, "Environmental Tobacco Smoke and Mortality in Chinese Women Who Have Never Smoked: Prospective Cohort Study", *British Medical Journal* 333, no. 7564 (2006): 376–379.

passive smoking in China was estimated based on epidemiological findings mainly from other countries. In a recent meta-analysis on passive smoking and IHD, He et al.[28] summarized 18 studies from eight countries [10 cohorts and eight case-controls, the two Chinese studies He[25] and He et al.[26] were also included in this meta-analysis). Their pooled RR estimates were 1.22 (95 percent CI: 1.10–1.35) for SHS-exposed men and 1.24 (95 percent CI: 1.15–1.34) for SHS-exposed women. CalEPA[29] found similar findings that passive smoking increased the lifetime odds of IHD by 30 percent.

The Passive Smoking Disease Burden Estimates

Passive smoking burden estimates of this study are summarized in Table 6, and for the purpose of comparison, the active smoking burden estimates are also presented in Table 7. All results presented here with 95 percent CI estimates were based on the 95 percent CIs of the RR estimates from the meta-analyses.

As the male smoking rate is extremely high and the female smoking rate is quite low in China, more than half of all male lung cancer deaths in 2002 were attributable to active smoking compared to only 9 percent among females. On the other hand, a significant proportion of lung cancer deaths among nonsmokers was caused by passive smoking (about 21 percent among non-smoking males and 26 percent among non-smoking females). Specifically, in the year 2002, 130,000 people in China, 88 percent of them men, died from lung cancer because of active smoking; 22,200 nonsmokers died from lung cancer because of exposure to SHS — 5,700 men and 16,500 women. The number of DALYs lost was also significant; overall active smoking caused the loss of over 1.1 million years of life from lung cancer, and passive smoking was responsible for the loss of 228,000 years of life from the same disease.

---

[28] He J, Vupputuri S, Allen K, Prerost MR, Hughes J and Whelton PK, "Passive Smoking and the Risk of Coronary Heart Disease a Meta-Analysis of Epidemiologic Studies", *New England Journal of Medicine* 340, no. 12 (1999): 920–926.

[29] Cal/EPA, *Proposed Identification of Environmental Tobacco Smoke as a Toxic Air Contaminant* (California Environmental Protection Agency Air Resources Board & Office of Environmental Health Hazard Assessment, 2006).

Table 6: Premature Deaths and DALYs Attributable to Passive Smoking in China in 2002 (in thousands) (95 percent CIs are in parenthesis)

	Male				Female				Total
	30–44	45–59	60–69	70+	Total	30–44	45–59	60–69	70+	Total	
Lung cancer											
Deaths	0.2	1.2	1.7	2.5	5.7	1.1	4.5	4.1	6.9	16.5	22.2
	(0.0–0.6)	(0.3–2.0)	(0.4–3.1)	(0.5–4.4)	(1.3–10.1)	(0.3–1.9)	(1.1–7.5)	(0.9–7.0)	(1.6–11.7)	(3.9–28.0)	(5.2–38.1)
DALYs	8.6	18.4	15.9	10.1	53.0	28.9	73.6	40.0	32.1	174.6	227.6
	(2.0–14.8)	(4.3–31.7)	(3.6–28.2)	(2.2–18.2)	(12.1–93.0)	(7.1–47.3)	(17.8–122.5)	(9.3–69.3)	(7.6–54.5)	(41.7–293.6)	(53.8–386.6)
IHD											
Deaths	0.3	0.9	1.3	3.9	6.3	0.9	2.6	3.9	20.0	27.5	33.8
	(0.1–0.4)	(0.4–1.3)	(0.6–1.9)	(1.9–6.0)	(3.0–9.6)	(0.6–1.2)	(1.7–3.6)	(2.6–5.4)	(13.0–27.1)	(17.9–37.3)	(20.9–46.9)
DALYs	7.1	14.6	12.0	16.1	49.9	25.3	46.6	40.4	92.9	205.2	255.1
	(3.4–10.8)	(7.0–22.1)	(5.7–18.3)	(7.6–24.6)	(23.7–75.7)	(16.6–34.0)	(30.5–63.0)	(26.2–55.0)	(60.5–126.1)	(133.8–278.1)	(157.5–353.8)

(Based on Gan et al.[10])

Table 7: Premature Deaths and DALYs Attributable to Lung Cancer and IHD Caused by Active Smoking in China in 2002 (in thousands)

	Male				Female				Total
	30–44	45–59	60–69	70+	Total	30–44	45–59	60–69	70+	Total	
Lung Cancer											
Deaths	3.2	26.4	41.4	43.7	114.7	0	1.1	4.3	10.0	15.3	130.0
DALYs	80.3	418.5	376.2	179.4	1,054.3	0.8	17.4	42.2	46.5	106.9	1,161.2
IHD											
Deaths	5.6	20.4	29.4	63.3	118.7	0.4	4.0	10.4	36.0	50.9	169.6
DALYs	155.9	344.2	276.7	260.1	1,036.8	12.3	70.9	107.1	167.3	357.7	1,394.6

(Based on Gan et al.[10])

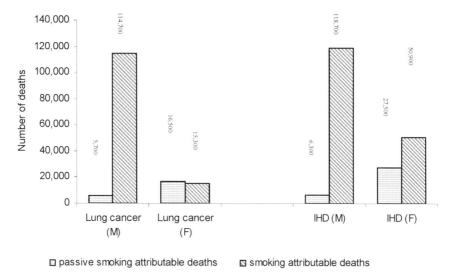

Fig. 1: Number of Premature Deaths Caused by Passive Smoking versus Number of Deaths Caused by Smoking by Disease and Gender.

Lung cancer was the first disease linked to smoking and passive smoking, but later research revealed that IHD caused more deaths than lung cancer.[29] The results from this study support this finding as well. As shown in Tables 6 and 7, active smoking caused about 40,000 more deaths from IHD than from lung cancer (169,600 versus 130,000), and the number of passive smoking-related IHD deaths also exceeded that of lung cancer (33,800 versus 22,200). Compared to lung cancer, the gender disparity in the IHD burden caused by active smoking is smaller: Among women, 30 percent of all the IHD deaths caused by smoking were among women while compared to only 12 percent of lung cancer deaths. Women shoulder most of the deaths caused by passive smoking, with 81 percent of IHD deaths and 74 percent of lung cancer deaths being attributable to it. Overall, 169,600 IHD deaths were caused by smoking and 33,800 IHD deaths were caused by passive smoking in 2002. In terms of DALYs, 1.4 millions years of healthy life were lost from IHD because of smoking, and about a quarter of a million years were lost because of passive smoking.

For lung cancer and IHD combined, mortality caused by passive smoking was around 19 percent of the mortality caused by active smoking. The total DALYs lost from these two diseases due to passive smoking combined were 19 percent of the total DALYs lost due to active smoking. Among males, the mortality caused by active smoking far exceeded that caused by passive smoking (Figure 1). Among females, however, IHD deaths attributable to SHS exposure were about two-thirds of the active smoking attributable IHD deaths; and lung cancer deaths attributable to SHS exposure even exceeded the smoking attributable lung cancer deaths (Tables 6 and 7; Figure 1). Overall, the number of deaths caused by passive smoking among females was about two-thirds of that caused by smoking, and the DALYs lost from passive smoking (379,800) were more than 80 percent of the DALYs lost from smoking (464,600) for females.

It is assumed in this study that the attribution is the same for YLLs and YLDs. However, the results show that YLDs made up only very small proportions of the total DALYs (less than 4 percent for both smoking DALYs and passive smoking DALYs). The proportion is even smaller for lung cancer (~1 percent), as few people survive lung cancer for long. Thus, the final DALYs estimates are not very sensitive to the assumption related to determining YLDs.

Added Risks from Passive Smoking upon Nonsmokers

Passive smoking causes around 56,000 deaths from lung cancer and IHD each year in China. The added risk that passive smoking puts upon exposed nonsmokers is around 200/100,000. To put this excess risk into context, the risk that one will die from traffic accidents in China is around 8/100,000, less than half that from passive smoking. And passive smoking causes more deaths than unsafe sex and twice as many deaths as illicit drug use in China in 2000.

DISCUSSION

Passive Smoking Prevalence in China

In the second National Smoking Prevalence Survey,[1] 53.5 percent of nonsmokers answered "yes" to the question, "Are you exposed to SHS at least 15 min/day for at least one day per week?", The question was formulated based on WHO's definition of passive smoking. Since most epidemiological studies[30–33] and major surveys in other countries[34,35] use a much more straightforward definition, which is simply based on the presence of a smoker in the household, we believe that the obscurity of the WHO definition and the direct application of it in the question may have led to significant number of missing answers and consequently considerably underestimated prevalence rate. Moreover, urinary cotinine measurements show that survey questionnaires tend to underestimate the actual exposure rate.[35] Thus the attributable estimate of the burden of disease from passive smoking in this paper should be considered as a conservative estimate of the actual burden from passive smoking, and is therefore probably an underestimate of the true burden.

Other Diseases Caused by Passive Smoking

The burden of disease caused by passive smoking was estimated for two major outcomes — lung cancer and IHD — because access to mortality and morbidity data for other diseases related to passive

---

[30] Wang LD, Lubin JH, Zhang SR, Metayer C, Xia Y and Brenner A, "Lung Cancer and Environmental Tobacco Smoke in a Non-Industrial Area of China", *International Journal of Cancer* 88, no. 1 (2000): 139–145.

[31] Stockwell HG and Lyman GH, "Cigarette Smoking and the Risk of Female Reproductive Cancer, *American Journal of Obstetrics Gynecology* 157, no. 1 (1987): 35–40.

[32] Gao YT, Blot WJ, Zheng W, Ershow AG, Cheng WH and Levin LI, "Lung-Cancer Among Chinese Women", *International Journal of Cancer* 40, no. 5 (1987): 604–609.

[33] Hirayama T, "Passive Smoking and Lung Cancer–Consistency of Association", *Lancet* 2, no. 8364 (1983): 1425–1426.

[34] Jarvis MJ, Goddard E, Higgins V, Feyerabend C, Bryant A and Cook DG, "Children's Exposure to Passive Smoking in England Since the 1980s: Cotinine Evidence from Population Surveys", *British Medical Journal* 321, no. 7257 (2000): 343–345.

[35] Pirkle JL, Flegal KM, Bernert JT, Brody DJ, Etzel RA and Maurer KR, "Exposure of the US Population to Environmental Tobacco Smoke: The Third National Health and Nutrition Examination Survey, 1988 to 1991", *Journal of the American Medical Association* 275, no. 16 (1996): 1233–1240.

smoking in China is limited. However, many of the diseases related to SHS exposure not estimated in this study have significant health consequences, especially among women and children. Recently, Cal/EPA[29] summarized previous scientific evidence regarding diseases related to passive smoking and found sufficient evidence to conclude that the following diseases could be caused by exposure to SHS: low birth weight, sudden infant death syndrome, a host of respiratory diseases including asthma, otitis media and lower respiratory infection, as well as breast cancer and nasal sinus cancer. Of particular relevance to the disease burden in China are breast cancer and lower respiratory infection. Cal/EPA[29] found that SHS-exposed pre-menopausal women had about twice the risk for breast cancer as did non-exposed pre-menopausal women, and young children exposed to SHS were at a 1.2 fold risk of acute lower respiratory infection (ALRI) than were non-exposed children. An estimated 34,000 pre-menopausal women died of breast cancer in China in 2002.[20] Assuming the same risk of breast cancer from passive smoking as in the United States, around 11,000 of the breast cancer deaths in China could be attributable to passive smoking. Applying the 1.5–2 fold risk of ALRI to the estimated 126,000 ALRI deaths in China in 2002, around 34,000 of these deaths could have been caused by passive smoking. If these two diseases had been included in our calculation of the disease burden of passive smoking, the total estimate would have nearly doubled.

Evidence has accumulated over the past decade that passive smoking might also be a risk factor for stroke. To date, three studies[36–38] have investigated this issue, including one study from Shanghai, China.[36] Zhang et al.[36] conducted a cross-sectional study based on the

---

[36] Zhang XL, Shu XO, Yang G, Li HL, Xiang YB and Gao YT, "Association of Passive Smoking by Husbands with Prevalence of Stroke Among Chinese Women Nonsmokers", *American Journal of Epidemiology* 161, no. 3 (2005): 213–218.

[37] Bonita R, Duncan J, Truelsen T, Jackson RT and Beaglehole R, "Passive Smoking as well as Active Smoking Increases the Risk of Acute Stroke", *Tobacco Control* 8, no. 2 (1999): 156–160.

[38] You RX, Thrift AG, McNeil JJ, Davis SM, Donnan GA, "Ischemic Stroke Risk and Passive Exposure to Spouses' Cigarette Smoking", *American Journal of Public Health* 89, no. 4 (1999): 572–575.

Table 8: Spousal SHS Exposure and Stroke Risk

Exposure	Cases/Total	OR (95 percent CI)	P for Trend
Cigarettes/day			
1–9	46/6,736	1.28 (0.92–1.77)	
10–19	77/11,233	1.32 (1.01–1.72)	
> = 20	116/14,316	1.62 (1.28–2.05)	0.0002
Duration (yrs)			
< = 17	25/16,245	1.13 (0.70–1.82)	
>17	214/16,042	1.47 (1.22–1.78)	0.0004
Pack-years			
< = 13	54/16,512	1.12 (0.82–1.54)	
>13	185/15,772	1.55 (1.27–1.90)	<0.0001

Source: Zhang *et al.* (2005) (refer foot note 36).

baseline data from the Shanghai Women's Health Study.[27] As seen from Table 8, the OR for stroke was elevated by SHS exposure, significantly so with higher or longer exposures. There were also significant exposure-response trends for both degree and duration of exposure. The findings were supported by two other studies in New Zealand and Australia,[37,38] which also observed elevated risks of stroke from SHS exposure. Overall, the evidence is suggestive of a causal relationship between SHS exposure and the risk of stroke, as was concluded by CalEPA.[29] Because of the limited evidence, disease burden from stroke was not estimated in this study. However, the issue of stroke being caused by passive smoking is of considerable significance in China, where stroke is one of the leading causes of death and disability, and where many more people die from stroke than from IHD.[36]

CONCLUSION

In this chapter, we addressed the types of diseases and the health burden that tobacco causes in China, from both active smoking and passive smoking based on the best available published evidence. We summarized the findings of previous studies related to disease burden caused by smoking. We also present the recent estimates of the disease burden caused by passive smoking (from two major diseases — lung cancer and IHD — among adults). The majority of the disease burden from tobacco results from active smoking, yet the passive smoking-related burden is also considerable and has significant policy implications. The passive smoking estimates presented begin the process of placing SHS health effects into context with other health risks in China. Children's health is impacted by SHS in many ways, but the burden of disease is not included here due to limited data.

Tobacco smoking is one of the leading causes of mortality and life lost in China. It caused about 1 million premature deaths and the loss of nearly 10 million years of life in 2000 in China, 12 percent and 5 percent of the national totals respectively. If the number of smokers continues to grow at present rates,[39] the smoking-related disease burden will double by 2020. Exposure to SHS also poses significant risks upon nonsmokers in China. Based on our analysis, an estimated 56,000 people died in China in 2002 from lung cancer (22,200) and IHD (33,800) because of exposure to SHS. The DALYs lost in 2002 from passive smoking from lung cancer and IHD combined was 482,700 years, about 19 percent of the burden of the same diseases caused by active smoking. Relatively few (5.4 percent) women smoke, but most live with a smoker. Passive smoking causes a surprisingly high portion of tobacco-related deaths in women — about two-thirds of deaths caused by active smoking.

More research should be conducted on the other diseases associated with passive smoking, e.g., breast cancer among pre-menopausal women and a number of childhood diseases, such as pneumonia, asthma and SIDS. Although the burden of these diseases from passive smoking was not estimated in this study, the potential magnitude is of serious concern given their importance in China.

Tobacco smoking causes as many as one million deaths a year in China and the smoking rate is expected to rise in the next decade.

---

[39] WHO, *Preventing Chronic Diseases: A Vital Investment*, (2006).

The Chinese government should realize that the fight against tobacco requires sustained efforts to invest in long-term comprehensive tobacco control programs, which are desperately needed. Smoke-free environment policies at work and public places have been shown to effectively reduce smoking and exposure to SHS. Such policies, however, cannot be successfully implemented without sufficient awareness of the harm of passive smoking among the public. Moreover, the current situation of poor compliance with smoke-free policies in China cannot be improved without raising awareness among the public and having their support for such policies. In light of the serious threat tobacco poses for the health of both smokers and nonsmokers in China, including children, we urge more resources be allocated to educate about the health impact of smoking and passive smoking and more stringent legislation be enacted to curb the nation's tobacco epidemic, one of the largest of any type in world history in terms of numbers of potential deaths.

ACKNOWLEDGEMENTS

The authors want to thank Dr. Yuan Jiang from China CDC for her kind help with the Chinese health survey data.

This study was supported by a grant from the United States National Institutes of Health Fogarty International Center (Grant No. RO1-TW05938).

Chapter 6

Economic Burden of Smoking in China*

Hai-Yen Sung, Liping Wang, Shuigao Jin, Teh-wei Hu and Yuan Jiang

China is the world's largest tobacco consumer, accounting for more than one-third of the world's tobacco consumption annually. In 2002, about 350 million adults aged 15 and older were ever-smokers and 300 million were current smokers.[1] China is considered to be in an early stage of a tobacco epidemic. The ever-smoking rates in 2002 were 66 percent for men and 3.1 percent for women of ages 15 years and older, slightly lower than the rates in 1996 of 66.9 percent for men and 4.2 percent for women. The prevalence of smoking in Chinese men seems to have leveled off but not yet dropped. The average cigarette consumption per smoker was the same in 2002 as that in 1996 — 14.8 cigarettes per day.

---

* This chapter originally appeared as Sung H-Y, Wang L, Jin S, Hu TW, Jiang Y, "Economic Burden of Smoking in China, 2000," *Tobacco Control* 15(Suppl 1) (2006): i5–i11. Copyright © 2006 by *British Medical Journal*. All rights reserved. Reprinted with permission from *Tobacco Control* and *British Medical Journal*.
[1] Yang GH, Ma JM, Liu N *et al.*, "Smoking and Passive Smoking in Chinese, 2002," (in Chinese), *Zhonghua Liu Xing Bing Xue Za Zhi* 26 (2005): 77–83.

Cigarette smoking is the leading cause of preventable deaths in the majority of high-income nations and increasingly in low- and middle-income nations,[2] and it also causes disability and productivity losses because of premature deaths.[3] One way to document and assess the adverse health effects of smoking on a society is to translate smoking-caused illnesses, premature mortality, and productivity losses into economic terms. In other words, the cost of smoking serves as a universal marker for measuring the adverse effects of smoking.

Only two studies have estimated the economic costs of smoking in China. Chen *et al.*,[4] using a medical cost accounting method to calculate the disease-specific medical costs, estimated the total medical costs attributable to smoking in 1988 as 2.3 billion yuan (US$0.3 billion using an exchange rate of 8.2784 yuan to US$1). Using a prevalence-based method, Jin *et al.*[5] estimated the total economic burden of smoking in 1989 at 27.1 billion yuan (US$3.3 billion), including 6.9 billion yuan (US$0.8 billion) in direct medical costs and 20.1 billion yuan (US$2.4 billion) in indirect morbidity and mortality costs. During the decade since these two studies, medical expenditures have risen dramatically, and smoking prevalence rates have also increased. To improve public health and reduce resources spent on smoking-caused illnesses, the progression of the economic burden caused by cigarette smoking must be numbered and the estimates for the costs of smoking must be updated.

The objective of this study is to assess the economic burden of diseases and deaths attributable to smoking on Chinese society in

---

[2] Jha P and Chaloupka, FJ, *Curbing The Epidemic: Governments and the Economics of Tobacco Control* (Washington, DC: World Bank, 1999).

[3] US Department of Health and Human Services, *The Health Consequences of Smoking: A Report of the Surgeon General* (Atlanta, Georgia: US Department of Health and Human Services, Centers for Disease Control and Prevention, National Center for Chronic Disease Prevention and Health Promotion, Office on Smoking and Health, 2004).

[4] Chen J, Cao JW, Chen Y *et al.*, "Evaluation of Medical Cost Lost Due to Smoking in Chinese Cities," *Biomedical Environmental Sciences* 8 (1995): 335–341.

[5] Jin SG, Lu BY, Yan DY *et al.*, "An Evaluation of Smoking-Induced Health Costs in China (1988–1989)," *Biomedical Environmental Sciences* 8 (1995): 342–349.

2000. The results may be used to justify the need for stronger tobacco control policies in China and guide health policy and planning.

METHODS

The economic burden of smoking comprises three components: direct medical costs of treating smoking-related diseases, indirect morbidity costs of smoking, and indirect mortality costs of premature deaths caused by smoking-related diseases. The prevalence-based, disease-specific approach[6–9] is used to measure the costs of smoking-related diseases and deaths in 2000 caused by current and past smoking. Three major categories of smoking-related diseases were considered: cancer (all types of malignant neoplasm (*International classification of diseases*, 9th revision (ICD-9) codes: 140–208)), cardiovascular diseases (stroke, ischaemic heart disease, rheumatic heart disease, etc. (ICD-9 codes: 390–414, 418–459)), and respiratory diseases (chronic obstructive pulmonary disease, respiratory tuberculosis, pulmonary heart disease, etc. (ICD-9 codes: 011–012, 018, 415–417, 460–519)). Because the effects of smoking will appear long after its onset, and because most smokers begin before age 20, this study included only persons aged 35 and older in the analysis.

Estimation of Smoking Attributable Fraction

For each of the three components of the economic burden of smoking, a smoking attributable fraction (SAF), also known as population attributable risk, was calculated by disease category, rural/urban district, gender, and age. The estimated SAF is then multiplied

---

[6] Luce BR and Schweitzer SO, "Smoking and Alcohol Abuse: A Comparison of Their Economic Consequences," *The New England Journal of Medicine* 298 (1978): 569–571.

[7] Office of Technology Assessment, US Congress, "Smoking Related Deaths and Financial Costs," *OTA Staff Memorandum* (Washington, DC: Health Program, OTA, 1985).

[8] Rice DP, Hodgson TA, Sinsheimer P *et al.*, "The Economic Costs of the Health Effects of Smoking, 1984," *Milbank Quarterly* 64 (1986): 489–547.

[9] Warner KE, Hodgson TA and Carroll CE, "Medical Costs of Smoking in the United States: Estimates, Their Validity, and Their Implications," *Tobacco Control* 8 (1999): 290–300.

by each cost measure of interest to derive the smoking attributable cost.[10] For example, the product of SAF and total inpatient hospitalization expenditures is smoking attributable hospitalization cost; the product of SAF and total morbidity cost is smoking attributable morbidity cost. The SAF is specified by the following epidemiological formula[11]:

$$\text{SAF}_{ijga} = \frac{(\text{PN}_{jga} + \text{PS}_{jga} * \text{RR}_{ijga}) - 1}{\text{PN}_{jga} + \text{PS}_{jga} * \text{RR}_{ijga}}, \quad (1)$$

where PN and PS denote the prevalence rate of nonsmokers and smokers, respectively; RR denotes the relative risk of mortality for smokers compared to nonsmokers; the subscript i is for disease category; j is for rural/urban district; g is for gender; a is for age classified into two groups, 35–64 and 65+. When RR is < 1, the corresponding SAF becomes negative, implying that smokers have a decreased risk of mortality compared with nonsmokers. This implication does not seem realistic, given the huge body of evidence linking smoking with multiple life-threatening diseases. Instead of employing negative SAFs, they are assumed to be zero.

SAFs were estimated using the RRs of mortality and then the same SAF estimates were applied to the total measure for all three components of the economic costs.

Data Source

The primary data source was the Second National Health Services Survey (NHSS) conducted by the Ministry of Health in China in 1998.[12] The NHSS is a national representative sample of 216,101

---

[10] Max W, Rice DP, Sung HY *et al.*, "The Economic Burden of Smoking in California," *Tobacco Control* 13 (2004): 264–267.
[11] Lilienfeld AM and Lilienfeld DE, *Foundations of Epidemiology*, 3rd edn. (New York: Oxford University Press, 1994).
[12] Ministry of Health, People's Republic of China, *Research on National Health Services — An Analysis Report of the Second National Health Services Survey in 1998* (Beijing: National Center for Health Information and Statistics, 1999).

individuals from 56,994 households extracted through a multi-stage random sampling method. Face-to-face interviews were conducted to collect detailed information about households and all household members. Such information includes age, gender, education, employment status, disease histories, health risk behaviors, and medical care utilization and expenditures including cause-specific outpatient visits and self-medication in the two weeks before the date of interview, as well as inpatient hospitalizations in the past 12 months before the date of interview. Self-reported days lost from work due to illness in the past two weeks before interview were also collected.

Smoking prevalence rates by rural/urban district, gender, and age came from the 1998 NHSS in which all the individuals of age 15 and older were asked their smoking status. Adults were classified as nonsmokers (never smoked) and smokers (current and former). Current smokers were not separated from former smokers because the RRs of mortality, needed in the calculation of SAFs, have not been estimated separately for former and current smokers in China.

The RRs of mortality for smokers were obtained from estimates published by Liu et al.,[13] population data from the 2000 Population Census,[14] 2000 mortality rates from China's Vital Registration system monitored by the Ministry of Health,[15] life expectancy from the 2000 China Life Tables reported by the World Health Organization,[16] and earnings data from the *China Statistics Yearbook*.[17]

---

[13] Liu BQ, Peto R, Chen ZM et al., "Emerging Tobacco Hazards in China: 1. Retrospective Proportional Mortality Study of One Million Deaths," *British Medical Journal* 317 (1998): 1411–1422.
[14] National Bureau of Statistics, People's Republic of China. *Tabulation On the 2000 Population Census of People's Republic of China* (National Bureau of Statistics: China Statistics Press, People's Republic of China).
[15] Ministry of Health, People's Republic of China, *China Health Statistics Yearbook 2001* (Beijing: Ministry of Health, 2001), 200–399.
[16] World Heath Organization, "Life Tables for 191 Countries, World Mortality in 2000," WHO website: http://www.who.int/country/chn/en/ (Accessed April 20, 2004).
[17] National Bureau of Statistics, People's Republic of China, *China Statistics Yearbook 2003*. (Beijing: China Statistics Press, 2004).

Direct Costs

Direct costs include all the health care expenditures for treating smoking-related diseases. China has three types of health care services: inpatient hospitalizations, outpatient visits, and self-medications. Hospitalization and outpatient costs include expenditures for prescribed medicine during the hospital stays or outpatient visits. Self-medications refer to medicine purchased by patients from a drug store without seeing a doctor.

Smoking attributable health care expenditure (SAE) for each subgroup stratified by disease category, urban/rural district, gender, and age (35–64 and 65+) was estimated by multiplying the SAF by the corresponding total health care expenditure (THE) according to the following formula:

$$\begin{aligned} SAE_{ijga} &= THE_{ijga} \times SAF_{ijga} \\ &= [PH_{ijga} \times QH_{ijga} + PV_{ijga} \times QV_{ijga} \times 26 \\ &\quad + PM_{ijga} \times QM_{ijga} \times 26] \times POP_{ijga} \times SAF_{ijga}, \end{aligned} \qquad (2)$$

where PH is the average expenditure per inpatient hospitalization; QH is the average number of hospitalizations per person in 12 months; PV is the average expenditure per outpatient visit; QV is the average number of outpatient visits per person in two weeks; PM is the average medication expenditure per person with positive self-medication expenditures in two weeks; QM is the proportion of persons with positive self-medication expenditures in two weeks; and POP is the 2000 population. The notation for the subscripts i, j, g, and a is the same as in Eq. (1).

The average expenditures and health care utilization rates were estimated from the 1998 NHSS data. In the NHSS questionnaire, respondents were asked to report the expenditures of inpatient hospitalizations and the amount paid by health insurance and by their own. Because of the logic of the questionnaire structure, the self-reported hospitalization expenditures were considered to represent actual expenditures including payment from insurance and out-of-pocket. For self-medications, the total expenditures were not likely paid by insurance since they were purchased without doctor's prescription. For two-week outpatient visits, respondents were asked to report the total expenditures without being probed for the out-of-pocket payment or health insurance payment.

To warrant that the self-reported health expenditures are a good proxy for actual expenditures, an adjustment process was undertaken. First, the average per capita health expenditure was estimated for each disease category by urban/rural district, gender and age from the 1998 NHSS data. Second, this number was multiplied by the population in 2000 for each subgroup and all the expenditures were added up across all subgroups to derive the estimated national health expenditure in 2000. The estimate is $40.2 billion, which is lower than the published figure of $55.4 billion.[18] Finally, an adjustment factor of 1.38 (55.4/40.2) was calculated and applied to the estimated average expenditures from the NHSS data.

Indirect Morbidity Costs

Indirect morbidity costs include expenditures for transportation and caregivers due to inpatient hospitalizations and outpatient visits as well as the value of lost productivity caused by smoking-related diseases.

Smoking attributable indirect morbidity cost (SAI) for each subgroup stratified by disease category, urban/rural district, gender, and age (35–64 and 65+) was estimated by multiplying the SAF by the corresponding total indirect morbidity expenditure (TIE) using the following formula:

$$\begin{aligned} SAI_{ijga} &= TIE_{ijga} \times SAF_{ijga} \\ &= [PHI_{ijga} \times QH_{ijga} + PVI_{ijga} \times QV_{ijga} \times 26 \\ &\quad + PW_{ijga} \times QW_{ijga} \times 26 \times Y_j] \times POP_{ijga} \times SAF_{ijga}, \end{aligned} \quad (3)$$

---

[18] China National Health Economic Institute, *China National Health Accounts Digest* (Beijing: China Statistics Press, 2004).

where PHI is the average expenditure on transportation and caregivers per inpatient hospitalization; PVI is the average expenditure on transportation per outpatient visit; PW is the average number of days lost from work due to smoking-related illness per employed person in two weeks; QW is the employment-population ratio which is defined as the proportion of the total population who are currently employed; and Y is daily earnings in 2000.

The expenditures for transportation and caregivers and the days lost from work were from the 1998 NHSS data. Since average earnings data were not available by age and gender, the work-loss days were evaluated using two sets of 2000 earnings data: Average annual wage of the staff and workers for urban residents, and per capita annual net income of rural households multiplied by the average number of rural residents supported by the rural working population.[17] Daily earnings were derived by dividing the annual earnings by 366 (number of days in 2000).

Indirect Mortality Costs

Human capital approach[19] was used to measure the expected value of lost future productivity caused by smoking attributable premature deaths in 2000. Smoking attributable deaths for each subgroup stratified by disease category, urban/rural district, gender, and age (35–64 and 65+) were estimated by multiplying the SAFs by the corresponding total number of deaths. Smoking attributable years of potential life lost (YPLLs) were estimated by the product of smoking attributable deaths and the average number of years of life expectancy remaining at the age of death. Life expectancy was obtained from gender and five-year age-specific life tables for China in 2000.[16]

Smoking attributable costs of premature deaths were estimated by multiplying smoking attributable deaths by the present value of forgone lifetime earnings (PVLE) for each person at the age of death.

---

[19] Rice DP and Cooper B, "The Economic Value of Human Life," *American Journal of Public Health* 57 (1967):1954–1966.

The PVLE is estimated by rural/urban district, gender, and five-year age groups based on the approach developed by Max et al.[20] which takes into account life expectancy for different gender and age subgroups, varying employment–population rates by rural/urban district, gender, and five-year age groups, and a discount rate of 3 percent to convert a stream of earnings into its current worth. To consider potential growth on future earnings, an annual productivity growth rate of 8 percent was assumed, that was approximately the average growth rate of gross domestic product (GDP) in China between 1998 and 2002. The employment–population rate was estimated from the 1998 NHSS data by dividing the number of currently employed persons by the total population. Definitions and calculation of earnings were the same as described earlier.

RESULTS

China had 1.243 billion people in 2000 — 427 million aged 35–64 years and 88 million aged 65+.[14] Among the 515 million people aged 35+, 323 million (63 percent) lived in rural areas and 192 million (37 percent) lived in urban areas. The prevalence of cigarette smoking in China is high. According to the 1998 NHSS data, 38 percent of the adults aged 35+ were ever-smokers including 34.5 percent as current smokers and 3.5 percent as former smokers. The ever-smoking rates among men in the urban areas were 75.3 percent for ages 35–64 and 61.0 percent for ages 65+, lower than the corresponding rates in the rural areas of 84.8 percent and 73.4 percent, respectively. The smoking rates among women in urban areas were higher than those in rural areas for both age groups (6.1 percent and 14.8 percent versus 5.3 percent and 10.3 percent). The smoking rates for men were higher among ages 35–64 than among the older group; the opposite was found for women.

---

[20] Max W, Rice DP, Sung HY et al., *Valuing Human Life: Estimating the Present Value of Lifetime Earnings, 2000* (Center for Tobacco Control Research and Education, Economic Studies and Related Methods, October 1, 2004), http://repositories.cdlib.org/ctcre/esarm/PVLE2000.

Table 1: Smoking Attributable Fractions (SAFs) of Mortality Associated with Smoking in China, 2000, by Disease, Urban/Rural District, Gender, and Age

Diseases	SAF(percent)			
	Male		Female	
	35–64	65+	35–64	65+
Urban				
Cancer	28.9	24.7	3.9	9.0
Cardiovascular diseases	10.0	8.3	0.8	2.0
Respiratory diseases	23.9	20.3	7.2	15.9
Rural				
Cancer	26.1	23.5	1.1	2.1
Cardiovascular diseases	9.4	8.2	0.0	0.0
Respiratory diseases	17.1	15.2	2.2	4.2

Based on the estimates of the smoking prevalence rates of this study and the RRs estimated by Liu et al.,[13] SAFs were calculated (Table 1). The SAFs are substantially smaller for women than for men, resulting from the much lower smoking prevalence among women. Cancer showed the highest disease-specific SAFs for men, while for women, respiratory diseases showed the highest SAFs. Note that the SAFs for rural female smokers were zero for cardiovascular diseases because the estimated RRs were less than one.[13]

Table 2 shows the SAEs of inpatient hospitalizations, outpatient visits, and self-medications by disease category, rural/urban district, gender, and age. The total SAE amounted to $1,705.7 million. Among the three disease categories, treating respiratory diseases cost the most for both urban smokers ($604.1 million) and rural smokers ($274.0 million) — $878.2 million, or 51 percent of the total SAE. The results from disaggregated analyses by the types of health care services show similar patterns except that for inpatient hospitalization, treating cancer cost the most for ages 35–64 for rural men and urban women and treating cardiovascular diseases cost the most for urban men aged 35–64, and that for self-medication, treating cardiovascular diseases cost the most for urban men aged 65+. The SAEs for treating

Table 2: Smoking Attributable Health Care Expenditures in China, 2000, by Service Type, Disease, Urban/Rural District, Gender, and Age (Unit: US$ 1,000)

Diseases	Inpatient Hospitalizations								Outpatient Visits								Self-Medication							
	Male			Female					Male			Female					Male			Female				
	35-64	65+	Subtotal	35-64	65+	Subtotal			35-64	65+	Subtotal	35-64	65+	Subtotal			35-64	65+	Subtotal	35-64	65+	Subtotal	Total
Urban																							
Cancer	61,275	52,339	113,614	13,834	8,277	22,111			37,239	9,156	46,395	2,398	2,569	4,968			4,524	0	4,524	23	0	23	19,1634
CV diseases	115,158	74,653	189,810	5,836	6,076	11,912			105,406	69,650	175,056	9,245	10,982	20,227			15,880	11,811	27,691	2,616	2,845	5,461	430,158
Resp. diseases	44,350	96,918	141,268	9,664	23,181	32,845			173,116	80,829	253,944	49,647	42,382	92,029			45,222	10,680	55,902	18,019	10,114	28,133	604,123
Subtotal	220,784	223,909	444,692	29,334	37,534	66,868			315,761	159,635	475,395	61,291	55,933	117,224			65,626	22,491	88,117	20,658	12,959	33,617	1,225,915
Rural																							
Cancer	35,600	12,280	47,880	1,000	263	1,263			49,072	8,892	57,964	671	53	723			332	440	771	1	5	6	108,608
CV diseases	24,268	15,291	39,559	0	0	0			36,391	16,555	52,945	0	0	0			3,046	1,600	4,645	0	0	0	97,149
Resp. diseases	30,131	18,297	48,429	3,437	2,284	5,720			132,524	34,464	166,988	17,437	10,272	27,709			15,538	5,481	21,019	2,814	1,356	4,170	274,035
Subtotal	89,999	45,868	135,867	4,436	2,547	6,983			217,986	59,911	277,897	18,108	10,324	28,432			18,915	7,520	26,435	2,815	1,362	4,177	479,792
Total	310,783	269,777	580,560	33,771	40,081	73,851			533,747	219,545	753,292	79,399	66,258	145,656			84,542	30,011	114,552	23,473	14,321	37,794	1,705,707

Source: Exchange rate of the Chinese yuan against US$ = 82.784 based on *China Statistical Yearbook*, 2003, Table 17.2; CV, cardiovascular; Resp, respiratory.

cancer and cardiovascular diseases were $300.2 million (18 percent) and $527.3 million (31 percent), respectively. In general, the middle age group incurred higher SAEs than the older group.

China had 688,512 deaths attributed to smoking in 2000 — 599,723 for men and 88,789 for women; 248,808 in urban areas and 439,704 in rural areas — accounting for 8.3 percent of all deaths. Table 3 shows that the YPLLs for these smoking attributable deaths were estimated as 9.7 million years — 8.6 million years for men and 1.1 million years for women; 3.4 million years for urban smokers and 6.3 million years for rural smokers. The disaggregated analyses by the underlying causes of death show that older women had higher total smoking attributable YPLLs than the middle age women except for the deaths caused by cancer in rural areas. The opposite is true for men in that the middle age group had higher smoking attributable YPLLs than the older group except for the deaths caused by respiratory diseases in both urban and rural areas. The average years of life lost per death was 14.1 years — 14.4 years for men and 12.2 years for women; 13.9 for urban smokers and 14.2 for rural smokers.

The estimated PVLEs for an average Chinese in 2000 by rural/urban district, gender, and age are shown in the Appendix. Table 4 shows the value of lost productivity caused by smoking-related deaths in 2000: $2,935.5 million — $2,816.3 million for men and $119.2 million for women; $790.4 million in urban areas and $2,145.1 million in rural areas. The value of lost productivity averaged $4,264 per death — $4,696 for men and $1,342 for women; $3,177 for urban smokers and $4,878 for rural smokers. The leading cause of smoking attributable mortality costs is cancer at $1,903.1 million (65 percent), followed by respiratory diseases at $534.4 million (18 percent), and cardiovascular diseases at $498.0 million (17 percent).

Table 5 shows that the smoking attributable transportation and caregivers costs were $122.5 million, much smaller than the direct medical costs of smoking. Productivity losses due to absence from work caused by smoking-related illness amounted to $270.6 million. Total indirect morbidity costs of smoking in 2000 amounted

Table 3: Smoking Attributable Years of Potential Life Lost (YPLL) in China, 2000, by Diseases, Urban/Rural District, Gender, and Age

Diseases	Male 35–64	Male 65+	Male Subtotal	Female 35–64	Female 65+	Female Subtotal	Total
Urban							
Cancer	1,179,329	568,724	1,748,053	113,417	152,301	265,718	2,013,770
CV diseases	322,819	287,313	610,132	18,205	78,012	96,217	706,350
Resp. diseases	167,638	292,788	460,426	36,876	228,890	265,766	726,192
Subtotal	1,669,786	1,148,824	2,818,611	168,498	459,203	627,701	3,446,312
Rural							
Cancer	2,372,443	816,935	3,189,378	64,682	51,212	115,894	3,305,273
CV diseases	583,184	542,704	1,125,888	0	0	0	1,125,888
Resp. diseases	593,305	892,537	1,485,842	63,760	272,176	335,936	1,821,778
Subtotal	3,548,933	2,252,176	5,801,109	128,442	323,388	451,831	6,252,939
Total	5,218,720	3,401,000	8,619,720	296,940	782,592	1,079,532	9,699,251

CV, cardiovascular; Resp, respiratory.

Table 4: Smoking Attributable Costs of Premature Deaths in China, 2000, by Disease, Urban/Rural District, Gender, and Age (Unit: US$ 1,000)

Diseases	Male 35–64	Male 65+	Subtotal	Female 35–64	Female 65+	Subtotal	Total
Urban							
Cancer	497,171	36,383	533,555	20,448	3,848	24,297	557,851
CV diseases	125,219	17,127	142,346	2,492	1,601	4,093	146,439
Resp. diseases	60,351	16,437	76,788	5,272	4,057	9,329	86,117
Subtotal	682,742	69,947	752,688	28,213	9,506	37,719	790,407
Rural							
Cancer	1,161,996	150,866	1,312,862	26,180	6,190	32,370	1,345,232
CV diseases	261,264	90,261	351,525	0	0	0	351,525
Resp. diseases	254,861	144,372	399,232	22,319	26,777	49,096	448,328
Subtotal	1,678,121	385,499	2,063,620	48,499	32,967	81,466	2,145,086
Total	2,360,862	455,446	2,816,308	76,712	42,473	119,185	2,935,493

Source: Exchange rate of the Chinese yuan against US$ = 8.2784 based on *China Statistical Yearbook,* 2003, Table 17.2. CV, cardiovascular; Resp., respiratory.

to $393.0 million — $344.5 million for men and $48.5 million for women; $175.8 million in urban areas and $217.2 million in rural areas.

Table 5 also summarizes the estimates for all the components of the economic burden of smoking. In 2000, the total economic cost of smoking in China was $5,034.2 million. A larger share of the total economic cost was borne by men than women ($4,609.2 million versus $425.0 million), and in rural areas than in urban areas ($2,842.1 million versus $2,192.1 million). Total annual economic losses averaged $25.43 per smoker among the 198 million smokers aged 35 and older in 2000 — $31.46 for urban smokers and $22.16 for rural smokers. Given that China's cigarette consumption in 2000 was 30.76 million cases (that is, 76.9 billion packs),[21] the economic cost of smoking averaged $0.07 per pack.

---

[21] Liu T and Xiong B, *Tobacco Economy and Tobacco Control* (in Chinese) (Beijing: Economic Science Press, 2004).

Table 5: Economic Costs of Smoking in China, 2000, Among Adults of Age 35 and Older (Unit: US$ 1,000)

Type of Costs	Urban Male	Urban Female	Urban Subtotal	Rural Male	Rural Female	Rural Subtotal	Both Areas Male	Both Areas Female	Total
Direct medical costs									
Inpatient	444,692	66,868	511,561	135,867	6,983	142,851	580,560	73,851	654,411
Outpatient	475,395	117,224	592,619	277,897	28,432	306,329	753,292	145,656	898,949
Self-medication	88,117	33,617	121,735	26,435	4,177	30,612	114,552	37,794	152,347
Subtotal	1,008,205	217,710	1,225,915	440,199	39,592	479,792	1,448,404	257,302	1,705,707
Indirect morbidity costs									
Transportation and caregivers	63,690	14,239	77,929	41,675	2,860	44,534	105,365	17,099	122,464
Absence from work	86,023	11,867	97,889	153,118	19,555	172,674	239,141	31,422	270,563
Subtotal	149,713	26,106	175,819	194,793	22,415	217,208	344,506	48,521	393,027
Indirect mortality costs	752,688	37,719	790,407	2,063,620	81,466	2,145,086	2,816,308	119,185	2,935,493
Total	1,910,606	281,535	2,192,141	2,698,612	143,473	2,842,085	4,609,218	425,008	5,034,226

Source: Exchange rate of the Chinese yuan against US$ = 8.2784 based on *China Statistical Yearbook*, 2003, Table 17.2.

Lost productivity caused by premature deaths accounted for the largest proportion of the total economic costs at $2,935.5 million (58 percent of the total), followed by the direct costs at $1,705.7 million (34 percent), and then indirect morbidity costs at $393.0 million (8 percent). Smoking attributable direct costs accounted for 3.1 percent of China's national health care expenditures in 2000 at $55.4 billion.[18] Outpatient visits accounted for the highest proportion of smoking attributable direct costs at $898.9 million (53 percent), followed by inpatient hospitalizations at $654.4 million (38 percent), and self-medication at $152.3 million (9 percent).

DISCUSSION

The results of this study indicate that the adverse health effects of smoking cause a huge economic burden to the Chinese society, reaching $5,034.2 million in 2000. Results also show that $1,705.7 million, 3.1 percent of the national health care expenditures, were spent on treating smoking-related diseases.

Compared to Western countries such as the United States where smoking attributable direct costs accounted for 6–8 percent of the national personal health care expenditures,[9] the estimates of the present study seem low, that are likely conservative for several reasons.

In this study first, the RRs from a retrospective mortality study of one million deaths by Liu et al.,[13] were used and their estimates were much lower than those from Western countries. For example, the RRs of lung cancer among men aged 35 and older were 2.98 for urban smokers and 2.57 for rural smokers in China compared to 22.36 for current smokers and 9.36 for former smokers in the United States.[22] The RRs of coronary heart disease among men aged 35–64 were 1.28 for both urban and rural smokers in China versus 2.81 for current smokers and 1.75 for former smokers in the United States.[22]

---

[22] US Department of Health and Human Services, *Reducing the Health Consequences of Smoking: 25 Years of Progress*, A report of the Surgeon General (Rockville, Maryland: Public Health Service, Centers for Disease Control, Office on Smoking and Health, 1989) (DHHS Publication No. (CDC) 89-8411).

Few studies have assessed the RRs of smoking for the Chinese population.[13,23-26] The estimates by Liu et al.[13] were chosen for this study because their study was based on a large national sample and was the only study providing the RR estimates by gender and rural/urban district. In general, the RRs estimated by Liu et al. were comparable to those from other Chinese prospective studies and case–control studies.[13] However, Lam et al.[26] have argued that most studies on smoking-related mortality in China tend to underestimate the RRs of smoking because of the short follow-up. They demonstrated that as the duration of follow-up period increased, RRs also increased. Based on 20 years of follow-up, their estimated RRs were similar to those in the United States and the United Kingdom. A sensitivity analysis was conducted here by using the RRs estimated by Lam et al.[26] while keeping the other data unchanged. The total economic costs of smoking more than doubled, from $5,034 million to $12,151 million, and the proportion of smoking attributable direct costs to the national health expenditures increased to 7.7 percent, comparable to that in the United States.

Second, when estimating PVLE, the earnings were assumed to be the same for all subgroups by age and gender because of the data limitation. As shown in the Appendix, the PVLE is the highest for persons < 1 year and decreases with age. Max et al.[20] found that the American males and females aged 20–24 have the highest PVLE at a discount rate of 3 percent given the varying earnings for each five-year age group. If the pattern of earnings by age in China is similar

---

[23] Yuan JM, Ross RK, Wang XL et al., "Morbidity and Mortality in Relation to Cigarette Smoking in Shanghai, China: A Prospective Male Cohort Study," *Journal of the American Medical Association* 275 (1996): 1646–1650.

[24] Chen ZM, Xu Z, Collins R et al., "Early Health Effects of the Emerging Tobacco Epidemic in China, A 16-year Prospective Study," *Journal of the American Medical Association* 278 (1997): 1500–1504.

[25] Niu SR, Yang GH, Chen ZM et al., "Emerging Tobacco Hazards in China: 2. Early Mortality Results From a Prospective Study," *British Medical Journal* 317 (1998): 1423–1424.

[26] Lam TH, He Y, Li LS et al., "Mortality Attributable to Cigarette Smoking in China," *Journal of the American Medical Association* 278 (1997): 1505–1508.

to that in the United States, the PVLE estimates of this study may be overestimated for persons younger than age 20 and underestimated for persons ≥20; therefore, the estimated indirect costs of smoking for persons aged 35 and older may be underestimated. Also, it was assumed that 8 percent was the annual growth rate in productivity that is lower than the average growth rate of GDP in China during 1979–2002 at 9.4 percent.[17] According to China's National Bureau of Statistics, the annual rates of GDP growth in 2003 and 2004 reached 10 percent. The estimated costs of smoking would be higher if the growth rate of 9.4 percent is assumed. However, if the growth rate in China is assumed to reduce to 5 percent beginning in 2006, the indirect mortality costs of smoking would be reduced from $2.9 billion to $2.2 billion.

Third, the smoking prevalence rates were estimated by using the 1998 NHSS data. Yang *et al.*[27] estimated that the prevalence rate of ever-smokers for persons aged 15–69 was 66.9 percent for men and 4.2 percent for women using the 1996 National Prevalence Survey. Applying the same age criteria, the corresponding rate was 57.5 percent for men and 3.8 percent for women from the 1998 NHSS data. In other words, our estimate was about 15 percent lower for men and 10 percent lower for women than the estimates by Yang *et al.* This could be due to an underreporting of smoking status among respondents in the 1998 NHSS. Another sensitivity analysis was conducted by increasing the smoking prevalence rate by 15 percent for each age group for men while keeping other things unchanged. The total economic costs of smoking increased by about 10 percent, from $5,034 million to $5,569 million.

Fourth, the calculation for the economic burden of smoking only considers the three major categories of smoking-related diseases. It did not include peptic ulcer diseases and liver cirrhosis, two diseases estimated to account for 14–19 percent of smoking attributable medical costs, YPLLs, and mortality costs according to two recent studies

---

[27] Yang G, Fan L, Tan J *et al.*, "Smoking in China: Findings of the 1996 National Prevalence Survey," *Journal of the American Medical Association* 282 (1999): 1247–1253.

in Asia.[28,29] Additionally, Yang et al.[29] found that kidney diseases caused the most smoking attributable medical costs. Further research is needed to examine the effects of smoking on the morbidity and mortality resulting from peptic ulcer, liver cirrhosis, and kidney diseases and their economic costs among the Chinese population.

Finally, this study did not count the days lost from work by the relatives taking care of patients with smoking-related illness, the health care costs of environmental tobacco smoke, and the deaths resulting from cigarette-caused fires and passive smoking. For persons younger than age 35, passive smoking is the main risk for diseases such as bronchitis and low birth weight. Yang et al.[1] estimated that more than 50 percent of Chinese nonsmokers aged 15 and older were passive smokers in 2002. Therefore, the true economic burden of smoking in China could be much higher than the estimates in this study, which only focuses on the evaluation of active smoking.

This study is based on the conventional epidemiological approach[6,7,29] which estimates the smoking attributable risks of mortality caused by the three major smoking-related diseases, and applies the attributable risks of mortality to the morbidity toll. In an alternative epidemiological approach,[8,28] the smoking attributable risks of health care utilization for smoking-related diseases are estimated and applied to health care expenditures. Several recent studies in the United States have developed the econometric approach[10,30–32]

---

[28] Kang HY, Kim HJ, Park TK et al., "Economic Burden of Smoking in Korea," *Tobacco Control* 12 (2003): 37–44.

[29] Yang MC, Fann CY, Wen CP et al., "Smoking Attributable Medical Expenditures, Years of Potential Life Lost, and the Cost of Premature Death in Taiwan," *Tobacco Control* 14, (suppl-I) (2005): i62–i70.

[30] Bartlett JC, Miller LS, Rice DP et al., "Medical Expenditures Attributable to Cigarette Smoking — United States, 1993," *Morbidity and Mortality Weekly Report* 43 (1994): 469–472.

[31] Miller LS, Zhang X, Rice DP et al., "State Estimates of Total Medical Expenditures Attributable to Cigarette Smoking, 1993," *Public Health Report* 113 (1998): 447–458.

[32] Miller VP, Ernst C and Collin F, "Smoking-Attributable Medical Care Costs in the USA," *Social Science Medicine* 48 (1999): 375–391.

which examines the relationship between smoking and health care expenditures in a multi-equation framework by adjusting other risk factors, health status, and individuals' taste for consuming health care. These econometric studies estimate smokers' total excess expenditures over those of nonsmokers by including all types of diseases. Warner et al.[9] anticipate that the econometric approach will become the norm in cost-of-smoking analyses. Due to the limitation of our data, neither the smoking attributable risks of health care utilization nor the econometric models are estimated in this study.

In conclusion, very conservatively estimated results of this study suggest that cigarette smoking costs an enormous economic burden in China through a huge number of preventable diseases, health care costs, premature deaths, and productivity losses. The total economic costs had grown from $3.3 billion in 1989[5] to $5.0 billion in 2000. Since the health effects of smoking on morbidity and mortality are cumulative, China will bear a much heavier economic burden from cigarette smoking in the future if the current trends in smoking behavior continue. The economic burden of smoking in the rural areas will be of special concern because of the large proportion of population, the high smoking prevalence rate, and poverty. To reduce the economic burden of smoking to the society, effective tobacco control programs and sustained efforts are needed in China to curb the tobacco epidemic. It is hoped that the results of this study will motivate policymakers in China to formulate a comprehensive health and economic agenda with adequate investment in research, public education, health providers' training, and intervention programs aimed at tobacco prevention and control.

ACKNOWLEDGMENTS

This study was supported by a grant from the Fogarty International Center (Grant No. R01-TW05938), National Institutes of Health. The authors are grateful for the comments provided by Professors Ming-Chin Yang, Gregor A. Franz, and Dorothy P. Rice. However, the authors alone are responsible for the findings.

APPENDIX

Present Value of Lifetime Earnings[a] in China, 2000, by Urban/Rural District, Gender and Age (Unit: US$1)

Age (years)	Urban Male	Urban Female	Rural Male	Rural Female
<1	238,235	158,620	189,567	185,462
1–4	218,518	145,609	173,878	170,249
5–9	177,523	118,246	141,258	138,256
10–14	140,524	93,525	111,817	109,351
15–19	110,887	73,636	88,027	85,974
20–24	85,897	56,320	68,479	66,757
25–29	64,626	41,330	52,623	51,202
30–34	47,457	29,258	40,011	38,830
35–39	33,848	19,679	30,042	29,042
40–44	23,051	12,136	22,181	21,315
45–49	14,466	6,669	16,011	15,249
50–54	8,050	3,361	11,207	10,543
55–59	3,843	1,718	7,522	6,979
60–64	1,769	972	4,842	4,395
65–69	1,014	575	2,981	2,649
70–74	632	335	1,751	1,548
75–79	382	174	1,005	857
80–84	216	53	583	437
85+	96	0	288	168

Source: Exchange rate of the Chinese yuan against US$ = 8.2784 based on *China Statistical Yearbook*, 2003, Table 17.2.

[a] Estimated by the authors with 3 percent discount rate and 8 percent productivity growth rate.

Section II

Demand for Cigarettes and Household Expenditures Analysis

Chapter 7

The Demand for Cigarettes in China

Zhengzhong Mao, Hai-Yen Sung, Teh-wei Hu and Gonghuan Yang

INTRODUCTION

Background and Importance

The tobacco epidemic is one of the most challenging public health problems in China. According to the 2002 National Smoking Prevalence Survey, among all Chinese adults aged 15 and older, the ever-smoking rates were 66.0 percent for men and 3.1 percent for women; about 350 million people were ever-smokers while 300 million were current smokers.[1] China's tobacco consumption accounts for more than one-third of the world's tobacco consumption annually. Smoking causes a huge health and economic burden to the Chinese society. In 2000, about 0.7 million deaths and an equivalent of 9.7 million years of potential life lost were attributable to smoking; the total economic costs of smoking amounted to

---

[1] Yang GH, Ma JM, Liu N and Zhou LN, "Smoking and Passive Smoking in Chinese, 2002" (in Chinese), *Zhonghua Liu Xing Bing Xue Za Zhi* 26, no. 2 (2005): 77–83.

$5.0 billion.[2] If current smoking patterns continue, it has been predicted that by 2025, China's annual death toll attributable to smoking-related diseases will exceed two million.[3]

To curb the tobacco epidemic and the associated health and economic burden, effective tobacco control programs are needed. China's tobacco control policies began in 1980 when the government enacted legislation banning smoking in public places and teenage smoking. However, the legislation provided no penalties for violating the bans. Thus, universal compliance with this legislation did not happen. Ten years later, in 1990, a nongovernmental organization, the China Association of Smoking and Health (now called the Chinese Association on Tobacco Control), was established to carry out tobacco control activities. In 1991, the Chinese government issued additional legislation banning cigarette advertising in the media and at sports events. However, this legislation contained loopholes that enabled cigarette companies to advertise their brand names in the media. Two years later, another law banned smoking in schools, but once again compliance was not achieved. Generally speaking, China's tobacco control policies have been limited to the areas of regulation and provision of consumer information.

On November 10, 2003, China signed the WHO Framework Convention on Tobacco Control (FCTC). On August 28, 2005, the People's Congress Standing Committee voted approval to ratify the FCTC, and then on October 11, 2005 China officially became an FCTC-ratified country. All the ratified countries are required to implement five key provisions of tobacco control that include banning smoking in public places, prohibiting cigarette sales to minors, banning cigarette advertisements, enlarging the health warning label on cigarette packages, and increasing tobacco taxes. The first four provisions are considered nonprice tobacco control schemes while

---

[2] Sung HY, Wang L, Jin S, Hu TW and Jiang Y, "Economic Burden of Smoking in China, 2000," *Tobacco Control* 15, Suppl. 1 (2006): i5–i11.

[3] Peto R and Lopez AD, "Future Worldwide Health Effects of Current Smoking Patterns", In Koop CE, Plarson CE Schwarz MR, eds., *Critical Issues in Global Health* (San Francsico: Wiley (Jossey-Bass), 2001): 154–161.

increasing tobacco taxes is a price-induced tobacco control scheme. The Ministry of Health has initiated activities to promote the four nonprice tobacco control schemes and to enforce the existing tobacco control legislation. However, the Chinese government has been slow in implementing the price-induced tobacco control scheme (i.e., increasing taxes on tobacco products).

A very large tobacco control literature has demonstrated that raising tobacco excise taxes is one of the most effective tobacco control tools to reduce cigarette consumption while raising tax revenue. Higher cigarette tax rates would lead to higher cigarette prices, which can cause some smokers to quit smoking, help prevent adolescents from initiating smoking, and reduce consumption among continuing smokers. Increasing tobacco excise taxes has not been considered in China mainly for economic reasons. Like many other countries in Asia, the Chinese government controls the production, manufacturing, and sale of tobacco products. As a state-run monopoly enterprise, China's tobacco industry has generated substantial profit and taxes, approximately 7.4 percent of the central government's total revenue in 2003.[4] Also, tobacco growing is an important source of income for farmers in the poorest provinces, such as Yunnan and Guizhou where tobacco taxes are the major source of revenue for local governments. It has long been a concern that raising tobacco excise taxes may harm the state economy and government revenue.

Another concern has been voiced that raising tobacco taxes may increase the financial burden of the poor or low-income smokers because they spend a greater proportion of their income on cigarette expenditures than do wealthier smokers. China has about 46 million people living below the poverty level. Studies from developed countries have found that compared with high-income people, low-income people are more likely to smoke and to consume more cigarettes. Opponents of raising tobacco taxes often argue

---

[4] Hu TW, Mao Z, Ong M *et al*, "China at the Crossroads: The Economics of Tobacco and Health," *Tobacco Control* 15, Suppl. 1 (2006): i37–i41.

that tobacco taxes are regressive because a disproportionate burden of cigarette tax increases would be borne by the low-income smokers.[5,6]

To prepare China for implementing the FCTC-required provision of increasing tobacco taxes in the future, it is important to investigate the responsiveness of cigarette demand to cigarette price increases in China especially among low-income people. A standard measure to quantify the price responsiveness on cigarette consumption is the price elasticity of cigarette demand. The estimates of price elasticities allow policy-makers to evaluate the effectiveness of cigarette taxation on reducing cigarette smoking as well as the impact on the government's tax revenue and the financial burden on smokers.

Previous Literature

The majority of the studies on price elasticity of cigarette demand have been conducted in developed countries. Estimates of the price elasticity for cigarette demand vary widely depending on the nature of the data (aggregated time-series data versus individual-level survey data), time period of the data, model specification, and estimation methodology,[7] but many fall within the narrower range from −0.30 to −0.50.[5,8] Almost all the literature on price elasticity of cigarette demand has focused on the general population. Only a few studies examined the price elasticities for different income groups. Townsend[9] found that among British men, cigarette taxes had the

---

[5] Chaloupka FJ and Warner KE, "The Economics of Smoking," In *Handbook of Health Economics*, ed. Culyer AJ and Newhouse JP (Amsterdam: Elsevier, 2000), 1539–1627.

[6] Remier DK, Poor Smokers, Poor Quitters, and Cigarette Tax Regressivity," *American Journal of Public Health* 94, no. 2 (2004): 225–229.

[7] Gallet CA and List JA, "Cigarette Demand: A Meta-Analysis of Elasticities," *Health Economics* 12, no. 10 (2003): 821–835.

[8] US Department of Health and Human Services (USDHHS), Reducing Tobacco Use: A Report of the Surgeon General, Atlanta, GA: Centers for Disease Control and Prevention, National Center for Chronic Disease Prevention and Health Promotion, Office on Smoking and Health 2000.

[9] Townsend JL, "Cigarette Tax, Economic Welfare, and Social Class Patterns of Smoking," *Applied Economics* 19 (1987): 355–365.

greatest impact on cigarette consumption among those in the lowest SES class. In contrast, another British study found no evidence of differential price elasticities across different SES classes for either men or women.[10] Using more recent data for British men and women, Townsend et al.[11] found that price elasticity was inversely related to SES, with the highest price elasticity in the lowest SES quintile (−1.0 for men and −0.88 for women), and the lowest price elasticity (not significantly different from zero) in the highest two quintiles. A study conducted in the United States[12,13] found that lower income adults were more price-responsive with price elasticity at −0.43, and higher income adults were not price-responsive at all.

Estimates of cigarette price elasticities for developing countries were scarce until recently.[14–16] A few of the published estimates pertain to China. Mao and Jiang[17,18] first analyzed the price-demand relationship for cigarettes in the Sichuan province by using both the

---

[10] Borren P and Sutton M, "Are Increases in Cigarette Taxation Regressive?" *Health Economics* 1 (1992): 245–253.

[11] Townsend JL, Roderick P and Cooper J, "Cigarette Smoking by Socioeconomic Group, Sex, and Age: Effects of Price, Income, and Health Publicity," *British Medical Journal* 309 (1994):923–927.

[12] Farrelly MC and Bray JW, "Response to Increases in Cigarette Prices by Race/Ethnicity, Income, and Age Groups — United States, 1973–1993," *Morbidity and Mortality Weekly Report* 47, no. 29 (1998): 605–609.

[13] Farrelly MC, Bray JW, Pechacek T and Woollery T, "Response by Adults to Increases in Cigarette Prices by Sociodemographic Characteristics," *Southern Economic Journal* 68, no. 1 (2001): 156–165.

[14] Chapman S and Richardson J, "Tobacco Excise Taxes and Declining Consumption: The Case of Papua New Guinea," *American Journal of Public Health* 80 (1990): 537–540.

[15] Tansel A, "Cigarette Demand, Health Scares and Education in Turkey," *Applied Economics* 25 (1993): 521–529.

[16] Van Kinh H, Ross H, Levy D, Minh NT and Ngoc VT, "The Effect of Imposing a Higher, Uniform Tobacco Tax in Vietnam," *Health Research Policy and Systems* 4 (2006): 6.

[17] Mao Z and Jiang JL, "Demand for Cigarette and Pricing Policy (in Chinese)," *Chinese Health Economics* 16, no. 6 (1997): 50–52.

[18] Mao Z and Jiang JL, "Determinants of the Demand for Cigarettes: A Cross-Sectional Study," (in Chinese) *Chinese Health Service Management* 13, no. 5 (1997): 227–229.

aggregated time-series data from 1981–1993 and the individual-level data from a 1995 survey. Their estimates of price elasticity ranged between −0.60 and −0.80. Later, another study[19] used the 1995 survey data conducted in Sichuan and Fujian provinces and estimated that the price elasticity of cigarette demand was −0.52. Instead of employing provincial data, Hu and Mao[20] used the national time-series data of annual cigarette sales from 1980–1996 to analyze per capita cigarette consumption in China with an estimated price elasticity of −0.54. Mao and Yang[21] estimated adults' demand for cigarettes stratifying by income and gender and using individual-level data from a 1998 survey collected from 16 counties in China. Their estimated price elasticity was −0.543 for all respondents, −0.507 for the group with family income of at least 500 yuan per month, and −0.775 for the group with family income less than 500 yuan per month. Lance et al.[22] used data from the 1993–1997 China Health and Nutrition Survey conducted in the following nine provinces: Guangxi, Guizhou, Heilongjiang, Henan, Hubei, Hunan, Jiangsu, Liaoning, and Shandong to examine the cigarette demand for Chinese males aged 13 and older. Their estimated price elasticity was −0.007 based on a community-level fixed effect model specification and −0.082 based on a heterogeneity-free model specification. Bai and Zhang[23] pooled the provincial time-series data of annual cigarette sales across all provinces in China from 1997 to 2002 and estimated that the price elasticity for the national aggregate cigarette demand was −0.84.

---

[19] Mao Z and Hsieh CR, Hu TW and Jiang J, "The Demand for Cigarettes in China, Chengdu, Sichuan: West China Medical Sciences University Working Paper, 2000.

[20] Hu TW and Mao Z, "Effects of Cigarette Tax on Cigarette Consumption and the Chinese Economy," *Tobacco Control* 11, no.2 (2002): 105–108.

[21] Mao Z and Yang GH, "Adults' Demand for Cigarettes and its Determinants in China" (in Chinese), *Soft Science of Health* 17, no. 2 (2003): 19–23.

[22] Lance P, Akin J, Dow W and Loh CP, "Is Cigarette Smoking in Poorer Nations Highly Sensitive to Price? Evidence from Russia and China," *Journal of Health Economics* 23 (2004): 173–189.

[23] Bai Y and Zhang Z, "Aggregate Cigarette Demand and Regional Differences in China," *Applied Economics* 37 (2005): 2523–2528.

As noted, the estimated magnitude of price elasticity ranged widely from −0.84 to −0.007 depending on the nature of the data (time-series versus cross-sectional), time period, and methods of estimation. Only one of these previous studies used individual-level national survey data; however, the data source was from the 1990s and covered only 16 counties.

Objectives

In this chapter, estimation is made on the price elasticities of adults' cigarette demand in China by income groups using the 2002 National Smoking Prevalence Survey and the implications for tobacco tax policy on the government's tax revenue and smokers' tax burden are assessed. Three issues are addressed: (1) whether or not low-income adults are more responsive to cigarette price increases in reducing cigarette consumption than high-income adults, (2) whether or not raising cigarette taxes will reduce government revenue, and (3) whether or not raising cigarette taxes will increase the disproportionate tax burden for low-income smokers. The results will provide empirical evidence to guide policy-makers in China to design appropriate tobacco tax policies in the future. Given that China is the largest cigarette consuming and producing country in the world, the results of this study will also provide important implications for international tobacco control.

METHODS

Demand Models of Cigarette Smoking

The cigarette demand theory generally assumes that quantity of cigarettes consumed is a function of cigarette prices, prices of all other goods, personal income, and other demand determinants.[5] These other determinants include demographic variables, cigarette advertising, anti-smoking regulations, interstate smuggling, perception of the health risk of smoking, and progression of addiction. Depending on the type of data, there are two fundamental methods to analyze the demand for cigarette smoking: one is based on aggregated time-series data, and the other is based on individual-level data taken from cross-sectional surveys.

Most previous cigarette demand studies have been based on aggregated time-series data. The unit of observation is either the whole nation or a single state. The measure of cigarette consumption is per capita cigarette sales. Several problems are inherent in using aggregated time-series data.[5,24,25] First, potential key determinants of cigarette consumption, such as race, gender, and education are typically omitted from the model due to the aggregation in the time-series data. Although these demographic variables influence individuals' smoking behavior, the aggregated values of these variables do not vary appreciably over time; so they do not show significant effect. Second, many of these key explanatory variables are correlated with the cigarette price variable. Including these variables can result in multicollinearity and an unstable estimate for the coefficient of cigarette price; excluding them can produce a biased estimate for the coefficient of cigarette price. Third, tax-paid cigarette sales data do not exactly reflect actual consumption. For example, cigarettes purchased from casual and organized smuggling are not counted in the cigarette sales. Failure to account for the potential of smuggling will produce upward-biased estimates for the impact of cigarette price on cigarette demand. Fourth, cigarette prices and cigarette consumption are simultaneously determined in the aggregated demand-supply framework. Failure to account for this simultaneity can lead to a biased estimate for the coefficient of price.

The use of individual-level cross-sectional survey data can avoid or mitigate some of the above-mentioned problems, although these data may be subject to potential reporting biases because individual-level surveys rely upon self-reported data. However, the most important

---

[24] Wasserman J, Manning WG, Newhouse JP *et al*, "The Effects of Excise Taxes and Regulations on Cigarette Smoking," *Journal of Health Economics* 10, no. 1 (1991): 43–64.
[25] Jha P and Chaloupka FJ, *Curbing the Epidemic: Governments and the Economics of Tobacco Control,* (Washington, DC: World Bank, 1999).

advantage of using individual-level data is the feasibility of addressing issues that cannot be addressed using aggregated data. First, using individual-level data allows for examining the separate effects of cigarette prices on smoking participation among all individuals and on smoking intensity among continuing smokers. Second, it allows for evaluating the effects of cigarette prices on cigarette demand for different demographic and socioeconomic subpopulation groups. Because the main objective of this chapter is to estimate the price elasticities of cigarette demand for different income groups, the cigarette demand analyses were conducted using the individual-level data method.

Specification of Econometric Model

A two-part model that has been used widely in the literature of health economics and the economics of smoking was employed.[24,26,27] The two-part model allows for examining the separate effects of price on the decision to become a smoker and on the quantity of cigarettes consumed among current smokers. The first part of the two-part model, called the smoking participation equation, estimates a discrete choice of whether an individual currently smokes or not. The second part of the model, called the smoking intensity equation or conditional cigarette demand equation, estimates the quantity of cigarettes smoked conditional upon those who continue to smoke. The probability of smoking participation is specified by a logit model, and the level of smoking intensity is specified by a linear regression as follows:

$$\text{Prob}(CS_i = 1) = \frac{1}{1 + e_1^{-(c_1 + \alpha_1 \ln P_i + \beta_1 X_i + \varepsilon_{1i})}}, \qquad (1)$$

$$\ln(Q_i / CS_i = 1) = c_2 + \alpha_2 \ln P_i + \beta_2 X_i + \varepsilon_{2i}, \qquad (2)$$

---

[26] Duan N, Manning WG Jr, Morris CN and Newhouse JP, "A Comparison of Alternative Models for the Demand for Medical Care," *Journal of Business and Economic Statistics* 1, no. 2 (1983): 115–126.

[27] Hu TW, Ren QF, Keeler TE and Bartlett J, "The Demand for Cigarettes in California and Behavioral Risk Factors," *Health Economics* 4 (1995): 7–14.

where CS_i is a binary variable which equals 1 if person i currently smokes and 0 otherwise; Prob($CS_i = 1$) is the probability that person i currently smokes; Ln ($Q_i/CS_i = 1$) are the packs of cigarettes smoked per month conditional upon smoking for person i; P_i is the price of cigarettes faced by person i; X_i is a vector of other explanatory variables including gender, age, education, annual family income, and smoking initiation age; ε_1 and ε_2 are random error terms. Because the distribution of cigarettes smoked per month is skewed, packs of cigarettes smoked are expressed in logarithm term. The price of cigarettes also is expressed in logarithm term.

The overall demand for cigarettes for person i can be obtained by multiplying the probability of smoking participation by the conditional cigarette demand as follows:

$$E(Q_i) = \text{Prob}(CS_i = 1) \times E(Q_i/CS_i = 1). \quad (3)$$

At the population level, the mean of the overall cigarette demand for all individuals is equivalent to the per capita cigarette consumption.

The total price elasticity of the overall demand for cigarettes, η, can be expressed by the sum of the price elasticity of smoking participation, η_{sp}, and the price elasticity of smoking intensity conditional upon current smokers, η_{si}, as below:[22,24,27]

$$\eta = \eta_{sp} + \eta_{si} = (1 - \overline{CS}) * \alpha_1 + \alpha_2, \quad (4)$$

where $\overline{CS}$ denotes the population mean of current smoking prevalence, α_1 is the price coefficient in Eq. (1), and α_2 is the price coefficient in Eq. (2). Note that the price elasticity of smoking participation equals the product of the price coefficient in Eq. (1) and $(1 - \overline{CS})$, while the price elasticity of smoking intensity equals the price coefficient in Eq. (2).

The standard error of the total price elasticity of the overall cigarette demand, s_η can be specified by:

$$s_\eta = \sqrt{(1-\overline{CS})^2 (s_{\alpha_1}^2) + (\alpha_1)^2 (s_{\overline{CS}}^2) + (s_{\alpha_1}^2)(s_{\overline{CS}}^2) + (s_{\alpha_2}^2)}, \quad (5)$$

where $s_{\alpha 1}$, $s_{\alpha 2}$, and $s_{\overline{CS}}$ denote the standard errors of the estimated parameters α_1, α_2, and $\overline{CS}$, respectively.

Data and Variables

With the exception of data on cigarette prices, the primary data source of the present cigarette demand analyses was the National Smoking Prevalence Survey (NSPS) conducted by the Chinese Center for Disease Control and Prevention in 2002. The NSPS is a national representative sample of 16,056 adults aged 16 and older who reside in the 130 counties and districts covering all the 27 province-level divisions (provinces, autonomous regions, and municipalities) in China. The survey was based on a multi-stage random sampling scheme. Face-to-face interviews were conducted to collect detailed information from each respondent about their history of smoking behavior including current smoking status, number of cigarettes smoked per day by current smokers, the age when smokers first smoked regularly (i.e., smoking initiation age); demographic characteristics, such as age, gender and educational attainment; and family characteristics, such as urbanization of residence and family income.

Smokers were also asked to list the brand of cigarettes they had smoked most often and to report the price per pack of that listed brand. To avoid the endogeneity problem that self-reported cigarette prices reflect the individual-level choices of cigarette quality and brands, the average of the self-reported cigarette prices was calculated among all smokers who resided in each of the 130 counties and districts. That was used as the average market price faced by all the adults in each county or district. Finally, the average market price was assigned to all the respondents (smokers and nonsmokers) by their residence location (county or district).

Although China does not impose provincial or local excise taxes on cigarettes, there still exists a cross-sectional variation of cigarette prices due to less integrated markets, difficult transportation, province-level trade barriers, and different input cost structures faced by cigarette factories.[22,28] Another important source of price variation is the huge geographical differentiation in the manufacturing of local brands as well as in the smoking habits of local smokers. Although more than 2,000 brands of cigarettes were available in China, cigarettes consumed in each county or district generally focused on a few brands distinct from those consumed in other counties and districts. Depending on the cigarette brands, cigarette prices per pack differed widely from less than 1 yuan to more than 100 yuan. Therefore, county- or district-level cigarette prices in China can provide legitimate cross-sectional variation to explain cigarette demand.

Income was measured by annual family income as reported in the 2002 NSPS. The respondents were classified into four mutually exclusive income groups: (1) poor group with annual income less than 5,000 yuan, (2) low-income group with annual income between 5,000 and 9,999 yuan, (3) middle-income group with annual income between 10,000 and 49,999 yuan, and (4) high-income group with annual income of at least 50,000 yuan. As it is common practice in the Chinese culture for people to avoid discussing their wealth when they are rich, those who refused to answer the income question were combined with the high-income group.

Both the age of respondents and smoking initiation age were measured by continuous variables. For the respondents' educational attainment, three mutually exclusive categories were defined: (1) poorly educated group, which includes the illiterate, those with primary school education, or those with unknown education, (2) moderately educated group for those with some middle school, high school, or vocational school education, and (3) highly educated group for those with at least some college education. In the cigarette demand analyses, it is assumed females, the poorly educated, and the poor were the omitted groups.

---

[28] Deaton, A, *The Analysis of Household Surveys: A Microeconometric Approach to Development Policy* (Baltimore: Johns Hopkins University Press, 1997).

Statistical Analysis

Equations (1) and (2) were estimated separately. First, a logit regression was used to estimate the smoking participation equation by including all the individuals in the study sample. Second, an ordinary least-squares regression was used to estimate the smoking intensity equation by including only those individuals who reported smoking currently in the study sample. Statistical significance was defined as P-value < 0.05. To test the null hypothesis that the total price elasticity was statistically different from zero, its 95 percent confidence interval (CI) was computed based on Eqs. (4) and (5). To test whether the total price elasticities between any two income groups were statistically different or not, their 95 percent CIs were compared. All statistical analyses were performed using STATA software version 7 (Stata Corporation, College Station, Tex).

RESULTS

Table 1 illustrates the frequency distribution of the 16,056 adults from the 2002 NSPS data by demographic characteristics. The majority of the respondents resided in the rural area (65 percent), were moderately educated (56 percent), and were male (51 percent). The middle-income group comprised 38 percent of the total sample; the poor and low-income groups each comprised one-fourth, and the high-income group (including respondents who refused to answer the income question) comprised about 10 percent.

The smoking prevalence rate among the 16,056 adults was 29.2 percent. Current smokers smoked an average of 14.2 cigarettes per day. As in many other Asian countries, smoking is mainly a habit for men in China. The gender gap in the smoking prevalence rate was very wide: 55.2 percent for men and 2.3 percent for women. Smoking prevalence rates were significantly different by educational attainment with the moderately educated adults having the highest smoking rate at 31.3 percent, followed by 27.6 percent for the poorly educated group, and 14.7 percent for the highly educated group. Smoking rates were higher in rural areas than in urban areas: 31.9 percent versus 24.2 percent, respectively.

Table 1: Distribution of Sample Size in the 2002 National Smoking Prevalence Survey Data by Demographic Characteristics

Characteristics	Sample Size	Percents of Total
All	16,056	100
Gender		
Male	8,178	51
Female	7,878	49
Family income (yuan per year)		
< 5000	3,977	25
5000–9999	4,147	26
10,000–50,000	6,084	38
> 50,000	666	4
Refuse to answer	1,182	7
Educational Attainment		
Primary school and below	5,095	32
Middle or high school	8,970	56
College and above	1,932	12
Unknown	59	0
Residence Area		
Urban	5,589	35
Rural	10,467	65

Table 2 shows the estimated smoking prevalence rates, amount of smoking intensity among current smokers, per capita cigarette consumption, and cigarette retail prices by income group based on

Table 2: Smoking Status and Average Cigarette Retail Price by Income Group in China, 2002

	Cigarette Retail Price (Yuan/pack)	Current Smoking Prevalence Rate (Percent)	Smoking Intensity by Smokers (Cigarettes/day)	Per Capita Consumption (Cigarettes/day)
All	4.62	29.2	14.2	4.1
Income Group:				
Poor	3.3	30.9	13.4	4.1
Low income	3.8	30.3	14.3	4.3
Middle income	5.6	28.8	14.2	4.1
High income[a]	9.2	23.0	14.6	3.4

[a] Includes those respondents who refused to answer the income question.

the 2002 NSPS data. The smoking prevalence rate was the highest for the poor group at 30.9 percent and decreased by income level: 30.3 percent for the low-income group, 28.8 percent for the middle-income group, and 23.0 percent for the high-income group. However, smoking intensity for the three higher income groups was about the same while the poor smokers had the lowest smoking intensity: 13.4 cigarettes per day. Overall, the per capita cigarette consumption among adults was 4.1 cigarettes per day for the entire sample. High-income adults had the lowest per capita consumption: 3.4 cigarettes per day. The average cigarette retail price for the entire sample was 4.62 yuan per pack, but it varied substantially across income groups: 3.3 yuan per pack for poor smokers, 3.8 yuan per pack for low-income smokers, 5.6 yuan per pack for middle-income smokers, and 9.2 yuan per pack for high-income smokers. Compared to the poorest, the wealthiest smokers spent almost three times as much money per pack of cigarettes. One explanation is that the wealthier smokers in China favor the more expensive brands of cigarettes.

The first two columns of Table 3 present the estimated coefficients from the two-part model of cigarette demand for all respondents. Cigarette prices had a significantly negative effect on both smoking participation and smoking intensity. Males were more likely than females to participate in smoking, and male smokers consumed more cigarettes than female smokers. The age of respondents showed a significant positive effect on both smoking participation and smoking intensity. Among current smokers, their smoking initiation age was inversely associated with smoking intensity, meaning that the younger they started to smoke regularly, the heavier smokers they tended to be. Higher education was associated with decreased propensity of smoking participation; however, among current smokers, the correlation between smoking intensity and educational attainment was not statistically significant. Income level had no significant impact on smoking participation but a positive impact on smoking intensity. Compared with the poorest, the smokers in the low-, middle-, and high-income groups consumed an average of 10 percent (= $e^{0.095} - 1$), 19 percent, and 20 percent more cigarettes, respectively.

Table 3: Estimated Coefficients for the Two-Part Model of Cigarette Demand by Income Group in China, 2002

Variable	All Smoking Participation	All Smoking Intensity	Poor (< 5,000 yuan) Smoking Participation	Poor (< 5,000 yuan) Smoking Intensity	Low Income (5,000–10,000 yuan) Smoking Participation	Low Income (5,000–10,000 yuan) Smoking Intensity
Constant	−3.923***	2.921***	−3.326***	2.908***	−3.893***	3.137***
Price (in natural log)	−0.091**	−0.090***	−0.692***	−0.111***	−0.286***	−0.035
Male	3.999***	0.230***	3.790***	0.196*	3.792***	0.142
Age	0.009***	0.009***	0.012***	0.005**	0.016***	0.011***
Smoking initiation age		−0.028***		−0.018***		−0.038***
Moderately educated	−0.197***	−0.025	−0.110	0.074	0.004	−0.028
Highly educated	−0.395***	−0.033	0.136	0.068	−0.527**	−0.323**
Low income	−0.013	0.095***				
Middle income	0.031	0.175***				
High income	−0.079	0.181***				

(continued)

Table 3: *(continued)*

Variable	Middle Income (10,000–50,000 yuan)		High Income (> 50,000 yuan)	
	Smoking Participation	Smoking Intensity	Smoking Participation	Smoking Intensity
Constant	−4.254***	3.063***	−4.836***	2.836***
Price (in natural log)	0.131**	−0.111***	0.441***	−0.083
Male	4.316***	0.379***	4.061***	0.369
Age	0.004	0.008***	0.010*	0.017***
Smoking initiation age		−0.030***		−0.037***
Moderately educated	−0.255***	−0.070	−0.420**	0.015
Highly educated	−0.505***	0.045	−0.432**	−0.047
Low income				
Middle income				
High income				

*, **, and *** indicate that the coefficient is statistically significant at *p*-values < 0.1, < 0.05, and < 0.01 of the two-tailed test. The omitted groups are females, poorly educated, and the poor.

The last eight columns of Table 3 contain the estimated coefficients from the two-part model for different income groups. The effect of cigarette prices on smoking participation was significant for all subgroups; however, the price effect was negative for the two lower income groups and positive for the two higher income groups. Among current smokers, the effect of cigarette prices on smoking intensity was negative for all subgroups but statistically significant only for the poor and middle-income groups. Similar to the pattern found in the model for all respondents, males and the age of respondent had the anticipated positive effect on both smoking participation and smoking intensity for all subgroups with two exceptions: the gender effect on smoking intensity was statistically significant only for the middle-income group, and the age effect on smoking participation was statistically significant only for the two lower income groups. Among current smokers, the negative effect of smoking initiation age on smoking intensity was the smallest (in absolute value) for the poor group. The effect of educational attainment on smoking participation was significantly negative for the two higher income groups but in general was insignificant for the two lower income groups. Generally speaking, educational attainment did not affect smoking intensity among current smokers.

Based on the estimated price coefficients from the two-part models and Eq. (4), the price elasticities of smoking participation and smoking intensity and the total price elasticity of unconditional cigarette demand by income group were calculated as shown in Table 4. For all respondents, the price elasticity of smoking participation was −0.064 (95 percent CI: −0.115, −0.013), and the price elasticity of smoking intensity conditional on current smokers was −0.09 (95 percent CI: −0.127, −0.053), both of which were statistically significant. The total price elasticity was statistically significant at −0.154 (95 percent CI: −0.217, −0.091), which suggests that a 10 percent increase in cigarette prices leads to a 1.54 percent reduction in per capita cigarette consumption. Approximately 42 percent (= 0.064/0.154) of the decline in per capita consumption was from decreased smoking participation and 58 percent from reduced smoking intensity among current smokers.

Table 4: Price Elasticities of Cigarette Demand by Income Group in China, 2002

Variable	Smoking Participation Elasticity		Smoking Intensity Elasticity		Total Elasticity	
	Elasticity	95 percent CI	Elasticity	95 percent CI	Elasticity	95 percent CI
All	−0.064	(−0.115, −0.013)	−0.090	(−0.127, −0.053)	−0.154	(−0.217, −0.091)
Income Group:						
Poor	−0.478	(−0.600, −0.356)	−0.111	(−0.191, −0.031)	−0.589	(−0.735, −0.443)
Low income	−0.199	(−0.310, −0.089)	−0.035	(−0.108, 0.038)	−0.234	(−0.367, −0.102)
Middle income	0.093	(0.009, 0.178)	−0.111	(−0.170, −0.052)	−0.018	(−0.121, 0.085)
High income	0.340	(0.172, 0.508)	−0.083	(−0.219, 0.053)	0.257	(0.040, 0.473)

In the separate demand analyses by income groups, the total price elasticities of cigarette demand were −0.589 (95 percent CI: −0.735, −0.443) for the poor group, −0.234 (95 percent CI: −0.367, −0.102) for the low-income group, −0.018 (95 percent CI: −0.121, 0.085) for the middle-income group, and 0.257 (95 percent CI: 0.040, 0.473) for the high-income group. These total price elasticities were all statistically different from zero except for the middle-income group. The negative total price elasticities diminished in absolute value as income level increased, but reversed to a positive effect for the high-income group. By comparing the 95 percent CIs across subgroups, the difference in total price elasticities was statistically different between the poor and all other income groups, and between the high- and low-income groups. The differential total price elasticities were mainly driven by the difference in price responsiveness on smoking participation. The price elasticities of smoking participation were −0.478 for the poor, −0.199 for the low-income group, 0.093 for the middle-income group, and 0.340 for the high-income group. All of the smoking participation elasticities were not only significantly different from zero but also different from one another except between the middle- and high-income groups. With respect to smoking intensity, the differences among income-specific price elasticities were not significant. Therefore, the poor group was the most responsive to price increases in reducing cigarette demand because they were more likely than all other groups to quit smoking and not to initiate smoking. In contrast, the high-income group positively responded to price increases in increasing cigarette demand because of their positive price responsiveness on smoking participation: A 10 percent increase in cigarette prices led to a 3.4 percent increase in smoking prevalence rate.

TAX SIMULATION

In 2002, the total government revenue from cigarette profits and taxes amounted to 140 billion yuan[29], and total cigarette sales were

---

[29] Lin T and Xiong B, *Tobacco Economy and Tobacco Control* (in Chinese), (Beijing: Economic Science Press, 2004).

34.7 million cases or 87 billion packs (1 case = 2,500 packs). Thus, it was estimated that the cigarette tax rate in China was approximately 1.61 yuan per pack or 35 percent of the cigarette price (=1.61/4.62). In other words, for every 10 yuan spent on cigarettes, Chinese smokers paid 3.5 Yuan on cigarette taxes. This rate is relatively low compared to the cigarette tax rates in other countries. For countries attempting to reduce tobacco use, it is recommended that the tax component account for two-thirds to fourth-fifths of the retail prices of cigarettes.[30] This suggests ample room in China for raising cigarette taxes.

To assess the potential impact of raising cigarette taxes on cigarette consumption, government's tax revenue, and smokers' tax burden in China, two simulation analyses were conducted based on the price elasticity estimates presented in the previous section. Notice that a part of China's cigarette tax is an *ad valorem* tax levied as a percentage of the wholesale price at the producer level. For the convenience of calculation, it is assumed that cigarette taxes are levied as a percentage of the retail price.

Implications for Government Revenue

In the first simulation analysis, the effect of tax increases on adults' cigarette consumption and government tax revenue for the general population was examined by considering different tax increases: 5, 10, 15, and 20 percents increases in the 2002 cigarette price. As shown in Table 2, before tax increases, smoking prevalence was 29.2 percent and per capita consumption was 4.1 cigarettes per day, an equivalent of 74.6 packs per year (= 4.1 × 365 / 20). Based on the 2002 adult population of 1.01 billion persons aged 16 and older in China[31], it was estimated that the total national cigarette

---

[30] Chaloupka FJ, Hu TW, Warner KE, Jacobs R and Yurekli A, "The Taxation of Tobacco Products," in *Tobacco Control in Developing Countries*, Jha P and Chaloupka F, eds. (New York: Oxford University Press, 2000): 237–272.
[31] National Bureau of Statistics, People's Republic of China, *China Statistics Yearbook 2003* (Beijing: China Statistics Press, 2004).

consumption per year would be 75.5 billion packs (=1.01 × 74.6). Multiplying the total adult population by smoking prevalence rate, a total of 295.4 million adults being current smokers were estimated. Similarly, multiplying the current cigarette tax rate of 1.61 yuan per pack by total national cigarette consumption, it was estimated that the total annual cigarette tax revenue would be 121.5 billion yuan.

Table 5 presents the simulation results. If cigarette taxes increase by 10 percent of the cigarette price, the cigarette tax per pack would increase from 1.61 yuan to 2.07 yuan (= 4.62 × 0.1 + 1.61). Consequently, the smoking prevalence rate would decrease from 29.2 to 29.0 percent, a reduction of 0.2 percentage point (= 0.292 × 0.064 × 0.1) based on the estimated price elasticity of smoking participation at −0.064, and the number of current smokers would be reduced by 1.9 million persons (= 1,011 × 0.2 percent). Overall, per capita annual consumption would decline to 73.5 packs (= 74.6 × (1−0.154 × 0.1)) based on the estimated total price elasticity at −0.154. In aggregated terms, total annual cigarette consumption would decrease by 1.2 billion packs (= 1.01 × (74.6−73.5)), and total annual government tax revenue would be 153.8 billion yuan (= 1.01 × 2.07 × 73.5), an increase of 32.3 billion yuan or 27 percent.

Even a smaller tax increase would have a substantial impact on curbing tobacco use. For example, a 5 percent increase in the cigarette price would lead to 1.0 million quitters, reduce total annual consumption by 0.6 billion packs, and increase total annual tax revenue by 16.3 billion yuan or 13 percent. The magnitude of the tax effect on cigarette consumption and government revenue multiplies as the increase in tax rates is elevated. If the cigarette tax increased by 20 percent of the cigarette price, the number of quitters would soar to 3.8 million persons, total annual consumption would drop by 2.3 billion packs, and total annual government tax revenue would increase by 63.5 billion yuan or 52 percent.

Simulation results of the present study show that raising cigarette taxes would increase the government's cigarette tax revenue. If the *ad valorem* tax rate increased by 10 percent of cigarette prices, total cigarette tax revenue would increase by about 27 percent.

Table 5: Simulated Impact of Cigarette Taxation on Cigarette Consumption and Government Tax Revenue in China for Different Tax Increases[a]

Indicator	No Change	5 percent Increase	10 percent Increase	15 percent Increase	20 percent Increase
Cigarette tax per pack (yuan)	1.61	1.84	2.07	2.30	2.53
Prevalence of current smoking (percent)	29.2	29.1	29.0	28.9	28.8
Per capita annual cigarette consumption (packs)	74.6	74.1	73.5	72.9	72.3
Total number of current smokers (million)	295.4	294.5	293.5	292.6	291.6
Total annual cigarette consumption (billion packs)	75.5	74.9	74.3	73.7	73.1
Total annual cigarette tax revenue (billion yuan)	121.5	137.8	153.8	169.5	185.0
Reduction in number of current smokers (million)	—	1.0	1.9	2.9	3.8
Reduction in total annual cigarette consumption (billion packs)	—	0.6	1.2	1.7	2.3
Increase in total annual cigarette tax revenue (billion yuan)	—	16.3	32.3	48.0	63.5

[a]The tax increase is measured by pecentage of the 2002 cigarette retail price in China, which was 4.62 yuan per pack.

Implications for Disproportionate Tax Burden

In the second simulation analysis, the effects of tax increases on cigarette consumption and smokers' tax burden for different income groups were examined by assuming an *ad valorem* tax increase of 10 percent of cigarette prices. Table 6 shows annual cigarette consumption and tax burden before and after the tax increase. Given the current 35 percent tax rate, cigarette taxes per pack were 1.155 yuan, 1.33 yuan, 1.96 yuan, and 3.22 yuan for poor, low-income, middle-income, and high-income smokers, respectively. Before estimating annual cigarette tax burden per smoker, the smoking intensity measure was first converted from cigarettes per day to packs per year. For example, for poor smokers, their smoking intensity of 13.4 cigarettes per day is equivalent to 244.7 packs per year. Then, multiplying the cigarette tax per pack by annual packs of cigarettes consumed per smoker, it was estimated that the annual tax burden per smoker was 282.6 yuan for the poor, 348.1 yuan for the low-income group, 507.0 yuan for the middle-income group, and 856.8 yuan for the high-income group. Even before the cigarette tax increase, the poorer smokers paid less cigarette taxes than the wealthier smokers although the proportion of their cigarette tax spending relative to family income might be substantially higher.

With a 10 percent increase in cigarette prices, the cigarette tax for the poor group would increase by 0.33 yuan per pack, about one-third of that for the high-income group. In response to the price increase, those continuing smokers in the poor group would reduce cigarette consumption by 2.7 packs per year (= 244.7 × 0.111 × 0.1) based on the estimated price elasticity of smoking intensity at –0.111. Consequently, their annual cigarette tax burden would increase by 76.7 yuan per smoker (= (244.7–2.7) × (1.155 + 0.33) – 282.6) or by 27 percent (= 76.7/282.6). For the continuing smokers in other income groups, after the tax increase, their annual cigarette tax burden would also increase by about 27 percent although the magnitude of the increment in tax burden would go up with a higher income level: 97.9 yuan for the low-income group, 137.6 yuan for the middle-income group, and 235.7 yuan for the high-income group.

Table 6: Simulated Impact of a Tax Increase of 10 percent of the Cigarette Price on Cigarette Consumption and Tax Burden by Income Group in China

Indicator	All	Poor	Low Income	Middle Income	High Income
Pre-taxation					
Cigarette tax per pack (yuan)	1.61	1.155	1.33	1.96	3.22
Annual consumption per smoker (packs)	255.4	244.7	261.7	258.7	266.1
Annual tax burden per smoker (yuan)	411.3	282.6	348.1	507.0	856.8
Per capita annual consumption (packs)	74.6	75.6	79.2	74.4	61.2
Per capita annual tax burden (yuan)	120.2	87.3	105.3	145.8	197.1
Post-taxation					
Increase in cigarette tax per pack (yuan)	0.46	0.33	0.38	0.56	0.92
Change in annual consumption per smoker (packs)	-2.3	-2.7	-0.9	-2.9	-2.2
Increase in annual tax burden per smoker (yuan)	112.7	76.7	97.9	137.6	235.7
Change in per capita annual consumption (packs)	-1.2	-4.5	-1.9	-0.1	1.6
Increase in per capita annual tax burden (yuan)	31.9	18.3	26.9	41.3	62.8

Furthermore, cigarette tax increases would not only cut down smoking intensity among continuing smokers, but also motivate some smokers to quit. Since quitters would no longer pay cigarette taxes, the full effect of taxation on the tax burden to a society should be measured by considering all adults regardless of whether they are continuing smokers or quitters. Therefore, the tax effects on the per capita cigarette tax burden were also simulated as shown in Table 6. For adults in the poor group, before the tax increase, per capita annual cigarette consumption was 75.6 packs, and per capita annual cigarette tax burden was 87.3 yuan (= 1.155 × 75.6). After the tax increase, their per capita annual consumption would drop by 4.5 packs (= 75.6 × 0.589 × 0.1) based on the estimated total price elasticity −0.589, and their per capita annual tax burden would increase by 18.3 yuan (= (75.6−4.5) × (1.155 + 0.33) −87.3) or by 21 percent. For the other subgroups, after the tax increase, per capita annual consumption would drop by 1.9 packs for the low-income group and 0.1 pack for the middle-income group, but increase by 1.6 packs for the high-income group. Per capita annual tax burden would increase by 26.9 yuan or 26 percent for the low-income group, 41.3 yuan or 28 percent for the middle-income group, and 62.8 yuan or 32 percent for the high-income group.

The above simulation results show that the additional tax burden measured either by per smoker or by per capita would be heavier for the wealthier adults. Therefore, raising cigarette taxes would not increase the disproportionate tax burden for poorer people.

CONCLUSION

In this chapter, attempt was made to assess the potential for raising cigarette excise taxes to reduce cigarette demand in China by estimating the price elasticity of demand for cigarettes. The empirical results indicated that adults' cigarette demand in China was responsive to price increases, with a total price elasticity of −0.154 (−0.064 for smoking participation elasticity and −0.09 for smoking intensity elasticity), and that more than half of the overall price effects resulted from the decline in the smoking intensity by current smokers. It was also found that the price effects on adults' cigarette demand varied significantly with income level. Price had its greatest negative effect (in absolute value) on cigarette demand for the poorest group with a total price elasticity of −0.589. Eighty-one percent of the overall price effect operated through reduced participation in smoking, while 19 percent was through cutting down smoking intensity. However, for the high-income group, price effect on the demand for cigarettes was positive with a total price elasticity of 0.257, attributable mainly to a positive smoking participation elasticity of 0.340.

The estimated total price elasticity of −0.154, in this study, is at the low end of the range of recent price elasticity estimates in the literature. Nonetheless, poor and low-income Chinese adults are much more responsive to the price increases with the price elasticity estimates similar to the pattern found in the developed countries. A recent study by Lance et al.[22] also yielded a low total price elasticity from individual-level survey data in China. They hypothesized that the lower price elasticity estimates in China may be due to stronger addiction to cigarette smoking and lack of cultural and institutional support for anti-smoking efforts compared to most of the developed countries.

With respect to the income effect, income appears to impact cigarette demand primarily by positively influencing the number of cigarettes consumed by smokers rather than the smoking participation rate. Interestingly, in responses to hypothesized price increases, current smokers with different income levels did not differ significantly in reducing the number of cigarettes smoked. However, adults with lower income were more price-responsive in reducing smoking participation. One of the explanations for differential price effects on smoking participation is that cigarette expenditures comprise a greater proportion of family income for those with lower income. As cigarette prices increase, affordability is likely to become a greater concern for poor and low-income people. This is evidenced by the fact that smokers in the poorest group consumed much cheaper cigarettes with an average price of 3.3 yuan per pack while smokers in the highest income groups consumed expensive cigarettes with an average price of 9.2 yuan per pack.

The results of the estimated price elasticities have several implications for future tobacco tax policies in China. First, a tobacco tax is effective in discouraging tobacco use in China. Based on the simulation of this study, if an *ad valorem* cigarette excise tax is levied by increasing the cigarette prices by 10 percent, 1.9 million smokers would quit smoking, per capita consumption would be reduced by 1.2 packs per pear, and total cigarette consumption would decrease by 1.2 billion packs per year. Moreover, the decrease in cigarette demand would be greater for the lower income groups. The adults in the poor group would reduce their per capita consumption by 4.5 packs per year, whereas those in the high-income group would increase their per capita consumption by 1.9 packs per year. Second, raising cigarette taxes would increase the government's cigarette tax revenue. If the cigarette tax increased by 10 percent of the cigarette price, total annual government tax revenue would increase by 32.3 billion yuan or by about 27 percent. Third, adults in all the income groups would experience an increase in cigarette tax spending per person; however, the poorest would have the least hit — a 21 percent increase — whereas the wealthiest will have the heaviest hit — a 32 percent increase. These results suggest that higher cigarette taxation in China will redistribute the relative tax burden across income groups in a progressive manner. The reason that cigarette taxation is not regressive in China is that the poorer smokers consume cheaper cigarettes and are more price-responsive. Therefore, raising cigarette taxes is expected to lead to more quitters, less smoking initiation, fewer cigarettes smoked, and less increase in tax burden for the poorer adults, hence mitigating the socioeconomic gap in the health and economic burden of smoking.

Considering the loss of employment and income for workers in the cigarette manufacturing industry and tobacco farmers, the government could decide to allocate a portion of the increased cigarette tax revenue to subsidize these workers or farmers and help them transfer to other manufacturing industries or crop growing. Also, allocating a portion of cigarette tax revenue to provide smoking cessation assistance to the poor smokers would further mitigate the income effects of tax increases. Finally, because of the positive price-responsiveness on smoking participation among the middle- and high-income adults, who constitute almost half of the Chinese adult population, it is important to implement other health education and anti-smoking campaigns targeted at these subpopulations to change their smoking attitudes and behaviors. The combined effects of the tax increase and the allocation of cigarette tax revenue to other tobacco control programs would lead to more quitters, which would have substantial health benefits and reduce the economic burden of smoking in China.

In high-income countries, the tax component often accounts for at least two-thirds of the retail price of a pack of cigarettes. In China, it accounts for only about 35 percent of the retail price. There appears ample room for raising cigarette taxes to reduce tobacco use in China. The simulation results of this study predict that raising the cigarette tax would not only curb tobacco use, but also raise government revenue and improve the disproportionate tax burden.

ACKNOWLEDGMENTS

This study was supported by a grant from the Fograty International Center (Grant No. ROI-TW05938), National Institutes of Health. The authors alone are responsible for the findings.

Chapter 8

Smoking, Standard of Living, and Poverty in China*

Teh-wei Hu, Zhengzhong Mao, Yuanli Liu, Joy de Beyer and Michael Ong

INTRODUCTION

Smoking increases the risk of incurring cancers, cardio vascular disease, and other smoking related illnesses that result in higher medical expenditures, lower productivity, and pre mature death. Many international studies have addressed this long term negative impact of smoking on health and

---

*This chapter originally appeared as Hu TW, Mao Z, Liu Y, de Beyer J and Ong M. "Smoking, Standard of Living, and Poverty in China," *Tobacco Control* 14 (2005): 247–250. Copyright © 2005 by BMJ (British Medical Journal). All rights reserved. Reprinted with permission from *Tob. Control* and BMJ.

personal welfare.[1-4] Smoking also has a short term immediate negative impact on household living standards, by diverting scarce household resources from essential expenditures. Cigarette expenditures can reduce the nutritional status of low income households by displacing expenditures on food.[5,6] A study conducted in the Minhang district near Shanghai (1995) reported that smokers in 2,716 households spent 17 percent of their household income on cigarettes.[7]

China is the largest cigarette consuming country in the world, with more than 320 million smokers.[8,9] In spite of recent rapid economic growth, China is still considered a low income country. Therefore, it is important to understand the relationships between smoking status, household standard of living, and poverty in China.

Low income and high income households differ in terms of the amount of tobacco consumed, types of cigarettes smoked (high price versus low price, foreign versus domestic brands), and cigarette expenditures. It has been asserted that, especially in developing

---

[1] Collins D and Lapsley H, "The Economic Impact of Smoking, 1997, http://www.globalink.org/tobacco/9910eco/ (accessed October 10, 2002).

[2] Rice D, Kelman S and Miller L, "Economic Costs of Smoking," In *Economic Costs, Cost-Effectiveness, Financing and Community Based Drug Treatment*. Cartwright WS and Kaple JM eds. NIDA Monograph Series. 113 (1991): 10–32.

[3] Miller LS, Zhang X, Rice DP, *et al.*, "State Estimates of Total Medical Expenditures Attributable to Cigarette Smoking, 1993," *Public Health Reports* 113 (1998): 447–458.

[4] Miller VP, Ernst C and Collin F, "Smoking-Attributable Medical Care Costs in the USA," Social Sciences and Medicines 48 (1999): 375–391.

[5] Siahpush M, Borland R and Scollo M, "Smoking and Financial Stress," *Tobacco Control* 12 (2003): 60–66.

[6] Efroymson D, Ahmed S, Townshend J, *et al.*, "Hungry For Tobacco: An Analysis of the Economic Impact of Tobacco Consumption on the Poor in Bangladesh," *Tobacco Control* 10 (2001): 212–217.

[7] Gong YL, Koplan JP, Wei Feng, *et al.*, "Cigarette Smoking in China: Prevalence, Characteristics, and Attitudes in Minhang District," JAMA 274 (1995): 1232–1233.

[8] Hu TW and Mao Z. Effects of Cigarette Tax on Cigarette Consumption and the Chinese Economy," *Tobacco Control* 11 (2002): 105–108.

[9] Bobak M, Jha P, Nguyen S, *et al.*, *Poverty and Smoking. Tobacco Control in Developing Countries* (Oxford: Oxford University Press, 2000), 41–61.

countries, smoking takes up a large portion of the household budget of low income households, thus depriving them of money for essential expenditures.[5,6,9] A concern is that an increase in the tobacco tax will increase the financial burden on low income smoking households. However, low income household smokers are likely to be more price sensitive; thus, they will quit or reduce their cigarette consumption by more than higher income households, so the increased burden of the tax will fall more heavily on high income households.[10] This chapter addresses the following two questions:

- What are the differences in smoking behavior and smoking expenditures between low and high income households in China?
- What is the impact of smoking on the standard of living of low income households in China?

This information will allow policymakers and the general public to understand better the trade-off between smoking and living standards in China. It also will allow them to estimate whether and, if so, to what extent additional tobacco taxes will raise the financial burden of low income households.

DATA SOURCES AND SAMPLE DESCRIPTIONS

Data were collected in Sichuan Province, Guizhou Province, and the municipality of Chungqing, all in western China. The research team identified a total of 36 townships/districts and 108 villages/communities in the three sampling sites and contacted the randomly selected households with assistance from local administrative officials. Data were obtained through personal interviews with the heads of the households. The total study sample was 3,404 households. Respondents were paid 5 yuan per interview; the non-response rate was less than 1 percent. The heads of the households were given a monthly diary for recording their household consumption and expenditures.

---

[10] Chaloupka F, Hu TW, Warner K, *et al.*, *The Taxation of Tobacco Products. Tobacco Control in Developing Countries* (Oxford: Oxford University Press, 2000), 237–272.

162 *Teh-wei Hu et al.*

Table 1 presents a sociodemographic and economic description of the study sample. A large majority of the heads of households were male, particularly in the rural households. A large majority of urban households had three members, while four to five was typical for rural households. One limitation of these data is that they do not include age information for each individual household member;

Table 1: Sociodemographic and Economic Characteristics of Study — Household Sample

	Urban ($n = 2,575$)	Rural ($n = 829$)
Head of household (%)		
Male	62.0	91.0
Female	38.0	9.0
Age of head of household (%)		
<30 years	34.3	26.9
30–50 years	54.9	58.4
50 years	8.8	14.7
Size of household (%)		
<2	14.0	4.9
3	59.0	15.1
4–5	24.2	63.7
6+	2.8	16.3
Education (%)		
Illiterate	0.7	12.4
Primary	4.7	52.3
Junior high	21.4	30.1
High school/vocational	34.4	4.6
College+	39.2	0.6
Smoking status (%)	44.0	79.7
Family monthly income (yuan)*	2254	872
Poor (%)	5.4	17.6
Near-poor (%)	18.1	18.7
Non-poor (%)	69.5	36.7

Urban: Poor: monthly capita < 143 yuan (or US$0.60 per day); near-poor: 144–286 yuan; non-poor: > 286 yuan

Rural: Poor: monthly capita < 54 yuan (or US$0.22 per day); near-poor: 53–83 yuan; near-poor: > 83 yuan: non-poor: > 83 yuan

*US$ = 8.23 yuan.

only the age of the head of the household was reported. A large majority of the heads of households was between the ages of 30–50 years. As expected, the heads of urban households had much higher education than the heads of rural households. Among urban households, 44 percent had members who smoke, while 79.7 percent of rural households had members who smoke. No information was collected about the number of smokers in each household. These data limitations mean that individuals could not be used as a unit of analysis. This chapter focuses on household cigarette consumption and overall household expenditures.

The mean monthly household income was 2,254 yuan (or US$274) for urban households and 872 yuan (US$106) for rural households. Since this chapter pays special attention to the impact of smoking on expenditures among poor households, three income groups are specified. The Chinese government has defined separate income poverty criteria for urban and rural populations based on the income levels needed to provide basic needs. The income poverty criteria vary by province. For example, in urban areas of Sichuan, poverty is defined as monthly per capita income less than 143 yuan (or US$0.60 per day).[11] In rural areas, poverty is defined as monthly per capita income less than 54 yuan (or US$0.22 per day). These poverty definitions are less than the World Bank's definition of US$1 per person per day. We further define near poverty as 200 percent of the poverty level definition (144–286 yuan for urban and 53–83 yuan for rural, depending on the province). Among the households surveyed, 5.4 percent of urban households and 17.6 percent of rural households met the poverty definition. About 18 percent of households in each area sample met the definition for near poverty.

Major household expenditures include food, housing, clothing, education, and other items. Cigarette consumption is not considered a necessity within the household consumption category. However, it is the focus of this study. Table 2 presents household expenditure

---

[11] Sunley E, Yurekli A and Chaloupka F, "The Design, Administration, and Potential Revenue of Tobacco Excises," in *Tobacco Control in Developing Countries* (Oxford: Oxford University Press, 2000), 409–426.

Table 2: Urban and Rural Household Monthly Income Expenditure Patterns and Smoking Information, 2002

	Urban			Rural		
	Poor (n = 140)	Near-poor (n = 463)	Non-poor (n = 1,972)	Poor (n = 146)	Near-poor (n = 149)	Non-poor (n = 534)
Income (yuan and smoking information)						
Income	502	780	2769	226	325	863
Cigarette expenditures (yuan)*	29	46	127	24	29	49
Percentage of income on cigarettes (%)	5.8	5.9	4.6	7.1	8.9	5.7
Cigarettes consumption (no of packs)	7.6	9.8	15.5	21.8	24.1	28.8
Price per pack (yuan)	3.8	4.7	8.2	1.1	1.2	1.7
Total expenditures (yuan)						
Total expenditures	441	689	1392	212	292	582
Food (%)	60.3	54.9	40.5	61.8	59.2	42.4
Housing (%)	3.6	4.2	8.8	2.3	2.4	7.7
Education (%)	6.6	5.4	11.0	9.5	10.6	15.5
Clothing (%)	5.7	4.5	10.3	5.7	6.5	6.7
Cigarettes (%)	6.6	6.7	9.1	11.3	9.9	8.4
Other (%)	17.2	24.3	20.3	9.4	4.9	19.3

Urban: Poor: monthly capita < 143 yuan (or US$0.60 per day); near-poor:144–286 yuan; non-poor: > 286 yuan.
Rural: Poor: monthly capita < 54 yuan (or US$0.22 per day); near-poor: 53–83 yuan; non-poor: >83 yuan.
*US$ = 8.23 yuan.

patterns for these major expenditures and cigarette consumption status by urban versus rural households and further separated by these income groups.

As shown in Table 2, for both urban and rural households, the higher the household income, the higher the cigarette expenditures. These higher cigarette expenditures are reflected in both the amount of cigarette consumption and the price per pack paid by different income households. For example, the urban poor households consumed 7.6 packs of cigarettes a month, the urban near-poor households consumed 9.8 packs a month, and the urban non-poor households consumed 15.5 packs a month. Overall, the rural households consumed more cigarettes than urban households: 21.8 packs a month for the rural poor households, 24.1 packs for the rural near-poor, and 28.8 packs for the rural non-poor.

However, significant differences are seen in the average prices paid per pack of cigarettes by smokers: 3.8 yuan for the urban poor households, 4.7 yuan for the urban near-poor households, and 8.2 yuan for the urban non-poor households. On the other hand, the price per pack in rural areas ranged from 1.1 yuan for the poor households to 1.7 yuan for the non-poor households, a much narrower price difference. As a result, monthly cigarette expenditures were much higher for non-poor than for poor households.

Table 2 indicates that urban higher income households spent more (four times) on cigarettes than low income urban households, largely because they purchased more expensive cigarettes, including foreign brands in some cases. Rural high income households spent more (two times) on cigarettes than rural low income households, largely because they consumed more cigarettes, with the price paid per pack showing less variation across rural income groups. Further, urban and rural smokers differed greatly in both the number of cigarettes consumed and price paid per pack: urban smokers smoked fewer cigarettes than rural smokers, and they paid much higher prices per pack.

Beyond understanding the differences in smoking behavior, it is useful to examine how cigarette expenditures differ as a percentage of total expenditures across the different household income groups as shown in Table 2. Among urban smoking households, cigarette expenditures accounted for an average of 6.6 percent of total expenditures of poor households, 6.7 percent for near-poor smoking households, and 9.1 percent for non-poor smoking households. Among rural smoking households, cigarette expenditures averaged 11.3 percent of the total household expenditures of poor households, 9.9 percent for near-poor smoking households, and 8.4 percent for non-poor households. These figures imply that in urban areas, cigarettes are a luxury good, with cigarette expenditures increasing as a percent of total expenditures as income increases. However, the opposite is true in rural areas — as income rises, cigarette expenditures decrease as a percentage of total expenditures, a so-called "normal good."

The patterns are more consistent across rural and urban areas when one looks at the percentage of total *income* (rather than expenditures) spent on cigarette consumption. In both urban and rural areas, this percentage is higher for poor households than for non-poor households, but highest of all for near-poor households. Urban poor households spent 5.8 percent of their reported income on cigarettes compared to 4.6 percent in urban non-poor households, and 5.9 percent in near-poor households. The differences are wider among rural households, with 7.1 percent spent in poor households, 8.9 percent in the near-poor households, and 5.7 percent for non-poor households.

REGRESSION ANALYSIS

Using the total sample of households, a regression model was used to estimate the impact of smoking status on total household expenditures minus cigarette expenditures. The main components of interest were food expenditures, housing expenditures, clothing expenditures, and education expenditures.

In examining the impact of smoking on household expenditures, a number of key explanatory variables help determine household expenditures. These include household income, size of the household, age and educational level of the head of the household, and smoking status. As income increases, urban households and rural households may show different patterns of change in spending on food, housing, and clothing because tastes and opportunities to expand income are quite different. Thus, an interaction term was introduced in the model. Smoking status was measured in two different forms: number of packs smoked per month and the amount of cigarette expenditures per month, by each household. The amount of household expenditures is directly associated with the size of the household; thus, both dependent variable expenditures and explanatory income variables were adjusted by household size. It would be ideal to use age adjusted equivalent weighted household size to analyze household expenditures functions. Unfortunately, the survey data do not include the age distribution information. A general regression model was specified as follows:

$$E_i = b_0 + b_1\text{SM} + b_2\text{In} + b_3\text{Age} + b_4\text{Ed} + b_5\text{HS} + b_6\text{UR} + b_7\text{UR}^*\text{ In} + U_i,$$

Where E_i: Per capita total household expenditures minus cigarette expenditures

Per capita food expenditures,
Per capita housing expenditures,
Per capita clothing expenditures,
Per capita educational expenditures,
SM: Smoking status — number of packs smoked,
In: Per capita household income,
Age: Age of head of household (years),
Ed: Years of education of head of household,
HS: Household size (number of individuals),
UR: Urban location (= 1) versus rural (= 0),
UR*In: Interaction term between urban and income,
U_i: Error terms.

The coefficient for smoking status, b_1, provides information about the magnitude of the impact of smoking status on household expenditures, holding other variables constant. Age, education, household size, and location (urban) are other important variables that could explain the household expenditure pattern.

168 *Teh-wei Hu et al.*

Table 3: Impact of Cigarette Consumption on Household Expenditures (*n* = 3,402)

	Total Expenditures (Minus Tobacco)	Food	Housing	Clothing	Education
Age	−1.27*	−0.01	−0.55*	−0.46*	−0.47*
Household size	−41.52*	−19.59*	−8.39*	−8.33*	−13.52*
Education level	33.30*	20.39*	4.00	4.07*	6.93*
Income per capita	0.06*	0.02*	0.01*	0.00	0.02*
Amount of cigarette consumption	−2.90*	−0.48*	−0.40*	−0.21*	−0.15*
Urban* income	0.16*	0.03*	0.02*	0.02*	0.00
Urban	−42.93*	28.11*	−5.02	−4.67	−4.67
Constant	318.79*	100.27*	63.68*	57.86*	57.94*
Adjusted R^2	0.4856	0.4511	0.1483	0.3575	0.2918

* Indicates coefficient is significant at $p<0.01$, two tailed test.

As shown in Table 3, on average, each additional pack of cigarettes per month would reduce other household expenditures by 2.9 yuan per capita (between 9 and 12 yuan per household) per month. The effect can be separately estimated for each major category of expenditures: each pack of cigarettes reduces expenditures by 0.5 yuan per capita per month on food, 0.4 yuan per capita per month on housing, 0.2 yuan per capita per month on clothing, and 0.15 yuan per capita per month on education. While the coefficients are small, the actual impact is quite considerable, since an urban household that buys 15 packs per month would spend 7.5 yuan per capita less on food, 6 yuan per capita less on housing, 3 yuan per capita less on clothing, and 2.25 yuan per capita less on education, controlling for the variables included in the regression. If rural households bought 20 packs per month, they would spend 10 yuan per capita less on food, 8 yuan per capita less on housing, 4 yuan per capita less on clothing, and 3 yuan per capita less on education. All these coefficients are significant at less than 1 percent level, two tailed test. The positive coefficient of the interaction term between income and the urban dummy variable shows that urban households tended to spend more when there was additional income than rural households. Also as expected, larger households had lower per capita household expenditures, after controlling for per capita income, reflecting scale economies in the household.

POLICY IMPLICATIONS

The survey results indicate that low income households bought much lower priced cigarettes than high income households in China. Lower income households also smoked fewer cigarettes than high income households, especially in rural households. However, given their relatively low income, households under the poverty level allocated a higher percentage of their income for cigarettes than did non-poor households. The analysis shows a clear reduction in spending on other goods in smoking households. Therefore, if households stopped buying cigarettes and spent the money on other goods instead, households could improve their overall standard of living. This is especially true for poor households.

One policy issue is the effect that higher cigarette taxes would have on low income households versus high income households — that is, whether higher taxes would impose an undue burden on low income households. Four factors would affect the tax impact: (1) cigarette prices paid by people with different income levels; (2) amount of cigarette consumption at different income levels; (3) their respective price elasticity of demand for cigarettes; and (4) the type of tax imposed on cigarette consumption.[10,11]

Smokers in lower income households in China paid less per pack and smoked fewer cigarettes than higher income smokers, and low income smokers had higher price elasticity than higher income smokers: −1.9 for low income households, −0.7 for middle income households, and 0.5 for high income households.[12] The additional financial burden caused by a tax increase would be much less for low income households than for high income households. If the tax is a fixed percentage of cigarette price, as with an

---

12 Mao Z, Yang GH, Ma JM, *et al.*, "Adult's Demand for Cigarettes and its Determinants in China (in Chinese)," *Soft Science of Health* 17 (2003): 19–23.

ad valorem tax, instead of a specific tax, which is a fixed amount on each pack regardless of its price, then the additional tax burden from a tax rate increase on low income households would be even lower. For instance, using Table 2 as an example, a 0.40 yuan specific tax increase per pack would become a 10.5 percent (0.40/3.8 yuan) per pack price increase for poor urban households, an 8.5 percent (0.4/4.7 yuan) price increase for near-poor households, and a 7.8 percent (0.4/8.2 yuan) increase for non-poor households. Given the different price elasticities, the poor smokers would reduce consumption by 20 percent, near-poor households by 5 percent, and non-poor households by only 2 percent. So the "average" poor household that bought 17 packs of cigarettes per month at 3.8 yuan per pack, or 64.6 yuan, when faced with a 10.5 percent price increase, would buy 14 packs per month at 4.2 yuan, and spend a smaller total of 58.8 yuan per month after the tax increase. An average non-poor household that bought 18 packs per month at 8.2 yuan, spending a total of 147.6 yuan, would decrease consumption very little after the tax increase. If these households bought the same number of packs each month, total spending would rise to 154.8 yuan; if they cut back by one pack per month, total spending would be reduced very slightly to 146.2 yuan per month. On the other hand, based on the average price per pack of cigarettes paid by different income groups, as shown in Table 2, the effect of an across the board 10 percent increase in price, such as an ad valorem tax, would be that poor household smokers would pay an extra 0.38 yuan per pack, near-poor household smokers would pay an additional 0.47 yuan per pack, and non-poor smokers would pay 0.82 yuan more per pack. The reduction in cigarette consumption, according to their different price elasticities, would be 19 percent for poor smokers, 7 percent for near-poor smokers, and 5 percent for non-poor smokers, respectively. Total monthly spending on cigarettes for the "average" poor smoker would fall from 64.4 yuan to 56.8 yuan (13.6 packs at 4.18 yuan each), whereas the average non-poor smokers would buy one pack less, but the price increase would mean total spending would increase from 147.6 to 153.3 yuan. The ad valorem type tax is more efficient at shifting the tax burden from poor to non-poor households.

Currently China levies a fixed 64 percent tax at the producer level, equivalent to a 38 percent tax at the retail level.[13] This is a relatively low rate compared to the cigarette tax rate around the world.[10] The analysis of these survey data suggests that raising cigarette tax rates in China would reduce consumption more among low income households than among high income households, increasing available household funds for other major household items, such as food, housing, clothing, and education. Furthermore, an ad valorem tax instead of a specific tax would lower the financial burden of a higher cigarette tax on low income households, and in this respect would be more "pro-poor".

ACKNOWLEDGMENT

This study was funded by the International Development for Research Center/Research Institute for Tobacco Control, the World Bank, Rockefeller Foundation, and Fogarty International Center/National Institutes of Health (Grant No. R01-TW05938).

---

[13] Hu TW, "Cigarette Taxation in China: Lessons from International Experiences," *Tobacco Control* 6 (1997): 136–140.

Chapter 9

Cigarette Smoking and Poverty in China*

Yuanli Liu, Keqin Rao, Teh-wei Hu, Qi Sun and Zhenzhong Mao

INTRODUCTION

Despite the overwhelming evidence of the harmful effects of smoking, tobacco use has increased in developing countries and become one of the most profound global health challenges.[1] With more than 320 million smokers consuming 30 percent of the world's cigarette production and three million of whom are new smokers each year, China is the world's largest producer and consumer of tobacco.[2] It is estimated that the upward spiral of tobacco consumption in China will result in three million tobacco-related deaths per year in China

---

*This chapter originally appeared as Liu Y, Rao K, Hu TW, Sun Q, and Mao Z, "Cigarette Smoking and Poverty in China," *Social Science and Medicine*. 63 (2006): 2784–2790. Copyright © 2006 by Elsevier. All rights reserved. Reprinted with permission from *Soc Sci Med* and Elsevier.

[1] Jha P and Chaloupka F, Curbing the Epidemic: Governments and the Economics of Tobacco Control. (Washington, DC: The World Bank, 1999).
[2] Mackay J, "Beyond the Clouds-Tobacco Smoking in China," *Journal of the American Medical Association*, 278 no. 18 (1997): 1531–1532.

by 2025, about 30 percent of the world's total number of tobacco deaths.[3] There is an estimated two million deaths per year from tobacco use for the entire developed world combined.[4]

Recently, China has made efforts to ban tobacco advertising and vending machines by ratifying the World Health Organization Framework Convention on Tobacco Control. However, due to the economic benefits (e.g., tax revenues) perceived by many policy makers, governments in developing countries like China are often reluctant to take decisive tobacco control measures. Hence, systematic studies on the economic consequences of smoking are critically important in informing and prompting policy makers and the public to take action.

Smoking can negatively affect income in several ways through productivity loss due to smoking-related diseases and deaths;[5-7] missed days of work, smoking-attributable medical spending,[8] and direct spending on tobacco products.[9] Furthermore, smokers have increased risks of incurring diseases, including lung cancer,

---

[3] Jin S, Lu B, and Yan DY, "An Evaluation of Smoking-Induced Health Costs in China (1988–1998)," *Biomedical and Environmental Sciences* 8 (1995): 342–349.

[4] Peto R, Lopez AD, Boreham J, Thun M, and Heath C, "Mortality From Smoking in Developed Countries 1950–2000, in *Indirect Estimates from National Vital Statistics* (New York: Oxford University Press, 1994).

[5] Efroymson D, Ahmed S, Townsend J, Alam SM, Dey AR, and Saha R. "Hungry for Tobacco: An Analysis of the Economic Impact of Tobacco Consumption on the Poor in Bangladesh," *Tobacco Control* 10, no. 3 (2001): 212–217.

[6] Kiiskinen U, Vartianen E, Puska P, and Pekurinen M, Smoking-Related Costs Among 25 to 59 year-old Males in a 19-year Individual Follow-up, *European Journal of Public Health* 12, no. 2 (2002): 145–151.

[7] Tsai SP, Wen CP, Hu SC, Cheng TY, and Huang SJ, "Workplace Smoking Related Absenteeism and Productivity Costs in Taiwan," *Tobacco Control* Supp 1 (2005): i33–i37.

[8] Centers for Disease Control and Prevention. "Cigarette Smoking-Attributable Morbidity — United States, 2000." *Morbility and Mortality Weekly Report* 52, no. 35 (2000): 842–844.

[9] Gong YL, Kaplan JP, Feng W, et al. Cigarette Smoking in China: Prevalence, "Characteristics, and Attitudes in Minhang District," *Journal of the American Medical Association* 274, (1995): 1232–1233.

emphysema, and cerebral vascular disease,[10] which can result in increased health expenditure. In addition to these health-related consequences, smoking can impose other direct economic costs. For example, tobacco expenditures represent a significant financial burden for low-income families,[11] and smoking may decrease productivity on the job. While the impact of smoking expenditures on household consumption has been examined in China,[12,13] further analysis on the impoverishing effect of smoking has not been made.

Primarily, based on the analysis of the 1998 China national health services survey data, the impact of smoking on poverty is estimated from: (a) the impoverishing effect of smoking-attributable medical spending and (b) the impoverishing effect of direct spending on cigarettes. Since the poverty line is calculated in different ways for urban and rural residents in China, the poverty impact of cigarette smoking for urban and rural populations is estimated separately. Poverty is defined as earning less than 54 yuan (US$0.22 per day) monthly capita in urban areas and less than 143 yuan (US$0.60 per day) monthly capita in rural areas.[14]

The 1998 National Health Services Survey

Using a multi-stage stratified random sampling framework, the 1998 national health services survey was conducted by the Chinese Ministry of Health. It included household interview surveys of

---

[10] US Department of Health and Human Services, "*Reducing the Health Consequences of Smoking. 25 years of Progress: A Report of the Surgeon General.* (Washington, DC: US Public Health Service, Centers for Disease Control, Center for Chronic Disease Prevention and Health Promotion, 1989), 89–8411.
[11] Hu TW, "Economic Analysis of Tobacco and Options for Tobacco Control: China Case Study," *Tobacco Control* 11, no. 2 (2002): 105–108.
[12] Hu TW, Mao Z, Liu Y, de Beyer J, and Ong M, "Smoking Standard, of Living, and Poverty in China," *Tobacco Control* 14, no. 4 (2005): 247–250.
[13] Wang H, Sindelar JL, and Busch SH, "The Impact of Tobacco Expenditure on Household Consumption Patterns in Rural China," *Social Science and Medicine* 62 (2006): 1414–1426.
[14] Li Q. Poverty Alleviation in China. (Kunming, China: Yunnan, 1997).

56,994 representative families (216,101 individuals) with a response rate of 99.9 percent.[15] As China is still a developing country with about 70 percent of its population living in rural areas and primarily engaged in agriculture, the household sample included 16,784 households from urban cities and 40,210 households from rural areas. In addition to demographic and socioeconomic data, the interviewers, who are trained medical professionals, also collected comprehensive information on self-reported health status, health care utilization (including outpatient and inpatient services), medical expenditures, and behavioral factors such as smoking and drinking.

Smoking Rate and Frequency

Based on the analysis of the 1998 China national health services survey data, the overall smoking rate is higher in rural than urban China, with the rural female smoking rate being slightly lower than that of the urban sample, as shown in Table 1. The percentage of male and female adults from the rural sample who are current smokers are 56.5 percent and 3.4 percent, respectively, slightly lower than from the most comprehensive study of tobacco use, the 1996 China national prevalence survey,[16] which shows 63 percent men and 4 percent of women are current smokers. The percentages of male and female adults from the urban sample who are current smokers are 51.7 percent and 5 percent, respectively. Moreover, both the male and female rates of former smokers in the rural sample are lower than that of the urban sample; 5.5 percent of the male smokers and 7.9 percent of the female smokers in the rural sample quit smoking. By comparison, 10.7 percent of the male smokers and 15.6 percent of the female smokers in the urban sample quit smoking. Since

---

[15] Gao J, Tang S, Tolhurst R, and Rao K, Changing Access to Health Services in Urban China: Implications for Equity, *Health Policy and Planning* 16, no. 3 (2001): 302–312.

[16] Yang GH, Fan XL, Tan J, Qi G, Zhang Y, and Samet JM, "Smoking in China: Findings of the 1996 National Prevalence Survey," *Journal of the American Medical Association*, 282, no. 13 (1999): 1247–1253.

Table 1: The Rate of Smoking and Quitting in China by Region and Gender

Region of China	Smoking Male (percent)	Smoking Female (percent)	Quitting Male (percent)	Quitting Female (percent)
Urban (n = 16,784)	51.7	5	10.7	15.6
Rural (n = 40,210)	56.5	3.4	5.5	7.9

Source: 1998 China national health services survey.
1. n = sample size (households). 2. Urban is defined as predominantly in the formal sector. 3. Rural is defined as predominantly in the informal and agricultural sectors.

the average income of rural residents is lower than that of their urban counterparts, these results are consistent with previous findings in the literature that the smoking rate in lower socioeconomic classes tends to be higher. Furthermore, while 62 percent of urban smokers reported smoking at least 10 cigarettes a day, the figure for rural smokers is 70 percent, indicating a higher level of cigarette consumption among rural smokers.

Expenditures on Cigarettes

The 1998 China national health services data only have information on the smoker's daily consumption of cigarettes. The smoker is asked to answer with one of the following categories: less than 10, 10–19, or more than 20 cigarettes per day. The group mean was used to approximate the smoker's daily consumption level to calculate his or her annual cigarettes consumption. For example, if the person indicates that he or she smokes 10–19 cigarettes a day, the person's daily cigarettes consumption level is set at 15. Very few people indicated smoking more than 20 cigarettes per day, the mean of which was set at 25. Information on prices of cigarettes was obtained from another household survey conducted in 2001.[17] Since

---

[17] Hu TW, Mao Z, and Liu Y, "Smoking, Standard of Living, and Poverty in China. Paper presented at the *International Health Economics Association Meeting*, held at Hilton San Francisco and Towers on June 15–18, 2003.

people of different income groups may buy different brand cigarettes, information on price per pack of cigarettes by income quintiles was compiled. Annual cigarette expenditure was estimated by using the 1998 annual cigarette consumption and average price paid by income quintile and regional (urban versus rural) in 2001, which was adjusted by the annual inflation rate from 1998 to 2001. On average, an urban smoker spent 448 yuan (12 percent of the household income) on cigarettes, whereas a rural smoker spent 87 yuan (5 percent of the household income) on cigarettes — the higher their income, the more smokers spent on cigarettes.

Medical Expenditures and Related Expenses

In 1998, the reported annual household income was 4,342 yuan (US$542) per capita in urban areas and 1,968 yuan (US$246) per capita in rural areas. Per capita medical spending was 247 yuan (7 percent of the income) and 134 yuan (9 percent of the income) in urban and rural areas, respectively. On average, the ever smokers in urban and rural areas spent 45 percent more and 28 percent more, respectively, on medical services than their non-smoking counterparts, indicating a higher need for medical care of the ever smokers. Smoking status is significantly correlated with the rate of chronic illness. But medical expenses are not only related to smoking status. Medical expenditures are found to vary with a number of variables, including age, income, gender, drinking, education, and insurance coverage.[18] To estimate medical expenditures attributable to smoking, confounding factors were controlled. It is worth noting that the majority of Chinese populations do not have health insurance coverage and that only 42 percent of the urban residents and 9 percent of the rural residents reported having any health insurance coverage in this survey.

---

[18] Newhouse J, *Free for all? Lessons from the Rand Health Insurance Experiment* (Cambridge, MA: Harvard University Press, 1996).

DATA AND METHODS

Estimating Medical Spending Due to Cigarette Smoking

Of the two main approaches to assess extra medical spending attributable to smoking, *inclusive* and *disease-specific*,[19] our study uses the former. The inclusive approach recognizes that the health effects of smoking are complex and may extend beyond what has been set forth by epidemiological research and thus, assesses the impact of smoking on all relevant types of medical spending, which may include inpatient care, outpatient care, long-term care, and other acute care services.

The excess use of medical services by current and by former smokers can be obtained using methods similar to that of Manning, Keeler, Newhouse, Sloss, and Wasserman.[20,21] In particular, the following regression equation of medical care utilization on smoking status (current, former, or never) is estimated:

$$\text{Log}[Y + 5] = b_1 * CS + b_2 * FS + XB + e, \qquad (1)$$

where Y is the annual medical expenditure, which might be zero (hence we make the dependent variable a positive number by adding 5 in this log-linear model); CS and FS are dummy variables equal to 1 if the individual is a current or former smoker; and X is the vector of demographic and individual covariates (age, gender, income, education, drinking, and insurance) with coefficient vector B; and e is a stochastic error term.

Using the coefficient estimates from the regression above, the value of the dependent variable for each individual in the sample

---

[19] Cutler, DM. *How Good a Deal was the Tobacco Settlement? Assessing Payments to Massachusetts* (Cambridge, MA: National Bureau of Economic Research, 2000).
[20] Manning WG, Keeler EB, Newhouse JP, Sloss EM, and Wasserman J, "The Taxes of Sin. Do Smokers and Drinkers Pay Their Way?," *Journal of the American Medical Association* 261 (1989): 1604–1609.
[21] Manning WG, Keeler EB, Newhouse JP, Sloss EM, and Wasserman J, *The Costs of Poor Health Habits.* (Cambridge, MA: Harvard University Press, 1991).

within each smoking group (current and former) can be predicted. Now, suppose that the current and former smokers had never smoked, what would their medical expenses have been? We estimate their medical expenses by using the same independent variables for each current and former smoker but setting the CS and FS variables to zero. The predicted expenditure of the smokers in the sample assuming they had not smoked is subtracted from the predicted expenditure given that they did indeed smoke. The difference of these two expressions is the predicted effect of smoking on medical care resource utilization:

$$\text{Excess use of CS} = \text{Average predicted use CS} \\ - \text{Average predicted use CS if NS}, \quad (2)$$

$$\text{Excess use of FS} = \text{Average predicted use FS} \\ - \text{Average predicted use FS if NS}, \quad (3)$$

where NS is a dummy variable equal to 1 if the individual is a never smoker. Thus, rather than taking the average medical care of non-smokers as the counterfactual, Eqs. (2) and (3) explicitly adjust for differences among individuals within each smoking group using the covariates in Eq. (1).

Estimating Impact on Poverty

The impoverishing effect of excessive medical spending attributable to smoking and direct tobacco expenditures is estimated using a poverty head count. The *head count* measures the number of individuals or households living below the poverty line as a percentage of the total population/households. The impact of a particular expenditure (in this case the excessive medical spending attributable to smoking and direct spending on cigarettes) on poverty is then measured by the change in poverty head count, after that expenditure is subtracted from the income. This method[22]

---

[22] Pen J, *Income Distribution* (New York, NY: Praeger Publishers, 1971).

has been used by others in estimating the impoverishing effect of medical expenses.[23]

RESULTS

Excessive Medical Spending and Impoverishment

Even though smoking attributable medical spending tends to be higher for the higher-income groups, this spending appears to impose higher financial burden on low-income families as shown in Table 2. For the urban sample, medical spending attributable to smoking as a percentage of income is 6.5 percent for the lowest income quintile, while it is 1.5 percent for the highest income quintile. A similar trend is also found for the rural sample, when excessive medical spending is compared to income levels. Therefore, it is not surprising to discover that the impoverishing effect of the excessive medical spending is mostly felt by people of low-income groups.

As indicated in Table 3, the urban poverty rate based on reported income alone is 58.3 percent for the lowest income quintile.

Table 2: Excessive Medical Spending Attributable to Smoking by Income Quintile and Region in China (Per Capita Spending and as Percent of Household Income)

Region	1 (Lowest Quintile)	2	3	4	5 (Highest Quintile)
Urban	88 yuan	99 yuan	111 yuan	124 yuan	130 yuan
(n = 16,784)	6.5%	3.6%	2.8%	2.3%	1.5%
Rural	22 yuan	21 yuan	22 yuan	24 yuan	25 yuan
(n = 40,210)	3.8%	1.8%	1.3%	1%	0.6%

Source: 1998 China national health services survey.
1. n = sample size (households). 2. Urban is defined as predominantly in the formal sector. 3. Rural is defined as predominantly in the informal and agricultural sectors.

---

[23] Wagstaff A, and Von Doorslaer E, *Paying for Health Care: Quantifying Fairness, Catastrophic, and Impoverishment, with Applications to Vietnam, 1993–1998*, (The World Bank Working Paper Series #2715, Washington, DC.

182 Yuanli Liu et al.

Table 3: Poverty Headcount by Income Quintile and Region in China Using Smoking Attributable Medical Spending (Pre-Subtraction versus Post-Subtraction of Medical Spending Attributable to Smoking from Income)

Region	1 (Lowest Quintile) (percent)	2 (Second Quintile) (percent)
Urban _n	58.3	0
(n = 16, 784)	65.4	0.5
Rural	29.6	0
(n = 40, 210)	32.2	0

Source: 1998 China national health services survey.
1. n = sample size (households). 2. Urban is defined as predominantly in the formal sector. 3. Rural is defined as predominantly in the informal and agricultural sectors.

After the excessive medical spending attributable to smoking has been subtracted from the income, the urban poverty head count increased more than 7 percent. Similarly, the rural poverty rate based on reported income alone is 29.6 percent for the lowest income quintile and increased to 32.3 percent. Given China's urban and rural populations as a percentage of the 1.29 billion total population (30 percent and 70 percent, respectively), the number of people who become impoverished because of the excessive medical spending attributable to smoking can be calculated. Each year, according to our estimate, 12.1 million people (5.8 million urban residents and 6.3 million rural residents) may have been driven into poverty due to smoking attributable medical spending.

Spending on Cigarettes and Impoverishment

Even though the smoking rate is higher for the lower-income groups than that for the higher-income groups, the lower-income smokers spent less (choosing cheaper cigarettes) on cigarettes due to ability to pay. On average, an urban smoker spent 448 yuan (12 percent of the household income) on cigarettes in 1998, whereas a rural smoker spent 87 yuan (5 percent of the household income) on cigarettes. However, cigarette spending constitutes a higher financial burden for the lower-income groups than the higher-income groups. Among the urban smokers, cigarette spending represents 7 percent of the household income for the highest 20 percentile of income groups, while it represents a stunningly 46 percent of the household income for the lowest 20 percentile of income groups. Among the rural smokers, cigarette spending represents 4 percent of the household income for the highest 20 percentile of income groups and 11 percent of the household income for the lowest 20 percentile of income groups.

While cigarette spending impoverished neither from the urban nor rural populations from the highest 20 percentile of income, it caused the poverty rate to increase by 19 percent and 8 percent for the lowest 20 percentile of income groups among the urban and rural, respectively, as indicated in Table 4. After cigarette spending is subtracted from income, the urban and rural head counts increased to 18.4 percent and 9.2 percent, respectively. Each year 41.8 million people (24.7 million urban residents and 17.1 million rural residents) may have been driven into poverty by cigarette spending.

Table 4: Poverty Headcount by Income Quintile and Region in China Using Direct Spending (Pre-Subtraction versus Post-Subtraction of Direct Cigarette Spending from Income)

Region	1 (Lowest Quintile) (percent)	2 (percent)	3 (percent)	4 (percent)	5 (Highest Quintile) (percent)
Urban	58.3	0	0	0	0
(n = 16, 784)	77.0	11	1.3	0.6	0
Rural	29.6	0	0	0	0
(n = 40, 210)	37.1	0.1	0	0	0

Source: 1998 China national health services survey; 2001 household survey on smoking in three provinces (data adjusted by the annual inflation rate from 1998 to 2001). 1. n = sample size (households). 2. Urban is defined as predominantly in the formal sector. 3. Rural is defined as predominantly in the informal and agricultural sectors.

DISCUSSION

According to our estimation, the excessive medical spending attributable to smoking caused the urban and rural poverty rates to increase by 1.5 percent (affecting 5.8 million urban residents) and 0.7 percent (affecting 6.3 million rural residents), respectively. Since the majority of the Chinese populations do not have health insurance coverage and such coverage is known to be closely correlated with health care utilization,[18,24] this estimate is likely to indicate a lower bound of the impact. In addition, the direct spending on cigarettes has a remarkable impact on poverty in China. Estimates indicate that cigarette spending caused the urban and rural poverty rates to increase by 6.4 percent (affecting 24.7 million urban residents) and 1.9 percent (affecting 11.7 million rural residents), respectively. The incidence of poverty due to excessive medical spending and direct cigarette spending falls disproportionately on low-income families.

From a policy perspective, reducing the smoking rate is not only an important public health issue, but also that of poverty reduction. It is clear from Tables 3 and 4 that the impoverishing effects caused by smoking-related medical expenditures and cigarette spending are mostly suffered by people in the lowest income bracket. Therefore, a lowered smoking rate would mean lower spending on cigarettes and result in less competition for the limited household budget of the low-income people. The lowered smoking rate would also reduce the risk of smoking-related illnesses and lower medical expenditures. Based on the estimates emerging from our analysis, if all else equal and the current smoking rate is halved in China, it may be that 28 million people can be lifted out of poverty.

However, there are several caveats regarding interpretations of our findings. First, as China is a large country with significant variation in income across regions, estimation from regionally adjusted poverty lines might be different from our results. Second, the 1998 China national health services survey did not collect information on household direct spending on cigarettes. Relevant information from another survey was used to calculate the expected spending on cigarettes for the smokers in our study sample. Third, our main results on medical impoverishment relied on the self-reported income data and expenditure data. There might be under-reporting of income and over-reporting of expenditures, which may bias the estimate of smoking-related medical impoverishment in rural China upwards. On the other hand, the "medical expenditures" only include direct expenses for health care services and drugs and not indirect costs such as transportation and lodging costs of the patients and their families, which are substantial in rural China.[24,25] Last but not the least, this study only examined the partial financial impact of smoking and not the effects of productivity loss due to smoking-related diseases and second-hand smoking, which may suggest an underestimation of results.

While China is the world's largest consumer and producer of tobacco, this impoverishing effect may also apply to other developing countries, whereby prevention is possible. Many studies have delved into the impact of tobacco consumption on expenditures, but few have looked at the link from smoking to poverty. Effective tobacco control measures, thus serve not only in health improvement purposes, but that of poverty alleviation.

ACKNOWLEDGMENTS

This study was funded by the Rockefeller Foundation. We would like to thank Dr. Anthony So for his support and guidance. Able research and editing assistance by Annie Chu was greatly appreciated. We remain responsible for the contents of the Chapter.

---

[24] Ministry of Health (PRC), *Research on National Health Services — An Analysis Report of the National Health Services Survey in 1993* (Beijing: Ministry of Health, PRC, 1994).

[25] Ministry of Health (PRC) *Reports on the 1998 National Health Services Survey Results* (Beijing: Ministry of Health, PRC, 1999).

Section III

Supply of Tobacco

Chapter 10

The Role of Government in Tobacco Leaf Production in China: National and Local Interventions*

Teh-wei Hu, Zhengzhong Mao, Hesheng Jiang, Ming Tao and Ayda Yurekli

INTRODUCTION

China is the largest producer of tobacco leaf in the world. In 2000, China produced 2.24 million tonnes of tobacco, or about one-third of world production.[1] China is also the largest consumer of cigarettes, with more than 320 million smokers, or approximately one-quarter of the world's smokers. These smokers consumed 1.7 trillion cigarettes in 2000. In addition, an estimated 440 million individuals,

---

*This chapter originally appeared as Hu TW, Mao Z, Jiang H, Tao M and Yurekli A, "The Role of Government in Tobacco Leaf Production in China: National and Local Interventions," *International Journal Public Policy*. 2, nos. 3–4 (2007): 235–248. Copyright © by Inderscience Publishers. All rights reserved. Reprinted with permission from *Int. J. Public Policy* and Inderscience Enterprises Ltd.
[1] Mackay J and Eriksen M, *The Tobacco Atlas* (Geneva: WHO, 2002).

comprised primarily of women and children, are exposed to smoking in the home. These individuals are called "environmental smokers" or "passive smokers". Chinese health officials and many top government officials are aware of the negative health consequences of smoking; therefore, for public health reasons, the government should assume an active role in tobacco control through effective economic measures such as increased tobacco taxes.

The Chinese government plays an important role in both tobacco and cigarette production through its national monopolies, the State Tobacco Monopoly Administration (STMA) and the China National Tobacco Company (CNTC). In 2000, the total profit and tax contribution of tobacco to the central government was 10.5 billion yuan.[2] Cigarette production is an important source of central government revenue, accounting for about 10 percent of total revenue[3]; therefore, any discussion of tobacco control in China requires a good understanding of tobacco production's impact on the country's overall agricultural economy and on government revenue, as well as the role the government plays in tobacco production. Income for tobacco farmers and job security for tobacco industry workers are also other major concerns of the Chinese government.

During the past three years, several external forces have affected China's leaf production and cigarette manufacturing, such as China's joining the World Trade Organization (WTO) in 2001 and its signing of the World Health Organization's (WHO) Framework Convention of Tobacco Control (FCTC) in 2003. China's participation in the WTO has had a direct impact on the trade in tobacco leaf and cigarette products and its signing of the FCTC could certainly have an affect on cigarette consumption should the government ratify and implement the agreement. This chapter describes Chinese government policies *vis-á-vis* tobacco production at both the central and local government levels and explains how government policy affected tobacco production and tobacco farmers during the 1990s.

---

[2] *China Statistical Yearbook* (2000–2001) (Beijing: China Statistical Bureau, 1990–2001).
[3] Hu TW and Mao Z, "Effects of cigarette tax on cigarette consumption and the Chinese economy," *Tobacco Control* 11 (2002): 105–108.

The chapter is organized as follows: the following section provides a description of the role of the central government in tobacco production; the second section examines the relationship between tobacco production, the government procurement price and tobacco's role in the agricultural economy; the third section discusses the role of local government, with a special focus on four major tobacco-producing provinces; the fourth section provides an analysis of household tobacco production and tobacco's role in sustaining household incomes; the fifth section provides a preliminary analysis of the potential impact of WTO membership on tobacco production in China; the sixth section examines China's potential to make a transition from tobacco production to other crops; the last section provides conclusions.

ROLE OF THE CENTRAL GOVERNMENT IN TOBACCO PRODUCTION

Before 1980, both tobacco production and cigarette manufacturing in China were decentralized, managed mainly by provincial and local governments. Local governments conducted their own planning with respect to tobacco production. Local governments strongly encouraged farmers to plant tobacco because a major source of government revenue was a special agriculture product tax on tobacco leaf. The results were large surpluses of tobacco leaf. In 1982, the central government decided to institute vertical and centralized management of cigarette production, allowing the CNTC to administer all aspects of the process — from the production, procurement and pricing of tobacco leaf, to the processing and marketing of cigarettes. In 1983, tobacco monopoly legislation was enacted, establishing the State Tobacco Monopoly Administration (STMA) as a tobacco monopoly agency and creating a link between the central government and the provincial governments to manage all tobacco leaf and cigarette production in China. In essence, CNTC and STMA were established to control the production of tobacco leaf and the manufacturing and marketing of cigarettes for the entire country.

STMA is a government agency that sets overall policies for tobacco production and cigarette manufacturing; it then delegates to CNTC full authority to:

- decide on the allocation of tobacco production quotas for each province,
- procure tobacco leaf,
- transport and store tobacco leaf,
- manufacture and sell cigarettes.

STMA sets overall government policy on tobacco, beginning with the allocation of tobacco production quotas among the provinces, the pricing of tobacco leaf, the setting of production quotas for cigarettes, and the managing of international trade. With the establishment of STMA, the policy, data collection and research functions with respect to tobacco production were removed from the jurisdiction of the Ministry of Agriculture and placed under the Ministry of Economics and Trade.

CNTC is an organization that can not only implement government (STMA) tobacco production policy, but also deal with foreign industries. Joint ventures with multinational tobacco companies, such as British American Tobacco, are carried out under the direction of CNTC. CNTC produces over 2000 brands and employs more than half a million people, or about 0.4 percent of total employment in China.[2]

The procurement of tobacco leaf is one of the CNTC's monopolistic functions. Public or private agencies or individuals are not allowed to purchase tobacco leaf or manufacture cigarettes without the CNTC's approval. Retailers also require CNTC's permission to sell cigarettes. Basically, CNTC controls the sources of production material (tobacco leaf), the allocation of production quotas and the marketing channels. While the private sector is not allowed to manufacture cigarettes, the government is nevertheless limited in its ability to fully enforce these regulations. One of CNTC's main challenges is the sale of the surplus leaf to private producers and the consequent growth of a black market for counterfeit cigarettes.

China is facing increasing international competition. For example, Zimbabwe and Brazil are capable of producing higher-quality tobacco leaf. Thus, one of CNTC's key missions is technological development for both tobacco production and cigarette manufacturing. In 2001, one billion yuan (8.23 yuan = US$1, 2001 exchange rate) was reportedly invested in research and development, or about 2.5 percent of industry profit. CNTC has a technology information network for insect disease prevention, quality improvement, and production forecasting, with two major research institutes (one in Henan and other in Yunnan), nine experiment stations and 15 extension stations. All of this technical information is delivered to local tobacco bureaus and tobacco companies through the CNTC network.

The 1991 tobacco monopoly implementation law dictates that only the Economic Planning Commission may determine the total amount of tobacco production, as well as the allocation of production quotas at the provincial and county levels. To help ensure the expected production quota is met, CNTC (or its affiliated companies) signs contracts with tobacco farmers specifying the amount of acreage that should be under tobacco cultivation and the price to be paid for different grades of leaf. CNTC is obligated to purchase the full amount of tobacco leaf produced under the allocated acreage at a predetermined price, while private companies are prohibited from purchasing tobacco leaf. One of STMA's key policy interventions is setting prices in order to control tobacco production. These prices are set according to the production location and quality. Each October, the STMA announces a list of 200 prices, covering five production regions and four grading categories; each quality category includes more than 10 detailed purchase prices. Table 1 provides selected sample procurement prices for the years 2000 and 2001.

Price varies widely among the five tobacco-leaf-growing regions and among the four grading categories. Yunnan belongs to Region 1, and the northern provinces belong to Region 5. Price variations between regions are narrower than the variation among the 40 grading levels. In 2000, Region 1's top grade tobacco could be sold at 835 yuan/per 50 kg, while the lowest grade could be

Table 1: Sample Tobacco Procurement Price List, yuan/50 kg, Years 2000 and 2001

Region	2000			2001		
	Plantation Area			Plantation Area		
	1	3	5	1	3	5
1	835	750	650	917	820	712
6	705	635	550	710	635	550
II	567	495	430	554	495	430
Mid (grade)						
1	565	490	425	593	530	460
8	413	370	325	347	310	270
17	288	260	225	235	210	182
Low (grade)						
1	155	150	140	112	100	87
10	85	85	75	62	55	48
Bottom (grade)						
1	60	58	60	37	33	30
2	38	35	32	22	20	17

Source: China Tobacco Almanac, edited by China National Monopoly Administration, 2000 and 2002.

sold only at 38 yuan/per 50 kg. A comparison of price lists for 2000 and 2001 reveals that the government raised the procurement price of top-grade tobacco leaf while at the same time decreasing the procurement prices of the lowest grades. This action was a strong signal that the government wanted to discourage the production of low-grade tobacco leaf.

One difficulty of using the price schedule to purchase tobacco leaf from farmers is the lack of a scientific benchmark, which often leads to disputes between tobacco fanners and agents. CNTC procurement agents may attempt to downgrade a farmers' product quality, based on a comparison of that farmers' tobacco leaf to the agents' samples, so that the agent may pay a lower price. Farmers may seek higher prices but the monopoly status of the CNTC puts farmers in a weak position for bargaining. In recent years, CNTC has tried to have a third party mediate price disputes by inviting tobacco farmers in the community to be members of a pricing committee. According to law, CNTC is the only legitimate buyer of tobacco leaf. In reality, farmers sell their leftover leaf to private cigarette companies, either for private local brands or for counterfeit brands. Counterfeit cigarettes are a serious challenge for CNTC as well as for the foreign brands, as they undermine the market share of both CNTC and the foreign companies. In fact, counterfeit cigarettes are an even greater challenge than smuggled foreign cigarettes. In 2000, the government confiscated 570,000 cases of counterfeit cigarettes.[4]

NATIONAL TOBACCO LEAF PRODUCTION AND ITS ROLE IN THE AGRICULTURAL ECONOMY

Although the amount of tobacco produced in 1990 and 2000 was virtually the same (2.259 tonnes versus 2.238 tonnes), this stability masked wide fluctuations during the decade, ranging from a low of 1.94 million tonnes in 1994 to a high of 3.91 million tonnes in 1997, more than a 100 percent difference (see Table 2).

The number of hectares under tobacco also fluctuated from year to year during the 1990s. In 1997, for example, the planting area was 2.16 million hectares — a year later it plummeted to 1.2 million hectares. These patterns indicate that the government experienced a large tobacco leaf surplus when production peaked, thus causing the government to reduce its tobacco allocation quota the following year. Comparing tobacco production volumes and hectares planted provides an estimate of average tobacco leaf yield. In 1990, the yield was 1.68 tonnes per hectare. In 2000, the yield was 1.76 tonnes per hectare, suggesting that there was little improvement in productivity in terms of yield per hectare.

The value of tobacco leaf went from 5.46 billion yuan in 1990 to 12.50 billion yuan in 2000, an increase of about 130 percent. However, when adjusted by the general inflation rate for farm products, the real increase was about 35 percent. The peak year for

---

[4] China Tobacco (2003) 1 October.

Table 2: Tobacco Farming in China, 1990–2000

Year	Tobacco Plantation Area (1,000 hectares)	Tobacco Leaf Production (1,000 tons)	Total Agriculture Areal Plantation Area (1,000 hectares)	Proportion of Tobacco Area to Total Area (percent)	Average Government Procurement Price (yuan/kg)	Gross Output Value of Fluecured Tobacco (million yuan)	Gross Value of Agricultural Output (billion yuan)	Proportion of Gross Value Tobacco Leaf to Total Agriculture (percent)
1990	1,342	2,259	148,362	0.90	2.42	5,462.26	459.43	1.19
1991	1,562	2,670	149,586	1.04	2.54	6,774.86	514.64	1.32
1992	1,849	3,119	149,007	1.24	2.58	8,040.78	558.80	1.44
1993	1,835	3,036	147,741	1.24	2.85	8,664.74	660.51	1.31
1994	1,302	1,940	148,241	0.88	3.13	6,079.36	916.92	0.66
1995	1,309	2,072	149,879	0.87	3.57	7,389.05	1,188.46	0.62
1996	1,683	2,946	152,381	1.10	5.15	15,159.95	1,353.98	1.12
1997	2,162	3,908	153,969	1.40	6.20	24,232.96	1,385.25	1.75
1998	1,200	2,088	155,706	0.77	5.54	11,562.02	1,424.19	0.81
1999	1,216	2,185	156,373	0.78	5.20	11,361.10	1,410.62	0.81
2000	1,269	2,238	156,300	0.81	5.58	12,497.79	1,387.36	0.90

Sources: China Statistical Yearbook, 1990–2001, China Statistics Bureau, Beijing.
China Industrial Statistical Yearbook, 1990–2001, China Statistics Bureau, Beijing.

value was 1997, when the gross value of tobacco was 24.2 billion yuan, four times higher than the value in 1990. Comparing the monetary value of tobacco production (the average government procurement price) and the amount of tobacco production during the decade, the value per kg was 2.42 yuan in 1990 and 5.58 yuan in 2000 — a real rate of increase of about 35 percent. The peak price was 6.20 yuan per kg in 1997, the year when tobacco leaf production was highest. After 1997, the price declined to between 5.20 yuan/kg and 5.58 yuan/kg, and tobacco production declined from 3.91 million tonnes to around 2.1 million tonnes, showing a clear and positive association between the amount of production and the price per kilogram. A comparison of the government's average procurement price and both tobacco production and the area under tobacco reveals positive associations, as shown in Table 2. The higher the tobacco procurement price, the greater the area planted and the more leaf produced. While the government can allocate acreage and set procurement prices for tobacco leaf, farmers can still respond by varying their production in the quantity and quality of tobacco leaf.

The area planted with tobacco fluctuated from 1.34 million hectares in 1990 to 1.27 million hectares in 2000. It reached a peak of 2.22 million hectares in 1997, a direct response to the high purchase price. Yet, as a percentage of total land under cultivation in China, tobacco accounts for only around 1 percent. The value of total agricultural output in China steadily increased from 459.4 billion yuan in 1990 to 1,387.4 billion yuan in 2000, a real rate of increase in output of about 75 percent. Yet the contribution of tobacco to total agricultural production value ranged from 0.62 percent in 1995 to 1.75 percent in 1997. Overall, tobacco's contribution to the total value of agricultural production has declined, from 1.19 percent of gross agriculture receipts in 1990 to 0.9 percent in 2000. These statistics indicate that tobacco leaf production makes a minimum contribution to China's agricultural economy, and both its production area and economic value have been declining. However, in some provinces, such as Yunnan and Guizhou, tobacco remains an important cash crop.

PROVINCIAL TOBACCO PRODUCTION AND THE ROLE OF LOCAL GOVERNMENT

Since the production of tobacco leaf is a source of tax revenue for local governments, 24 out of 31 provinces in China grow tobacco. China has about five million farm households engaged in growing tobacco, or about 2 percent of total farmers.[2] Almost all farm households growing tobacco also produce other crops. Of the 24 tobacco-producing provinces, Yunnan, Guizhou, Henan, and Sichuan are the four most important in terms of both growing tobacco and manufacturing cigarettes. Together, these four provinces produce about 51 percent of China's total tobacco output, and in 2000 accounted for one-third of the country's 343 cigarette factories, producing 61.15 billion packs of cigarettes or about 30 percent of the country's total production.[2]

Of the four provinces, Yunnan had 330,000 hectares under tobacco in 2000, followed by Guizhou with 193,400 hectares, Henan with 163,300 hectares and Sichuan with 54,600 hectares. As the first two provinces are located at high altitudes with plenty of rainfall and warm weather, Yunnan and Guizhou produce a higher quality tobacco leaf with a greater yield. In fact, Yunnan is considered to have the best soil and weather for tobacco production and is the location for the country's largest tobacco company, Hong-Ta-Shan, Yunnan, and Guizhou also have a greater proportion of their total agricultural land devoted to tobacco (5.7 percent and 4.1 percent respectively) than do Henan and Sichuan (1.2 percent and 0.6 percent, respectively). The rest of the provinces, which grow tobacco, have less than 1 percent of their agricultural land under tobacco. Following the national trend, the amount of area under tobacco in those provinces fluctuated between 1990 and 2000, peaking in 1997 and drastically declining, due mainly to the reduction in purchase price decreed by STMA and reduced quota allocation for tobacco production. In 2000, Yunnan produced 646,070 tonnes of tobacco leaf, compared to 310,940 tonnes in Guizhou, 271,770 tonnes in Henan, and 97,300 tonnes in Sichuan. The peak production year was 1997, in which Yunnan produced almost one million tonnes of tobacco leaf.

It was shown that Yunnan's production of tobacco in 2000 was worth 3.6 billion yuan, or 8.7 percent of the total value of the province's agricultural output. In the peak year of 1997 tobacco leaf contributed 15 percent of the total value of agricultural production in Yunnan. Tobacco production in 2000 contributed 6.2 percent of the value of agricultural production in Guizhou, 1.2 percent in Henan, and 0.69 percent in Sichuan. Any change in tobacco control policy could therefore have an important impact in both Yunnan and Guizhou provinces, but particularly in Yunnan.

While the procurement price is set by the central government, local tobacco companies engage in the actual procurement. Procurement practices vary by company: some companies are more active in providing tobacco farmers with assistance (financial credit, fertilizer, and seeds). These companies, which use the crop as collateral to enable early purchasing, seek a higher-quality tobacco leaf and are more likely to assist those farmers who can provide them with high-quality tobacco.

The use of price to control production volume is not always effective, as tobacco-tax–dependent local governments often encourage or even require farmers to produce tobacco. Furthermore, there is a time lag between the time the crop is planted and the setting of the price. Even preannounce production quotas set by CNTC cannot guarantee production volumes will be on target. The government experienced chronic shortages of tobacco leaf prior to 1997; however, the peak price in 1997 induced a major increase in the production of tobacco, leading to a major surplus. After 1997, the government reduced the procurement price; hoping annual production would fall to around two million tonnes. Since then, the government has been accumulating surpluses, sometimes equivalent to one year's worth of cigarette production.

Two reasons account for this surplus phenomenon: one is the decline in the amount of tobacco leaf used per cigarette owing to technological innovation. In 1999, the cigarette industry used 39.5 kg to produce one case of cigarettes (5,000 pieces). By 2002, the industry had reduced that amount to 38.4 kg to produce the same number of cigarettes, meaning a savings of approximately 37,000 tonnes, or 2 percent of total production.[4] The second reason for the surplus is the significant contribution of tobacco leaf makes to local (county) and provincial tax revenues. Before 2003, local governments imposed a 27 percent to 31 percent tax on tobacco leaf, much higher than the tax of 8 percent of production value for other agricultural products. When CNTC purchased tobacco leaf from farmers, it withheld 31 percent of the payment as the farmers' contribution to the local tobacco tax. Therefore, a very strong incentive existed for local governments to encourage or sometimes require farmers to produce tobacco leaf.[5]

No official statistics are available on the exact amount of tobacco tax revenue collected by local governments. However, one can estimate the amount by multiplying the value of tobacco leaf produced in each province by 31 percent. For instance, during 2000, Yunnan's local and provincial governments collected about 1.11 billion yuan from tobacco leaf production, or about 70 percent of their total provincial tax revenues. Guizhou collected 538 million yuan, followed by Henan with 470 million yuan, and Sichuan with 168 million yuan.

No official statistics exist on the private market for tobacco, as it is not legal for farmers to sell their leaf to anyone other than the CNTC. However, in reality, a private market exists; given the amount of counterfeit cigarettes available on the market, private tobacco leaf markets are clearly operating.

TOBACCO LEAF PRODUCTION AND REVENUE BY HOUSEHOLD

Before addressing which policies might encourage a transition from tobacco, it is important to first understand tobacco farmers' cost, productivity, and revenue from tobacco as compared to other crops. The STMA has estimated that 20 million farmers, or about five million farm households, engage in tobacco production in 24 provinces

---

[5] Peng Y, "The Politics of Tobacco: Relations Between Farmers and Local Governments in China's Southwest," *The China Journal* 36 (1996): 67–82.

in China. However, very limited information is available to the public about tobacco production, cost, and overall household economic status. Yunnan is the most important province for obtaining household production and revenue information. However, it was not possible to obtain permission from the Yunnan local government to conduct a survey in 2002. With permission from local officials in Sichuan, Guizhou and a special district of Chongqing, 1015 rural household surveys were obtained through personal interviews in tobacco-growing counties in 2002.[6] About one-third of those farm households had less than half a hectare of farmland; another third had between half a hectare and one hectare; the other third had more than one hectare. In other words, Chinese farming households have very little cultivatable land. Within these survey households, 20 percent did not plant any tobacco, while 20 percent planted more than 50 percent of their land with tobacco. In addition to tobacco, these households also planted grain, beans, oilseed and fruit.

The survey collected information on the cost of producing each crop and the revenue received so economic returns could be compared; however, most farmers do not keep accounting records. To help farmers recall their costs and revenues, the survey developed a resource-accounting framework, which asked farmers specific questions about the type, amount and unit cost of each input. Costs included rent, hired labor (full time or part time), cost of curing tobacco and market transportation costs. Detailed questions were asked regarding the quantity and type of crop each household sold to the market (or government) and the average unit price they received.

Table 3 provides a summary of total costs and revenue for each crop by farm size. According to some interviews in Sichuan and Guizhou counties, citrus is a speciality and had high market value; thus, fruit produced the highest revenues, followed by tobacco. While tobacco was the second-highest revenue producer, it was equal to only about two-thirds of fruit revenue for small farms, one-half of

---

[6] Hu TW, Mao Z and Yurekli A, "Tobacco Farmers in China: Their Economic Status and Alternative Options," *Report Submitted to the World Bank*.

Table 3: Revenue to Cost Ratios by Major Crops by Size of Farm

	Small (<= 0.5 hectare) (n = 302)	Middle (0.5–1.0 hectare) (n = 361)*	Large (> 1.0 hectare) (n = 340)	Total Sample (n = 1,003)
Grain	2.5	2.3	2.6	2.5
Tobacco	2.4	2.6	2.8	2.6
Beans	3.0	5.9	2.9	4.3
Oil seed	3.1	4.0	3.7	3.7
Fruit	4.7	3.4	3.7	3.7

Note: *one mu = hectare/15.

fruit revenue for medium farms, and one-third of fruit revenue for large farms. If one measures the ratio between revenue and costs of each crop, it can be seen that, along with grain production, tobacco had a lower return than oilseeds, beans or fruit. These ratios imply that for every yuan farmers spent, they received on average 3.7 yuan for fruit. Small farmers benefited even more, as they received 4.7 yuan per yuan spent for fruit. On the other hand, for every yuan farmers spent on tobacco production, they received only 2.4–2.8 yuan. This return is smaller than returns from other crops, such as beans or oilseeds. Obviously, there are many reasons why farmers do not simply plant fruit instead of tobacco, including different land endowments, prior capital investments in tobacco, rainfall and temperature, marketing, assurance of government purchase of tobacco leaf, and government tobacco quotas assigned to some farmers.

Another way to compare revenue is by the percent of land devoted to tobacco. The categories are 0 percent (about 20 percent of the total sample, $n = 212$), greater than 0 but less than or equal to 30 percent ($n = 298$), greater than 30 percent but less than or equal to 45 percent, and greater than 45 percent. Table 4 provides the costs and revenue by percent of tobacco plantings. Among those farms that did not produce tobacco, the highest net revenue came from fruit production, which had the highest net revenue among all farm households, including those that planted tobacco. The return for fruit is about 4 yuan in revenue for every 1 yuan in cost. The return on fruit is even higher for farms that devoted between 0 percent and

Table 4: Revenue to Cost Ratio Cent of Tobacco Plantation

	Percent = 0 (n = 212)	Percent ≤0.3 (n = 298)	Percent ≤0.45 (n = 248)	Percent >0.45 (n = 245)
Grain	2.4	2.6	2.4	2.5
Tobacco	—	2.5	2.9	2.6
Beans	1.7	5.6	3.7	4.3
Oil seed	3.9	3.9	3.9	2.7
Fruit	3.9	5.1	5.7	1.1

45 percent of the land to tobacco, although the return on fruit is lower for farms that devoted more than 45 percent of their acreage to tobacco. This is likely because labor and capital resources were diverted to produce tobacco.

The data source of this study is limited to Sichuan and Guizhou provinces and Chongqing special district. Nevertheless, this study suggests that those farmers may do better growing crops other than tobacco. Compared to fruit production, tobacco showed decreasing returns to scale. Fruit had the highest net revenue of the five major crops studied. Returns from fruit, oilseeds, and beans were higher than from tobacco per unit cost. Farms that produced fruit and not tobacco had the highest returns, both in terms of net revenue and in terms of the revenue-to-cost ratio. Even those farms that planted a high percentage of tobacco had a very modest return and their revenue-to-cost ratio was less than the ratio for many alternative crops. Producing fruit or beans and not planting tobacco may provide greater revenue. These findings imply that there are promising alternative crops to tobacco. However, there are many institutional, governmental, and technical barriers preventing farmers from shifting from tobacco to other cash crops.

A study comparing the economic return to tobacco farmers and the economic return to the Chinese cigarette industry concluded that tobacco farmers have benefited the least from the cigarette industry.[7] The finding that tobacco may not always produce the best

---

[7] Lien J, "Who Will Curb China's Tobacco Industry?," *China International Business*, October 2002, 20.

economic returns is not unique to China.[8] A study from India indicates the following revenue-to-cost return ratios: 4.01 for safflower; 1.33 for mustard; and 1.2 for flue-cured tobacco.[9] Tobacco farming is often labour-intensive and requires equipment to cure the leaf, which reduces the net return. Therefore, alternative crops sometimes yield greater revenue-to-cost ratios than tobacco.

As indicated by STMA, the relatively low return from tobacco production could be due to an oversupply of tobacco.[10] The government does not have a price subsidy policy for tobacco. In fact, the overall farm-product price index in China did not increase during the last decade even though the general consumer price index did.[11] If tobacco does not provide a better economic return than other crops, why do farmers continue to plant it? One reason is the historical dependence of local governments on tobacco taxes. The second reason is that the ongoing arrangement with STMA assures revenue from tobacco without considering storage or marketing problems. Under the agreement, STMA provides technical assistance and guarantees the purchase. The third reason is, in the provinces in question, the soil and weather are ideal for cultivating tobacco. Finally, some farmers may not be aware of alternative crop options.

The new listing of CNTC's procurement prices sends a clear message to tobacco farmers to cut back their production of low-quality leaf. If there is an elimination of the special tobacco tax, local governments should have less incentive to force farmers to plant

---

[8] Kweyuh PHM, "Does Tobacco Growing Pay? The case of Kenya', in *The Economics of Tobacco Control: Towards an Optimal Policy Mix.* Abedian I van der Merwe R Wilkins N and Jha P (Cape Town: Medical Association of South Africa Press, 1998), 245–250.

[9] Chari MS and Kameswara RBV, "Role of Tobacco in the National Economy: Past and Present," *Control of Tobacco-Related Cancers and Other Diseases: International Symposium 1990* eds. in Gupta PC Hammer JE and Murti PR (Bombay: Oxford University Press, 1992.

[10] Chen Y, "From Monopoly to Consolidation," *China International Business,* October, 2002.

[11] *China Agricultural Yearbook* (1990–2000) (Beijing: China: Ministry of Agriculture, 2001).

tobacco; therefore, this is a critical time for Chinese tobacco farmers to re-evaluate their tobacco cultivation plans. The Chinese government should be more proactive by eliminating production quotas and providing economic incentives and technology to help tobacco farmers wishing to transfer from tobacco to other cash crops.

POTENTIAL IMPACT OF WTO MEMBERSHIP ON TOBACCO PRODUCTION

In 2000, China imposed a 40 percent tariff on tobacco leaf imports; as a result of the 2002 WTO trade agreement, China promised to reduce said tariff to 10 percent by 2004, even lower than the 17 percent tax rate on other imported agricultural products. In 2000, it was estimated that, with the 40 percent tariff, the average market price for tobacco was about 30 percent lower than the leaf imported from Zimbabwe. However, the reduction in the import tariff is expected to make domestic tobacco prices quite comparable to that of imported tobacco from countries such as Zimbabwe or Brazil. Yet the quality of Chinese tobacco is generally lower than that from those countries.[12]

Currently, China imports 300,000 tonnes of tobacco, or the equivalent of about 13 percent of total domestic production. Under the WTO agricultural framework agreement, exporting countries cannot provide government subsidies in the form of research and development, poverty-relief programmes in less developed regions, environmental protection projects or export loans. Currently, China has two forms of export subsidies:

1. an export rebate policy for exported flue-cured tobacco, tobacco leaf, and cigarettes,
2. an export bounty, which is a reward for exporting cigarettes.

Each province may set different bounty rates; they average three cents (yuan) per US$1 worth of exports. In Yunnan, the bounty rate

---
[12] Wang QJ, "Memorandum on Control Tobacco Leaf Production," *China Tobacco Biweekly*, May 2003, 11–23.

was six cents (yuan) for US$1 worth of exported goods. All these subsidy practices will have to stop now that China has joined the WTO, making China's tobacco leaf and cigarettes even less competitive in the world market and reducing the country's ability to export tobacco.

Finally, the WTO requires reduced tariffs on imported cigarettes. Before joining the WTO, China set the import quota at between 1 percent and 3 percent of domestic consumption. In 2000, the tariff was 65 percent for imported cigarettes; in 2004, the tariff rate fell to 25 percent. China's retail prices vary widely: with low tariff rates and smuggled foreign cigarettes, popular foreign brands are about 10–15 yuan (including the 25 percent tariff rate), no more expensive than some domestic Chinese brands such as Zhonghua or Hung Ta Shan. Thus, a lower import tariff will make foreign brands more competitive, reducing even further the market share for domestic cigarettes. While there are differences in taste between Chinese and foreign cigarette brands, foreign brands have more effective promotion schemes, particularly those geared towards the young and female populations in China. In addition, foreign brands are trying to make their taste suitable for Chinese smokers. The reduced market share for domestically produced cigarettes will soon translate into reduced demand for Chinese tobacco.

As a result of the WTO agricultural framework agreement in 2003, the STMA has stopped issuing special tobacco retail certificates, one of the mechanisms used to control retail sales of foreign cigarettes. Their removal will enhance the selling of foreign cigarette brands, which will have a negative effect on domestic tobacco production by reducing the competitiveness of local or low-quality brands, thus reducing the demand for low-quality tobacco leaf. Even with its membership in the WTO, China does not currently allow foreign companies to directly invest in tobacco or cigarette production. On the other hand, STMA allows foreign investors to participate in joint ventures with existing Chinese tobacco companies. For example, RJR and British American Tobacco (BAT) have recently signed investment agreements with STMA on a limited scale.

Top officials in the Chinese tobacco industry acknowledge the worldwide increase in anti-smoking attitudes, especially due to the WHO/FCTC agreement. Chinese government officials realize that rapid developments in the automobile, computer, and telecommunications industries will eventually lead to a decline in tobacco's contribution to government revenue, which is now about 10 percent. Some officials acknowledge that tobacco is going to be a "sunset" industry, meaning its role in the Chinese economy will decline. As foreign cigarettes increase their market share in China, top officials realize that eventually the Chinese tobacco monopoly system will be privatized and decentralized, a transition that may take five to six years according to some officials. In the meantime, *CNTC* is trying to reduce the number of cigarette factories by eliminating the inefficient plants, reducing the surplus supply of tobacco leaf (especially low-grade leaf), and lowering the procurement price.[13] The local government should remove tobacco quotas and allow tobacco leaf prices to be a market signal for tobacco farmers to consider the transition to other crops.

CONCLUSIONS

Tobacco has been considered a very attractive value-added product for the Chinese economy. Tobacco production is also a major source of local and central government tax revenue. The main factors behind the Chinese government's reluctance to use economic means, i.e., taxation, to control cigarette smoking are its concerns about lower tax revenue from tobacco leaf for local governments and lower revenue for the cigarette industry. This chapter has shown that the contribution of tobacco leaf to the Chinese agricultural economy is very minimal, except in Yunnan and Guizhou provinces. Historically, given the wide fluctuation in tobacco leaf production over the last decade, price setting is not an effective way to stabilize

---

[13] Nie HP, "How to Deal with WTO — Issues of China Tobacco Leaf [in Chinese]," *China Tobacco* 183, 7 (2000): 21–22.

tobacco leaf production. Since 1997, the peak year for production, tobacco production has been declining. The recent agricultural tax reform, which replaced the special tobacco leaf tax (31 percent) with a general agricultural product tax (8 percent), should remove the economic incentives for local governments to encourage farmers to plant tobacco leaf, thus helping to reduce the problem of surplus production.

The household survey of tobacco farmers indicated that many Chinese tobacco farmers operate on a small scale (less than one hectare per household), and income from tobacco generally constitutes less than 20 percent of their income. Compared to other cash crops, such as fruit, sugar, oilseeds or grain, and to livestock, tobacco has the lowest rate of economic return (revenue minus cost per mu). Dealing with large-scale tobacco farms would be a more cost-effective way for STMA to produce a large quantity of tobacco leaf. Therefore, the government should discourage those provinces that have less production or are not profitable in tobacco production. China's entrance into the WTO poses the threat of high-quality foreign tobacco entering China's market, with which low-quality tobacco will not be able to compete.

Crop substitution is an often-cited option for tobacco farmers; however, important factors must be considered. Even if an alternative crop can be identified, the transition takes time and requires economic resources, including the initial investment in the alternative crop; also, the size of the potential market for the alternative crop, its sensitivity to price changes, access to markets, production costs and the soil and climate of the area must be acknowledged.[14,15] Further research is needed on these important policy issues that affect the economic well being of farmers in China.

Currently, STMA is in charge of the planning of tobacco production, in place of the Ministry of Agriculture. The two organizations

---

[14] Jacobs R, Gale H, Capehart T, Zhang P and Jha P, "The Supply-Side Effects of Tobacco-Control Policies," *Tobacco Control in Developing Countries*, 2002.

[15] Skolnick AA, "Answer Sought for Tobacco Giant China's Problems," *Journal of the American Medical Association* 275 (1996): 1220–1221.

should work together to promote the economic welfare of farmers. The Ministry of Agriculture should provide information to farmers about alternative crops, which can be produced, as well as technical assistance on making a transition from tobacco production to those crops. The new administration in China has made the improvement of farmers' economic well being its top priority. It is of prime importance for the Chinese government to help the 20 million tobacco farmers improve their livelihood by providing information and technology for growing other crops. The government's concern over the possible negative economic impacts on tobacco farmers caused by imposing additional cigarette taxes appears to be unfounded, as such impacts would be minimal. In fact, an additional cigarette tax might stimulate farmers to seek more productive and profitable crops. International organizations, such as the Food and Agriculture Organization and the World Bank, should develop polices to help tobacco farmers make the transition from tobacco to other crops.

ACKNOWLEDGMENTS

The International Development Research Center/Research Initiative funded this study for Tobacco Control, World Bank and Fogarty International Center/National Institutes of Health (NIH/FIC lROlTW05938). The authors are grateful for suggestions and comments from Frank Chaloupka, Ross Hammond, Hana Ross, Shangan Shui, Thomas Wan and Kenneth Warner.

Chapter 11

China's Tobacco Industry and the World Trade Organization

Elisa Tong, Ming Tao, Qiuzhi Xue and Teh-wei Hu

INTRODUCTION

China is the world's largest consumer and producer of cigarettes. From the mid-1980s through the mid-1990s, smoking increased in China with little general knowledge of the health effects of smoking,[1] and by 2004 China had 350 million smokers nationwide.[2] The number of Chinese smokers may still grow significantly as the smoking prevalence among women (6.9 percent) was much lower than among men (60.2 percent) in 2001.[3] China's state-owned tobacco

---

[1] Yang G, Fan L, Tan J, *et al.*, "Smoking in China: Findings of the 1996 National Prevalence Survey," *JAMA* 282, no. 13 (1999): 1247–1253.
[2] Yang G, "The Epidemiological Investigation of the Smoking Behavior Among Chinese Population in 2002 (in Chinese)," *Chinese Smoking and Health* (2004): 7–18.
[3] Gu D, Wu X, Reynolds K, *et al.*, "Cigarette Smoking and Exposure to Environmental Tobacco Smoke in China: The International Collaborative Study of Cardiovascular Disease in Asia," *American Journal of Public Health* 94, no. 11 (2004): 1972–1976.

monopoly has been highly profitable, producing 1.7 trillion cigarettes in 2002 and generating 8 percent of the central government's revenue.[4]

In December 2001, China's entry into the World Trade Organization (WTO) lowered international trade tariffs and opened the market gateway for transnational tobacco companies (TTCs). TTCs have been eager to recapture China's large tobacco market, ever since China reopened its doors to foreign companies in 1979.[5,6] The potential impact of this market liberalization on consumption and market share is of great concern to public health in China. The entry of TTCs (and their foreign cigarettes) into the markets of Taiwan, Thailand, South Korea, and Japan in the mid-1980s resulted in a 10 percent increase in smoking consumption. Subsequent government priorities for tobacco control also dictate the long-term impact of market liberalization: Thailand is considered a model of tobacco control with strong national regulation,[7] whereas Japan has learned from other TTCs and is now the third largest producer in the world.[8] The entry of TTCs into China's tobacco market may escalate the current smoking-related epidemic of morbidity and mortality and raises questions about the future of tobacco control in China.

In this chapter, we examine how China's tobacco industry is being affected by entry into the WTO. First, we describe the structure of the Chinese tobacco monopoly and its importance to the economy. Next, we discuss China's schedule of agreements with the WTO and relative competitiveness with the TTCs. We then examine how China's

---

[4] China National Statistics Bureau, *China Statistical Yearbook 2000–2003* (Beijing: China Statistics Bureau, 2003).

[5] O'Sullivan B and Chapman S, "Eyes on the Prize: Transnational Tobacco Companies in China 1976–1997," *Tobacco Control* 9, no. 3 (2000): 292–302.

[6] Lee K, Gilmore AB and Collin J, "Breaking and Re-Entering: British American Tobacco in China 1979–2000," *Tobacco Control* 13, (Suppl. 2) (2004): ii88–95.

[7] Chantornvong S and McCargo D, "Political Economy of Tobacco Control in Thailand," *Tobacco Control* 10, no. 1 (2001): 48–54.

[8] Iida K and Proctor RN, "Learning From Philip Morris: Japan Tobacco's Strategies Regarding Evidence of Tobacco Health Harms as Revealed in Internal Documents from the American Tobacco Industry," *Lancet* 363, no. 9423 (2004): 1820–1824.

tobacco monopoly is reorganizing to compete with the TTCs and the challenges it faces with market liberalization. Finally, we address the greater implications for the future of tobacco control in China.

CHINA'S TOBACCO INDUSTRY STRUCTURE

National Level

The Chinese tobacco industry consists of a state monopoly with a centralized and vertical management of cigarette production. In 1982, the state council set up the China National Tobacco Company (CNTC) as an official government agency under the administration of the Ministry of Economics and Trade.[9] In 1984, the State Tobacco Monopoly Administration (STMA) was established, with all levels of the local government setting up provincial, district, and county bureaus. STMA sets the overall government tobacco policy beginning with the allocation of tobacco production quotas among the provinces, pricing of tobacco leaf, production of cigarettes and international trade. With the establishment of the STMA, the policy, data collection and research functions related to tobacco leaf production were separated from the jurisdiction of the Ministry of Agriculture.

Since 1991, STMA has delegated authority to the CNTC for the administration of all aspects of tobacco: (1) deciding a tobacco leaf production quota allocation for each province, (2) procuring tobacco leaf, (3) transporting and storing tobacco leaf, and (4) producing and marketing/selling cigarette products. To ensure the expected production quotas (approximately 34 million cases nationally), CNTC or its affiliated companies sign contracts with tobacco farmers regarding the amount of cultivation acreage. CNTC is obligated to purchase the full amount of tobacco leaf, with predetermined purchase price schedules based on tobacco leaf grades. CNTC approval is required for public or private agencies or individuals to purchase tobacco leaf or produce cigarettes and for retailers to sell cigarettes.

---

[9] Han B and Tao M, *The Analysis of the Government Role in the Restructuring Process of the Tobacco Industry (unpublished),* (Shanghai, China: Fudan University, 2006).

CNTC can also act in a non-official government capacity in dealing with non-governmental functions and foreign industries.

Regional Level

Even though CNTC is a monopoly, it has numerous company branches throughout the provinces that vary in size and act as competitors. The regional CNTC branches develop the sales plan, set factory production orders and prices, and are subsequently responsible for distribution. Each branch company is decentralized in that it must be self-sufficient and is allowed to retain its profits. Since local governments benefit from tobacco production through taxes and employment, each province and municipality has a cigarette factory. In 2001, CNTC oversaw about 140 regional companies located in almost every province and four major cities: Shanghai, Beijing, Tianjin, and Chongqing.[12] The top five cigarette manufacturing provinces in 2000 were Yunnan, Henan, Shangdong, Hunan, and Hubei.

The top cigarette companies in China do not have significantly concentrated market shares. In 2001, the top 10 companies had a 31 percent total market share, the top four companies had a 17 percent total market share, and the largest tobacco company, Hong-Ta-Shan, had only about 3 percent of the domestic market share.[10] Figure 1 demonstrates the low market ratio concentration for individual CNTC manufacturers (described on the x-axis as enterprise number) in 2001.[11] The market ratio concentration reflects the cumulative proportion of the production, sales, assets, and employees of each additional enterprise against the total production, sales, assets, and employees of the whole market. It takes 30 Chinese tobacco enterprises before the market concentration ratio reaches approximately 60 percent.

---

[10] China National Tobacco Corporation, *China Tobacco Statistics 2000–2005* (Beijing).

[11] Tao M, *China Tobacco Industry Under Monopoly System: Theory, Problem, and System Reform (in Chinese)* (Shanghai, China: Xiulin (Academic) Press, 2005).

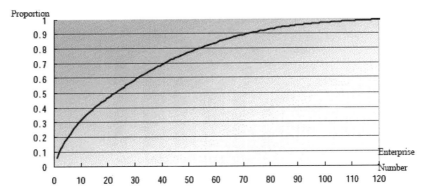

Fig. 1: Low Market Ratio Concentration for CNTC Manufacturers[13]

Contribution of China's Tobacco Industry to the Economy

China's tobacco industry has been a lucrative source of taxes for China's governments at all levels. Figure 2 demonstrates CNTC's growth in overall production and sales from 1999 to 2004.[11,12] For 15 consecutive years, the tobacco industry ranked first among all the sectors of the national economy in paying taxes.[11] Among the list of China's Top 100 Taxpayers 2003, the tobacco industry ranked first with 34 cigarette factories paying a total tax of 85.1 billion yuan. The tobacco tax has amounted to over 10 percent of China's total revenue, with special taxes on tobacco leaves, the value-added tax, the enterprise income tax, the urban maintenance and construction tax, and the education tax. From 1994, when China implemented a new taxation and financial distribution system to 2002, the tobacco industry produced an accumulated consumption tax of 311.2 billion yuan, or 62 percent of China's total consumption tax during that period. In tobacco-growing provinces such as Yunnan, the taxation from the tobacco industry amounted to about 70 percent of the financial revenue for the province.

---

[12] Philip Morris International, The China National Tobacco Corporation and Philip Morris International Announce the Establishment of a Long-term Strategic Cooperative Partnership, http://philipmorrisinternational.com/pmintl/pages/eng/press/pr_20051221.asp (accessed February 2007).

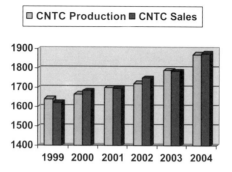

Fig. 2: Increase in CNTC Production and Sales in Billions of Cigarettes[13,14]

CNTC employs more than half a million people, about 0.4 percent of China's total employment. Approximately 500,000 persons are employed in the tobacco manufacturing industry (0.51 percent of total employment in the manufacturing industry). More than 20 million farmers also grow tobacco. About 3.5 million persons are engaged in retail cigarette sales,[10] about 0.6 percent of the total employed population. However, few retailers engage solely in cigarette sales.

Most cigarettes are sold domestically; less than 1 percent of the total is exported.[11] China is a major exporter throughout Asia, with 20 of the 43 countries and regions receiving exported Chinese cigarettes. In 2003, these exports totaled 18.4 billion cigarettes worth approximately $24 million dollars.

Tobacco Tax Structure for Chinese Central and Local Governments

As a state enterprise, the Chinese central and local governments profit from the tobacco industry's tax revenue. The governments levy two taxes on producers: a producer value-added tax, about 17 percent of the producer price, and a consumption tax, an additional 50 percent of the wholesale price. From the producers' point of view, the tax paid to the government is 67 percent of the producer price, but the effective tax rate is 38 percent if the amount of tax paid by the producer is compared to the retail price of cigarettes.[13] In addition, the local government levies an additional tax on tobacco leaves, especially for farming provinces, as their major source of tax revenue. The local governments "share" the revenue with the state, receiving on average 38 percent of the tax on tobacco leaves and over 50 percent of the product tax on cigarettes.[11] On average, the tobacco industry makes about a 10 percent profit on its total sales, profits then transferred to the government. Due to these financial incentives, non-profitable companies still exist because the local governments are willing to subsidize them for the sake of employment and tax revenue.

China's Tobacco Products

China's tobacco industry produces six types of tobacco products:[11] (1) Virginian-type cigarettes, which comprise 95 percent of the total domestic market, (2) sun-cured type cigarettes, (3) blend-type cigarettes which are popular in foreign countries and account for 70 percent of the international market (excluding the Chinese market), (4) exotically fragrant cigarettes, (5) medicinal or "new" blend cigarettes with Chinese herbal medicines added to promote health, and (6) cigars.

The Chinese flue-cured cigarettes are Virginian-type, but differ greatly from British Virginian-type. The raw materials for the medium- and high-grade cigarettes are mainly from imported American flue-cured tobacco. For low- and medium-grade cigarettes, flue-cured tobacco from Henan, Shandong, and Anhui is mixed into the formula in different proportions. Chinese cigarettes are characterized by their high tar and sugar, low ash, softer smoke, fragrance, clean mouth sensation, and sweet aftertaste. The high tar content has been difficult to reduce with Chinese tobacco science and technology, and tobacco leaf production has not focused on quality development, such as for aromas.

---

[13] Hu TW and Mao Z, "Effects of Cigarette Tax on Cigarette Consumption and the Chinese Economy," *Tobacco Control* 11, no. 2 (2002): 105–108.

Chen *et al.*[14] have described the development of the unique fifth category of cigarettes from China. These herbal-tobacco cigarettes were initially produced by China in the 1970s and required a prescription. Sales of these products were introduced to Japan and the transnational tobacco companies in the 1980s, but the transnational tobacco companies' analyses of the products suggested that they were not palatable and had potentially toxic cardiovascular effects. By the late 1990s, China began producing more herbal-tobacco cigarettes in a renewed effort to reduce the harmful constituents in cigarettes. Tobacco companies from Korea, Taiwan, and Thailand made similar attempts after 2000, perhaps in conjunction with the transnational tobacco companies' renewed interest in harm reduction cigarette products, but they encountered resistance because of concern about the health claims made by the products. Many products claimed to relieve respiratory symptoms and reduce toxins, with only four herb-only products advertised for smoking cessation. The scientific medical literature does not support these health claims. China continues to promote these brands, and in 2005 STMA included herbal-tobacco brands *Zhongnanhai* and *Jinsheng* among its "Top 36 Chinese Cigarette Brands" designated for further development.[15]

CHINA'S ENTRY INTO THE WORLD TRADE ORGANIZATION

Terms

During the first half of the 20th century, British American Tobacco (BAT) dominated the Chinese market with an 82 percent market share as early as 1924, and China became BAT's largest source of foreign earnings.[6] However, the Chinese market was closed to foreign companies, after the establishment of the People's Republic of China

---

[14] Chen A, Glantz SA and Tong EK, "Asian Herbal-Tobacco Cigarettes: 'Not Medicinal, but Less Harmful'?", *Tobacco Control* 16, no. 2 (2007): e3.

[15] Fell J, Khoo E and Adelman D, *China: The Final Frontier (Tobacco Industry Overview)* (Morgan Stanley, July 26, 2005).

in 1949. China officially asked for resumption of its membership into the post-World War II General Agreement on Tariffs and Trade (GATT) on July 10, 1986.[11] The principles of GATT are now enforced by the World Trade Organization, which was established in 1995 with 148 member nations.[16] The basic principle of WTO is non-discrimination between domestic and foreign goods. Included are tariffs, import quotas, laws, and regulations. Terms from the WTO can supersede local, state, and national decisions.

In December 2001, China gained entry into the World Trade Organization after negotiating over the years with 37 of more than 130 WTO members and reaching different trade agreements.[11] With China's entry into the WTO, tariff concessions immediately reduced tax rates with further reductions scheduled in the future; non-tariff measures (e.g., licenses and quotas) and government subsidies were scheduled for cancellation. Government subsidies for the tobacco industry totaled zero in 1990–1993, 1.2 billion yuan in 1994, 8.62 million yuan in 1995, 926 million yuan in 1996, 1.025 billion yuan in 1997, and 883 million yuan in 1998.

Implementation of China's tobacco agreements under WTO were delayed so its industry could improve its competitiveness before full trade liberalization. The reduction of import tariffs over a four-year period addressed tobacco leaf, cigarettes, and other related products are seen in Table 1.[11] The timetable for significantly increasing cigarette import quotas was left unclear. The export rebate was eliminated for flue-cured tobacco leaf and cigarettes, as well as the export bounty for cigarettes.

Comparing China's Tobacco Monopoly with Transnational Tobacco Companies

The timetable delay for full market liberalization under WTO reflects CNTC's competitive disadvantage compared with the TTCs. Although

---

[16] Shaffer ER, Brenner JE and Houston TP, "International Trade Agreements: A Threat to Tobacco Control Policy," *Tobacco Control* 14, Suppl 2 (2005): ii19–ii25.

Table 1: Tariff Reduction Schedule for Tobacco-related Products[11]

Product Name	Day of Entry to WTO percent	2002	2003	2004	2005
Tobacco leaf	28.0	22.0	16.0	10.0	
Cigarettes	49.0	35.0	25.0		
Cigars	49.0	41.0	33.0	25.0	
Cut tobacco for smoking	65.0				
Reproduced cigarettes	65.0				
Thread tobacco	9.0	7.0	5.0	3.0	
Acetate cellulose	10.3	8.4	6.5		
Filters	25.0	21.8	18.5	15.3	12.0
Cigarette paper	32.5	26.3	20.0	13.8	7.5
Essence and spice	35.0	30.0	25.0	20.0	15.0
Art/printing paper	8.5	6.8	5.0		
Cigarette machines	10.4	8.6	6.8	5.0	
Cigarette packers	12.0	10.0			
Inspection instruments	6.0	3.0	0.0		

China's state tobacco monopoly has the largest smoking market in the world, CNTC and its individual companies have not had the economic resources or capacity to compete on an individual company basis or as an entity with the TTCs. Table 2 compares CNTC and the Hongta Group (CNTC's largest manufacturer) with the top three transnational tobacco companies. Although CNTC's sales were almost twice that of Philip Morris or British American Tobacco (BAT), CNTC's revenue was two to four times lower. In 2001, the largest tobacco company in China, the Hong-Ta-Shan Group, produced 95 billion cigarettes, about 5 percent of total Chinese production. This production capacity is only about 10 percent that of Philip Morris, 12 percent of British American Tobacco (BAT), and 20 percent of Japan Tobacco levels.[10] Due to the large Chinese market in 2005, China had 30 percent of the global market selling 1874 billion cigarettes, whereas Philip Morris International had 14.5 percent of the global market selling 761 billion cigarettes.[12] However, CNTC

Table 2: Comparison of CNTC and the Hongta Group (CNTC's leading manufacturer) with the Top Three Transnational Tobacco Companies[19]

	Hongta Group	CNTC	Philip Morris	BAT	Japan Tobacco
Revenue (US$100 M)	18.4	203.7	804.1	389.7	371.4
Capital (US$100 M)	43.7	260.7	754.0	257.3	250.4
Returns (US$100 M)	3.5	19.3	111.0	20.4	30.0
Sales (10,000 cases)*	190.2	3399.6	1829.4	1554.6	907

*50,000 cigarettes per case.
Source: State Tobacco Monopoly Administration, *Economic Research*, (Beijing, 2002).

taxes and profits totaled $25.6 billion, whereas Philip Morris International's net revenues were $39.5 billion.

Imports and Exports

From 1995 to 2000, total official cigarette imports and exports comprised only 0.8 percent of the domestic Chinese market.[10] By early 2000, foreign products had about 3 percent of the Chinese market. The CNTC anticipates that before the end of the decade, foreign products may reach 8 percent to 10 percent of the Chinese market.[17] Cigarette imports into China are mostly from the United Kingdom (52.3 percent), the United States (24.5 percent), and Japan (10.7 percent).[11]

The WTO import tariff reductions on tobacco leaf and cigarettes are increasing the price competitiveness for foreign tobacco products. The tariff on tobacco leaf has gradually been reduced from 64 percent in 1999 to 25 percent in 2003 to 1 percent in 2004.[10] This tariff reduction has made foreign tobacco leaf as competitive as Chinese domestic tobacco leaf, and China's tobacco farmers already face a

---

[17] Liu TN and Xiong B, *Tobacco Economy and Tobacco Control* (Economic Science Press (Chinese), 2004).

tobacco leaf surplus. The tariff on cigarette products was 49 percent before 2001 but was reduced to 25 percent in 2003.[10] China's cigarette imports have increased by 37 percent — from 68.51 million packs in 2002 to 93.92 million packs in 2003.[10] Prior to 2003, foreign brands such as Marlboro or 555 cost about 20 yuan (US$2.50) per pack. The current market price is now 12 yuan (US$1.50) per pack, similar to popular domestic brands such as "Hong-Ta-Shan," which costs about 10 yuan. As the Chinese economy is growing with higher personal income, the demand for foreign brands is increasing, particularly among urban young adult male smokers.[2]

Total Chinese tobacco exports account for only 1.8 percent of the world's total exports.[10] China exports mostly to Southern Asia (e.g., Burma, Singapore, Malaysia, and Mongolia). With cooperative agreements with TTCs,[12] CNTC will be increasing exports globally.

Non-Tariff Financial barriers

Some Non-Tariff Financial Barriers in China have been eliminated. For example, the "Special Tobacco Retail Sale Permit" for imported cigarettes was eliminated in late 2003, and now four million retailers can sell imported cigarettes with only a general permit.[11] This agreement was a result of earlier negotiations with the European Union to reform the monopoly management license. A transition period of two years was agreed upon to unify the license procedures without regard to country of origin.

The United States tried to negotiate with China further in opening China's cigarette distribution system and allowing tobacco companies from other countries to establish their own sales system. Instead, tobacco was deemed an "exception" to the opening of wholesale commodities and the establishment of distribution systems. Joint ventures are another special tobacco exemption, in which retail and distribution of tobacco products are not permitted to have foreign majority ownership in joint venture retail enterprises as of early 2005.[10]

CHINA'S TOBACCO MONOPOLY REORGANIZATION

In anticipation of WTO membership and the effects of market liberalization, STMA announced four modernization goals in 1999[18]: consolidate; acquire new technology, diversify; and internationalize; Given the numerous manufacturing companies and brands throughout the regions, CNTC does not have the economy of scale needed to compete with the transnational companies' products; hence the need to consolidate. Acquiring new technology will assist with efficiency and achieving international product standards. Diversification will allow the companies to grow and stabilize with revenue from other sectors. Internationalization will expand the current markets for future growth beyond China.

Consolidation of Companies and Brands

Through merger and integration, STMA hopes to achieve economic efficiency in cigarette production, pricing, and marketing by closing inefficient and small cigarette factories. The purpose of merging has not been to acquire the benefits of collaborating on a management or financial level. While maintaining the quota system, STMA has sought to achieve economy of scale by ultimately reducing its operations to 30–50 factories with six to eight large inter-regional tobacco groups.[9] Whereas provincial governments previously could expect a local regional monopoly, CNTC seeks to establish mergers within provinces first and then have regional companies compete against each other.

The number of regional companies decreased from 185 in 2001 to 62 in December 2004.[10] This rapid reduction in companies was accomplished by merging and integrating smaller companies into larger ones. In 2002, China had 123 factories. Based on production levels, the 36 smallest companies (less than 5 billion cigarettes) were phased out by 2004; the 35 medium-sized companies (5–15 billion

---

[18] Bennett C, Biggest in the World: An overview of the STMA and the Chinese Cigarette Industry, *Tobacco Reporter*, 1999.

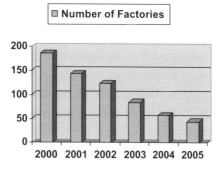

Fig. 3: STMA Reduction of Factories to Achieve Economy of Scale[10]

cigarettes) were reorganized by merger; the 52 large companies (> 15 billion cigarettes) remained, with 12 very large companies (> 30 billion cigarettes). Figure 3 demonstrates the reduction of companies from 2000 to 2005. As a result of this merging, certain provinces/factions have come to dominate the production scales: Yunnan (6 million cases), Shanghai (4–5 million cases), and Hunan (3 million cases).[11]

Case examples demonstrate how the government facilitated the merging process[9]:

(1) Unpaid state asset transfer: Without any payments to the companies, STMA transferred the Beijing Tobacco Company and the Tianjin Tobacco Company to the Shanghai Tobacco Company, and the Xunyang Tobacco Company to the Baoji Tobacco Company.

(2) Stakeholding with joint funds for tobacco companies and local governments not in the same provinces: The Inner Mongolia Kunming Tobacco Company Limited was formed by combining the Kunming Tobacco Company and the Huhehaote Tobacco Company, and the Hongta Liaoning Tobacco Company Limited was formed by combining the Hongta corporation, the Shenyang Tobacco Company, and the Yingkou Tobacco Company. In the latter example, the Shenyang Tobacco Company and the Yingkou

Tobacco Company invested their net assets for a 49 percent share, and the Hongta Corporation put in the remaining 51 percent investment.

(3) Assuming the debts of another company: the Xuzhou Tobacco Company absorbed the Chengcheng Tobacco Company; the Changde Tobacco Company absorbed the Qidong Tobacco Company; the Hongta Corporation absorbed the Changchun Tobacco Company, and the Qujing Tobacco Company absorbed the Wulanhaote Tobacco Company.

(4) Canceling the corporate status and changing into a manufacturing facility: The impact of the noted mergers reflects a change in brand names more than the actual activities of the company. In Guangdong province, six former tobacco companies merged into one company. In Hunan province, nine former tobacco companies merged into four companies. In the above example of The Hongta Liaoning Tobacco Company Limited, the Shenyang and Yingkou tobacco companies dropped their own corporate status and became the manufacturing facilities for the Hongta Corporation.

The local governments have played an important role in coordinating these mergers within and between provinces.

Besides consolidating companies, STMA has also reduced the number of domestic cigarette brands. In 2001, 1,049 brands produced 1,722 billion cigarettes. Only three brands had annual sales of over 50 billion cigarettes representing 10 percent of the market[17]: Honghe, Baisha, and Hongmei, which have licensed joint ventures with manufacturers in non-neighboring regions. By June 2004, the number was reduced drastically to 370 brands. Figure 4 demonstrates the reduction of domestic cigarette brands from 2002 to 2005. In 2004, STMA earmarked the top 100 Chinese brands and 36 brands designated for further development. STMA's five-year plan for 2006–2010 will control product expansion, with 10 brands slated to produce more than 50 billion cigarettes and 35 percent of the market, and three to four brands slated to produce more than 100 billion cigarettes.

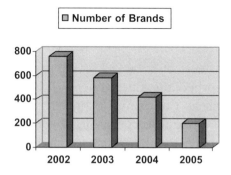

Fig. 4: STMA Reduction of Domestic Cigarette Brands[10]

Taxation and profit increased during this period from 111 billion yuan in 2000 to 240 billion yuan in 2005 and amounted to one tenth of the central government's revenue.[10] From 2002 to 2004, the top four companies increased their market share from 16 percent to 24 percent, and the top four brands increased their market share from 8 percent to 11 percent. These market shares likely will continue to increase as barriers resulting from local protectionism are eliminated.

Previously, provincial tobacco companies enacted local protectionism by setting trade barriers for out-of-province cigarettes.[19] This practice was encouraged by the local governments who benefited from the tobacco revenue. STMA seeks to reduce this local protectionism by two mechanisms.[9]

The first mechanism is removing the local governments' tobacco revenue (Fig. 5). The manufacturing and commercial sectors were separated at the provincial level in the period 2003–2005. The provincial company now acts as the CNTC subsidiary, the district company serves as the key operations level, and the county-level company's corporate status has been cancelled. As a result, the role of the 16 provincial companies has changed from administrative to asset management, and from manufacturing and operation activities to supervision and personnel management; this consolidation may streamline implementation of plans by STMA and CNTC. The district

---

[19] Tuan, "WTO and Yunnan Tobacco," *China Tobacco (Chinese)* 7, (2000): 25.

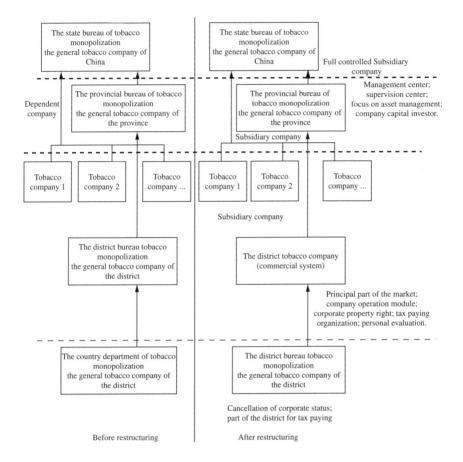

Fig. 5: The Different Government Levels and Role of the Tobacco Companies Before and After Restructuring[9]

companies continue to have corporate property rights, assuming the responsibility of their operational assets. The 1,317 county-level companies no longer have corporate status, meaning they no longer legally own capital, and the local county governments no longer benefit from tobacco revenue; many county companies have since changed their name to reflect a county-level tobacco sales or manufacturing department.

The second mechanism to reduce local protectionism is price unification.[9] By 2006, price unification will have been phased in at the provincial level and will subsequently be followed at the national level. These mechanisms will reduce the economic incentives of the local governments to prevent growth of companies and brands that do not provide a local tax or employment benefit.

Product Standards and Technology

STMA considers acquiring new technology as a high priority and has instituted a "Technology Innovation System" to promote quality and innovation. A key feature of this system is the Zhengzhou Tobacco Research Institute, whose website describes it as "an innovative and modernized research institute which includes scientific research, popularization, quality supervision and test [sic], information, standardization, and training center" on tobacco.[20] The staff of 231 persons is composed of engineers, scientists, and technicians. Research from this institute has been used, for example, to help demonstrate that Chinese herbal-tobacco cigarettes such as *Wuyeshen* and *JiangShan* and *QunYingHui* have reduced toxic substances compared to other cigarettes.[14] Other features of the Technology Innovation System includes technology centers, laboratories, and model counties.

Improving tobacco leaf quality has been of great importance since China is the largest producer of tobacco leaf in the world, accounting for about one third of leaf output. The best quality areas for tobacco leaf in China are the southwestern provinces where major rivers are adjacent, including Yunnan, Guizhou, south of Sichuan, west of Hunan, southwest of Hubei, and southwest of Guangxi.[11] Part of STMA's new technology initiative is to implement changes in growing and processing tobacco leaf. Other leaf processing considerations in order to compete with international products include producing blend type cigarettes, improving paper production for high quality products, incorporating additives including spices, and reducing the high proportion of tobacco leaves used for one case of cigarettes.

---

[20] Zhengzhou Tobacco Research Institute of CNTC, Orientation Goal and Foreground, http://www.ztri.com.cn/eng/eng01.htm (accessed February 2007).

Cigarette product improvement has also been important in anticipation of CNTC competing with foreign brands. Chinese cigarettes used to have a high tar content between 14 and 15 mg. However, beginning in July 2004, China prohibited the sale of cigarettes with more than 15 mg.[11] By 2005, cigarette manufacturers were to reduce tar content to 12 mg. Manufacturers are now required to use new technology to reduce the tar content to meet the international standard of 11.2 mg. Exports to European Union nations may not exceed 10 mg starting in January 2005. Machinery also needs to be upgraded for these new standards. Other quality improvements include changes in the packaging of cigarette products, the paper quality, and printing.

TTCs have been key in helping the Chinese tobacco industry acquire technology through the limited joint ventures and cooperative agreements.[11] Under these arrangements, the TTCs may provide technical experience, joint development of new products, and licensed production of foreign cigarette brands. The technology transfer can include tobacco leaf production and development, fragrance, flow training, and production management. In exchange, the TTCs gained an early foothold in the Chinese market and distribution channels controlled by the government.

Another forum in which STMA may have acquired ideas from transnational tobacco companies about scientific developments and new technology is the Asia Regional Tobacco Industry Scientist Team (ARTIST).[21] ARTIST was established in 1996 by Philip Morris initially as a vehicle to include Asian tobacco companies and to implement strategies against global smoke-free areas. Representatives from STMA, Zhengzhou Research Institute, and the China Tobacco Society were invited members. By 2001, ARTIST had evolved into a forum to discuss scientific and regulatory issues faced by the TTCs, and Philip Morris hoped ARTIST would help reach out to the public health and regulatory community. At the meetings,

---

[21] Tong EK and Glantz SA, "ARTIST (Asian Regional Tobacco Industry Scientist Team): Philip Morris' Attempt to Exert a Scientific and Regulatory Agenda on Asia," *Tobacco Control* 13, Suppl 2 (2004): ii118–ii124.

scientific publications related to industry interests were discussed, TTC-developed technologies for indoor air ventilation (which have not been shown effective) were introduced, and strategies to limit smoke-free regulations were presented.

Diversification

In the early 1990s, the larger companies began to diversify industries. The rationale for diversification beyond tobacco was to increase profits, stabilize operations, and improve the local economy.

The Hongta Group is an example of such diversification. According to its website in 2005,[22] Hongta Group had 69 enterprises, 16,500 employees, and a $1 billion yuan total industry production value. Besides tobacco manufacturing, enterprises included energy production of hydroelectric power, transportation development with an automobile factory and highways, finance and banking, and real estate with hotels. STMA urged other tobacco manufacturers to follow the Hongta Group's example of diversification.[19]

However, an analysis of 2002 data demonstrates that while the Hongta Group ranked first among all tobacco companies in realizing tax profits, it ranked second in net profit.[11] Furthermore, in calculating the economic value added (value after subtracting the cost of operations and the lost opportunity of investing consumed resources elsewhere), the Hongta Group would not be among the top 10 companies. The enormous capital scale of the Hongta Group may suffer from lack of efficiency, decreasing the appreciation value added of its capital.

Internationalization

Opportunities for TTCs to gain a foothold in the Chinese tobacco market have been carefully restricted by STMA. The TTC official

---

[22] Hongta Group, Diversified Hongta (company website), http://www.hongta.com/model_ht_en/MixedInvestment/index.jsp?ID=130500000000000000 (accessed June 2006).

import quota for cigarettes has increased slowly. The import quotas increased from 1.4 billion cigarettes in 2002 to 1.9 billion cigarettes in 2003 to 2.1 billion cigarettes in 2004. Current estimates are that TTCs have 3 percent domestic market share; STMA projects that this will increase to 8–10 percent by 2010.[15] Licensing between transnational tobacco companies and Chinese manufacturers to produce foreign brands is also limited due to quotas. These companies include British American Tobacco, Philip Morris, Reemtsma, Japan Tobacco, Imperial Tobacco, and Seita.[11]

Joint venture factories with TTCs have been heavily restricted.[11,15] In 1988, RJ Reynolds International (now owned by Japan Tobacco) created a joint venture with Fujian China American Cigarette Factory. The joint venture creates 2.5 billion cigarettes a year of *Camel*, *Winston* and the joint venture brand *Golden Bridges*. Rothmans International (now owned by British American Tobacco) in Shandong province produced joint venture brands *Horseman* and *Neptune* at a similar volume. However, STMA later proclaimed that no further joint ventures or new cigarette factories would be allowed due to excess production capacity in the Chinese market.

Subsequent joint ventures reflect long-term cooperation to foster goodwill for future business but are not guaranteed footholds into China's tobacco market. In 2003, Imperial Tobacco Company agreed to a 10-year cooperation deal with Yuxi Hongta Group. In return for the production of Imperial's *West* cigarettes at 10 million cigarettes a year, Imperial agreed to invest $8–10 million a year for infrastructure and marketing. In 2003, Gallagher Tobacco Company agreed to a reciprocal license with Shanghai Tobacco Group. Gallagher's *Memphis* will be manufactured and distributed by Shanghai Tobacco Group in China, and in return Gallagher will make and distribute the Chinese brand *Golden Deer* in Russia. British American Tobacco announced plans for a joint venture twice. In 2001, British American Tobacco announced plans for a new factory in Sichuan, and in 2004, British American Tobacco announced plans for a factory that would produce 100 billion cigarettes a year with HK China Eastern Investments. STMA later denied approval for both BAT announcements.

Most recently, Philip Morris International and CNTC announced an international joint venture described on Philip Morris' website as a "long-term strategic partnership ... not expected to have material impact on immediate financial results."[12] Starting in 2006, the licensed manufacturing and sales of Marlboro in China will be allowed. In return, an international equity joint venture company will be established in Lausanne, Switzerland, where Philip Morris International is headquartered. This joint venture will distribute Chinese brands in global markets in 2006, expand exports of tobacco products and tobacco materials from China, and explore business development opportunities. With China claiming 30 percent of the global market and Philip Morris International claiming 14.5 percent of the global market, this joint venture may have a large impact on increasing tobacco consumption in China and around the world.

CHALLENGES OF CHINA'S TOBACCO INDUSTRY REORGANIZATION AND MARKET LIBERALIZATION

Tobacco Leaf Production

Although China is the largest producer of tobacco leaves in the world, China has been dependent on its domestic market. The total export of Chinese tobacco leaves accounted for only 3.5 percent of the world's total, and the total export of cigarettes accounted for only 1.8 percent of the world's total.[11] In 2002, China's import of tobacco leaves was 550,000 tons, ranking 10th in the world, and China's export of tobacco leaves was 169,000 tons, ranking second in the world. The amount of tobacco leaves annually purchased by the Chinese government from the farmers is approximately 2 million tons.

As the price of high quality leaves from other nations drops because of the elimination of tariffs, the high quality leaves from select provinces in China may be able to compete, but leaves grown for tax and quota purposes will not. China has 32 provinces and autonomous regions/municipalities due to China's quota system for purchasing tobacco leaves. Tobacco is cultivated in 22 of these provinces (152 prefectures and cities and 532 counties), but only five southwestern provinces are considered to produce high-quality leaves. High-quality tobacco leaves from Zimbabwe presents an example of how foreign competition will increase. Imported leaves from Zimbabwe in 1999 cost 65,000 yuan/ton while domestic leaves cost a third less at 20,000 yuan/ton. With tariffs dropping to 10 percent by 2004, imported tobacco leaves would be 20,000 yuan lower. This price may drop further as more Zimbabwe tobacco leaves is imported and increases in supply. Argentina is another growing import source of high-quality tobacco leaves.

Further affecting the domestic tobacco leaves market is China's system of determining the purchase price of tobacco leaves based on price parity between tobacco and grain. When the price of grain rises, the farmers have less incentive to grow tobacco, and the area of tobacco cultivation declines. For example, in 2003, the rice in Guizhou was 1.2 yuan/ton and the output value was 800 yuan/hectare. The price of tobacco leaves was 4.8 yuan/ton, and the output value was less than 1,000 yuan/hectare. While the rate of return for tobacco compared to grain was 1.2:1, more workdays are required to cultivate tobacco. Farmers can more easily cultivate grain and spend the off-season making money in the cities. With a rise in the grain price in 2003 and 2004, STMA raised the purchase price of tobacco by 10 percent and encouraged more cigarette factories to build a cultivation base. To compete internationally, China will need to consider the international pricing and market demand for tobacco leaves.

Companies

Whether China's merging and restructuring process will allow CNTC to compete with the transnational tobacco companies remains to be seen, since the strong government role may offset reforms to become more competitive.[9] The reforms have not resulted in a true tobacco oligarchy, since there is not a true open market nationally. However, opening the sales and distribution networks would create access for the transnational tobacco company products before full trade liberalization under WTO. Local governments still retain a large amount of control due to the unchanged sales system, and tobacco companies will continue to find it difficult to operate out of the province. The fiscal revenue system remains essentially unchanged; while no more county revenue is obtained from sales of cigarettes made locally, an additional tax has been substituted to help ease the transition, and local governments still benefit. Another problem is that the local governments have historically received large tax revenue from cigarettes from these local enterprises and have disregarded state planning efforts; these factories may continue to develop and are difficult to ban by the state. Whether this distribution network issue may be offset by the development of new sales channels with large retailers is unclear.[15]

Company property rights and asset management are also not separate from central administrative interests, which may not encourage internal reform of management or operations.[9] While some companies may have adopted a corporate management structure, the companies still operate under old operations; the management positions are jointly held by members of the company's party council without clearly defined responsibilities; the board of supervisors is selected internally rather than by external investors; and the company's rights of decision, operation, and supervision are also highly centralized. Central and local government interests may conflict. The central government seeks to cultivate the top national brands (which already conflicts with its interest in protecting the public health of its citizens), and the local governments seek to protect their local tax and revenue income. Furthermore, beyond reducing the numbers of companies and brands, no guidelines exist for enacting or evaluating these changes to promote CNTC's competitiveness.

An unintentional consequence of these consolidating reforms is that local protectionism may even increase. For example, the relationship between the Guangdong China Tobacco Industrial Company and the Guangdong Tobacco Company is similar to that between STMA and CNTC.[9] Before the restructuring of the tobacco industry, the Guangdong China Tobacco Industrial Company supervised the operations of six tobacco companies in Guangdong province. Since

Guangdong China Tobacco Industrial Company and these Guangdong tobacco companies became one after restructuring, this entity controls not only the manufacturing, but also the selling of the tobacco products. As a result, the new Guangdong Tobacco Company is strengthening its monopolizing of the tobacco market within Guangdong province.

Products

The Chinese cigarette industry does not have any powerful brands on the domestic or foreign market to compete with TTC brand leaders. The top Chinese brand leader *Hongtashan* has a domestic market concentration ratio of 3 percent compared to *Marlboro's* 38.8 percent in the US market; its respective brand value of $5.56 billion compares to $24.2 billion for Marlboro in 2002. Output of Chinese brands is relatively low: *Hongtashan* has an annual output of 800,000 cases compared to *Marlboro's* 2.9 million cases. Also, while there are 2,198 varieties of 1,149 Chinese cigarette brands, this diversification is not concentrated by brand: *Hongtashan* has only five varieties, while *Marlboro* has more than 80. However, STMA is now focusing more on brand operation than general product sales, and domestic cigarette consumers may perceive improved quality and acceptance of brands. Average cigarette sales increased from 2002 to 2005 by 2.46 percent, and in 2002 the sales of the 36 designated famous and high quality cigarettes increased 15.6 percent from the previous year to 6.976 million cases.

The type of cigarettes typically produced by China may not be palatable for the international market. China's cigarette production has focused on the Virginian-type cigarettes (95 percent domestic market), whereas blend-type cigarettes comprise 70 percent of the international market (excluding the Chinese market) and are increasing by 14.3 percent annually.[11] The blend-type cigarettes produced in China are at the low–medium price range and do have market potential. However, the TTCs already dominate these product lines, and the Chinese domestic tobacco leaf currently grown cannot meet the demand for the production of the blend-type cigarettes.

236 *Elisa Tong et al.*

The pricing of cigarettes is a challenge as foreign brands are becoming more competitive with domestic brands. How the companies will respond to capture the large low-grade rural smoker market remains to be seen. Foreign cigarettes are priced mostly at 10 yuan/pack, similar to the domestic medium- and high-grade cigarettes. The medium- and high-grade cigarettes produced in China represent a smaller proportion (35 percent) of cigarettes than the proportion in developed countries (85 percent). Chinese tobacco companies have also been concentrating on profits from high-priced cigarettes, leaving a serious shortage in the supply of low-priced cigarettes.[11] In 2002, sales of cigarettes priced over 100 yuan/carton reached 570,000 cases, accounting for only 1.7 percent of the total sales but 31.8 percent of the total profits of the cigarette industry. This profit focus on high-priced cigarettes may be backfiring. In early 2003, among the 36 designated famous brands and high-quality cigarettes, sales of eight of the brands decreased, six of them dropping by over 10 percent. Rural smokers in China far outnumber those in the cities, and in 2003 they smoked cigarettes averaging 2.04 yuan/pack versus 4.87 yuan/pack in 2001. However, the increase in rural consumption was less than 50 percent the increase in urban areas. As a result, 80 percent of the low-grade cigarettes have been produced in underground and unplanned cigarette factories not controlled by STMA.

Import/Exports

With the decrease in import tariffs for cigarettes from 65 percent before China's accession to WTO to 25 percent in 2003, imports are increasing. Figure 4 demonstrates cigarette product import and export data from China customs statistics from January 1997 to May 2003.[11] As seen in Fig. 6, before 1999, export of Chinese cigarettes was very high, but imports were low. Starting close to and after China joined the WTO in 2001, the balance of import to exports changed. Most notably, cigarette imports in 2003 increased by 37 percent compared with 2002.

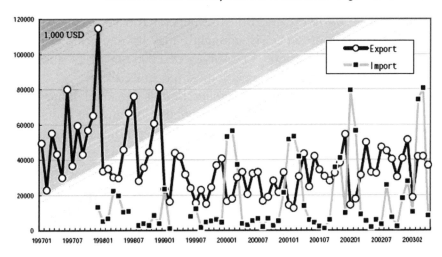

Fig. 6: Monthly Figures for Import and Export of Chinese Products of Cigarettes and Cigarette Substitutes from 1997–2003[11]

Smuggling and Counterfeiting

Smuggling and counterfeiting of cigarettes are important issues in China, and STMA estimates that 100 billion cigarettes a year are now smuggled or counterfeit.[15] Between 1988 and 1992, the number of smuggled cigarettes confiscated by customs officials escalated up to 26 billion.[23] In 1998, a national anti-smuggling campaign was instituted with regular seizures of millions of cigarettes. In 1994, the yuan depreciated significantly, and the cost of importing foreign cigarettes increased with a tariff rate as high as 150 percent and an actual tariff rate of 430 percent.[11] Official foreign cigarette imports halted, and tariff rates progressively decreased from 150 percent to 65 percent in 1995 to 1998 with an overall rate as high as 283 percent due to the increase in the rate of the consumption tax. Up to 50 billion smuggled cigarettes were believed to be foreign by the late 1990s,[23] with the top smuggled brands being British American Tobacco's 555,

---

[23] Lee K and Collin J, "Key to the future: British American Tobacco and Cigarette Smuggling in China," *PLoS Medicine* 3, no. 7 (2006): e228.

Philip Morris' *Marlboro,* and British American Tobacco's *Hilton.* This increased market presence by smuggling may have affected Chinese recognition of these brands. In a survey of 2,000 university students, these brands were among the eight most recognized.[24]

In 2003, 46 percent of the smuggled brands remained domestic.[11] Domestic smuggling is even more profitable because of costs and taste preference by Chinese smokers. Exported domestic cigarettes are exempted from taxes, and smugglers can obtain these cigarettes at prices nearly 50 percent lower than on the domestic market. State taxes (e.g., value-added tax (VAT), consumption tax), which are higher than the value of the cigarettes themselves, can be evaded. Other taxes for state certification and high-rate custom tariffs can be avoided if cigarettes are smuggled through irregular channels. An example is the case of "Chunghwa" cigarettes, which have a factory price for external sale at 2,100 yuan/case and a factory price for domestic sale at 2,500 yuan/case.[11] If the 17 percent VAT and 40 percent consumption tax are added, the after-tax factory price for external sale is 4,000 yuan/case, and the retail price on the domestic market is 15,000 yuan/case. The difference between the factory price for external sale and domestic sale is 12,900 yuan. If a 40-foot container holding 880 cigarette cases is successfully smuggled, a profit of 11,080,000 yuan can be made. Smuggling one container of domestic cigarettes can result in the equivalent of becoming a millionaire.

British American Tobacco has used smuggling to re-enter the Chinese market. This tactic has been described in the European markets by Philip Morris and British American Tobacco.[25] Lee and colleagues[6] analyzed tobacco industry document files made available from litigation at the Guildford Depository in England operated by British American Tobacco. The documents suggest that British American Tobacco, frustrated by STMA's restrictions in gaining market access, relied on illegal imports and exploited inconsistencies in the

---

[24] Zhu SH, Li D, Feng B, Zhu T and Anderson CM, "Perception of Foreign Cigarettes and their Advertising in China: A Study of College Students from 12 Universities," *Tobacco Control* 7, no. 2 (1998): 134–140.

[25] Joossens L and Raw M, "Cigarette Smuggling in Europe: Who Really Benefits?," *Tobacco Control* 7, no. 1 (1998): 66–71.

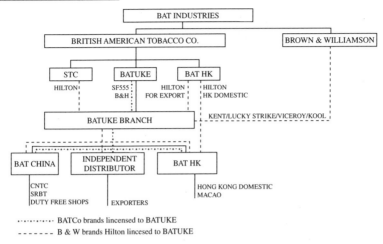

Fig. 7: BAT Internal Document Demonstrating Planned Restructuring of Operations to Separate Supply of "Independent Distributors" to China[23] [redrawn from original].

local enforcement of advertising bans to expand the market presence of key brands. In 1991, 25 percent of BAT's profits came from the illegal "transit trade" to China. Figure 7 is a BAT internal memo demonstrating an organizational graph of how BAT reorganized its operations in 1991 to include "independent distributors" to China. These "independent distributors" would allow BAT full control at an arms-length basis while allowing deniability of the operations. This restructuring was approved by BAT Chairman Sir Patrick Sheehy and reviewed internally and by Price Waterhouse to determine the optimal location of the companies to minimize tax liability.[24] Only when risks to contraband sales increased did the company make greater efforts to establish a legal presence by concomitantly pursuing official distribution networks through joint ventures in the mid-1990s.[6] Table 3 demonstrates how internal British American Tobacco company documents describing exports to China differed widely from total official government import numbers. The British American Tobacco numbers far exceeded the imports allowed by the Chinese

Table 3: Official Chinese Imports and Cited BAT Exports of Cigarettes to China, 1982–2004[23]

Year	Total Official Imports (Million of Sticks)	Exports Cited in BAT Documents	
		Millions	Context
1982	202	811	Total sales of BAT brands made in Hong Kong, or shipped by the brand owners through Hong Kong, into the southern provinces of China
1984	547.7	2,653	For BATHK (China)
1985	433	6,101	Total volume
1990	10,551	20,300	Total volume
1994	9,000	46,290	Total planned volume
1995	26,372	39,700	Forecast sales
1996	17,960	21,297.8	State Express 555 sales
		2,852.8	kent sales
		17,691.7	Hilton sales
		230.8	John Player, Gold Leaf sales
2000	25,353	39,700	Forecast sales
2003	1,878	107,245	
2004	2,134	113,919	

government from 1982 to 2004, with 2003–2004 exceeding the official imports by a factor of over 50. The supply and price of both legal and illegal products were carefully controlled to compete with other competitors like Philip Morris and RJ Reynolds.[23] British American Tobacco has not yet been held accountable for these and other similar actions. An investigation by the UK Department of Trade and Industry was abandoned without a decision in 1994.

From 1994 to 1998, a special anti-contraband effort was launched by STMA, the General Administration of Customs, the Ministry of Public Security, and the State Administration for Industry and Commerce. In recent years, the Chinese government has taken further steps to reduce smuggling by strengthening the customs department and smuggling penalties, in an effort to recoup the estimated

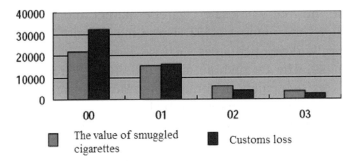

Fig. 8: Value of Smuggled Cigarettes (and Amount of Tax Evasion) Seized by China Customs from 2000 to 2003[11]

1.8 billion yuan in lost tax revenue annually.[23] The number of smuggled cigarettes seized has been declining, as seen from Chinese customs data in Fig. 8.[11]

Counterfeiting of cigarettes is rampant and profitable in China. In 1999, around 2 million cartons of counterfeit cigarettes, both domestic and international brands, were sold in China, double the amount in 1997. Raids of factories and workshops in 1998 collected 3.15 billion cigarettes.[23] In 2003, 5.3 billion cigarettes were collected — 2,575 tons and 1,531 machines seized; this was 0.3 percent of the estimated total national output of 1,789 billion cigarettes.[11] During this period, 3,539 lawbreakers were detained, with 956 sentenced and 263 re-educated through labor. In fact, 70 percent of the cities or counties in Guangdong province had counterfeiting operations in 2003. These operations are easy to conduct and highly profitable, with one machine producing 300 cases a day and the equivalent of $15,000. If one machine operates for over 10 days, the money principal used to buy the machine can almost be recovered. Furthermore, the highest penalty for counterfeiting cigarettes is only two years of imprisonment.

Markets also exist for the distribution of these counterfeit cigarettes. In urban and rural areas of China, wholesale and retail sites of counterfeit cigarettes are often seen. In 1993, there were nearly 300 such markets across the country. STMA has taken steps to eliminate the free wholesale cigarette market and with difficulty has reduced the number to 52. These markets are mainly in the economically developed areas such as Liaoning, Beijing, Zhejiang, and Jiangsu. The free wholesale markets of cigarettes occur as (1) markets spontaneously formed by relatively concentrated cigarette retailers, and (2) markets run by local governments or relevant administrative departments. To some extent, these markets are legal with standardized administration, but it remains a free wholesale market and does not solve the problem of illegal operations participating in the trade.

FUTURE TOBACCO CONTROL IN CHINA

China's entry into the WTO has not led to transnational tobacco companies' immediately overtaking the Chinese market. As China's general economy changes with trade liberalization, tobacco control efforts may benefit in that the tobacco industry's relative contribution to employment or government tax revenue is declining. The industrial manufacturing sector (e.g., textiles, electronics and automobile products) is developing rapidly. The value of Chinese cigarette production increased from 8 billion yuan (US$1 = 8.23 yuan) in 1981 to 130 billion yuan in 1997, and 169 billion yuan in 2002.[10] However, in terms of its relative share of the total value of national industrial production, the tobacco industry contributed only 1.57 percent in 1980, and that figure decreased to 1.14 percent by 1997. In 1997, cigarette tax and profit revenue was 90 billion yuan, about 11 percent of the central government's tax revenue. By 2002, the tax and profit revenue was 140 billion yuan,[17] but despite the increase in profits, the relative share of government revenue had decreased to 8 percent by 2000. With these reductions in the government's dependence on tobacco tax revenue, along with the reduction in demand for domestic cigarette leaf, the importance of the tobacco agricultural sector is declining.

Understanding these changing economic priorities and tobacco industry within China can help identify new solutions for tobacco control. The impact of additional tobacco taxes will have smaller negative effects for China's tobacco industry as the number of regional tobacco companies is reduced. Instead, the central government could remove its special tobacco leaf tax as demand for domestic cigarette leaf is reduced, and instead impose an additional cigarette product tax. Thus, the central government and the local governments can share the revenue income, resolving the concern for replacing lost government revenue. At the same time, this strategy will free tobacco farmers to plant any product they desire, and help resolve the domestic tobacco leaf surplus problem resulting from increased importation of higher quality foreign leaf.

The World Health Organization (WHO) Framework Convention on Tobacco Control (FCTC) will bring new opportunities for tobacco control in China. Governments that have ratified the FCTC will be responsible for implementing tobacco control provisions, such as advertising bans, rotating health warning labels, increasing tobacco taxes, and combating smuggling. China signed the FCTC in November 2003 and ratified it in 2005.[26] An intergovernmental working committee, reviewing the impact of China's ratification, has recommended that the China People's Congress ratify the FCTC treaty. The committee acknowledged that smoking has a negative impact on health and that ratification would help China's international image and social responsibility.

The FCTC provisions may help to restrict the transnational tobacco companies' activities and market growth in China, but the WTO impact of transforming China's tobacco industry into a global competitor remains to be seen. Japan Tobacco's development into the world's third largest tobacco company, with two thirds still owned by Japan's Ministry of Finance, may bring some insightful lessons.[27] Tobacco control in Japan after market liberalization has

---

[26] Hu TW, Mao Z, Ong M, *et al.*, "China at the Crossroads: The Economics of Tobacco and Health," *Tobacco Control* 15, Suppl 1 (2006): i37–i41.
[27] Sato H, "Policy and Politics of Smoking Control in Japan," *Social Science Medicine* 49, no. 5 (1999): 581–600.

been limited because of conflicting government interests,[28,29] and Japan Tobacco has also learned from Philip Morris about strategies to minimize public concerns regarding health risks.[8] STMA is poised to become a global industry leader through transnational collaborations rather than a casualty from WTO market entry, and it may respond to tobacco control efforts similarly to other transnational tobacco companies.

China stands at an economic and public health crossroads with respect to tobacco control. China's entry into the WTO could enrich the transnational tobacco companies or help propel China into becoming a leading transnational company. China's ratification of the FCTC may encourage the local and central governments to recognize the declining contributions of the tobacco sector and present new opportunities for novel tobacco control solutions. Sustained collaborative efforts with tobacco control colleagues in China can help identify and construct the direction in which China is heading.

---

[28] Sato H, Araki S and Yokoyama K, "Influence of Monopoly Privatization and Market Liberalization on Smoking Prevalence in Japan: Trends of Smoking Prevalence in Japan in 1975–1995," *Addiction* 95, no. 7 (2000): 1079–1088.

[29] Tobacco Free Japan, *Tobacco Free Japan: Recommendations for Tobacco Control Policy* (Tokyo, Japan: INKS, Inc, and Institute for Global Tobacco Control, Johns Hopkins Bloomberg School of Public Health, 2003).

Section IV
Cigarette Taxation

Chapter 12

Effects of Cigarette Tax on Cigarette Consumption and the Chinese Economy*

Teh-wei Hu and Zhengzhong Mao

INTRODUCTION

China has a very high prevalence of cigarette smoking. According to a 1996 Chinese national survey, 63 percent of adult males (age 15 years and) and 3.8 percent of adult females were current smokers.[1] These prevalence rates indicate that there are over 320 million cigarette smokers in China.[1] Given the size of its smoking population, it comes as no surprise that China consumes more cigarettes than any other country in the world.

---

*This chapter originally appeared as Hu TW and Mao Z, "Effects of Cigarette Tax on Cigarette Consumption and the Chinese Economy," *Tobacco Control* 11 (2002): 105–108. Copyright © 2002 by BMJ (British Medical Journal). All rights reserved. Reprinted with permission from *Tob. Control* and BMJ.
[1] Chinese Academy of Preventive Medicine, "*Smoking and Health in China: 1996 National Prevalence Survey of Smoking Patterns* (Beijing: China Science and Technology Press, 1997).

It is well known that cigarette smoking is a major health hazard. Many government officials in the Ministry of Health and public health professionals in China have recognised the importance of tobacco control; they have made a substantial effort to discourage cigarette consumption through a public health campaign. However, they have been unable to convince the Ministry of Finance, Ministry of Economics and Trade, or the Ministry of Agriculture to support tax increases as a means to control tobacco. Obviously, there is a policy conflict between public health concerns and the economic benefit of tobacco production. In China, tobacco production is a state run enterprise that provides substantial revenue for the government. Also, tobacco cultivation is a major income source for farmers in many poor regions. This conflict of interests among policymakers in public health and economics constitutes a major dilemma for the Chinese government.

In this chapter we address this policy dilemma by describing and then analyzing the economic consequences of a tax increase on cigarette consumption in the Chinese economy.

CIGARETTE TAX AND GOVERNMENT REVENUE

In China, the cigarette tax is considered a product tax that is levied on manufacturers or during importation. Cigarettes are valued (for tax purposes) at the producers level, not by the consumers. Value added tax is levied on retailers, since there is no sales tax collection system in China. This taxation practice, perhaps owing to the fact that cigarette production is a state run enterprise, is different from standard international practices, where tax rates are expressed as a percentage of the retail price. In China, the state enterprise is directly responsible for collection of the tax revenue when the product is shipped to market. The government levies two components of taxation on producers: the producers value added tax, which is about 17 percent of the producer price, and an additional approximate 50 percent of the wholesale price as consumption tax. Thus, from the producer's point of view, the tax paid to the government is 67 percent of the producer price. However, if the amount of tax paid by the producer is compared to the retail price of cigarettes, the effective tax rate is 38 percent.[2]

In 1997 China collected 90 billion yuan in cigarette taxes and profit earned by the Chinese National Tobacco Company, about 11 percent of central government revenue.[3] In short, cigarette tax revenue and profits are an important and reliable source of funds for the central government.

The importance of the role of cigarette taxes is further amplified by other factors: (1) local government levied tax on tobacco leaves, especially in those farming provinces (Yunan, Guizhou), is a major source of tax revenue; (2) both local and central government share cigarette tax from product tax; and (3) the China National Tobacco Company, which is a state enterprise, provides much value added profit as well as taxes to the central government.

Therefore, a recommendation to raise the cigarette tax rate would lead to a reduction in the demand for tobacco leaves and cigarette production, which is perceived by both the local and central governments as resulting in less government revenue. The subsequent section of this study will provide detailed analyses to show that the concern surrounding the issue of less tax revenue can be alleviated if additional tax is levied.

PRICE ELASTICITY, CONSUMPTION, AND ITS IMPACT ON GOVERNMENT REVENUE

To address the issue of the impact of tax on cigarette consumption and its subsequent impact on government revenue and tobacco leaf production, an analysis of the relation between price and consumption of cigarettes is required. This demand analysis is based on national aggregate time series data between 1980 and 1996.

Price elasticities are particularly important since they measure the effect of change in cigarette price on changes in cigarette

---

[2] Hu TW, "Cigarette Taxation in China: Lessons from International Experiences," *Tobacco Control* 6 (1997): 136–140.
[3] China Statistics Bureau, *China Statistical Yearbook* (Beijing: China Statistical Publishing House, 1986–1998).

consumption. Price elasticities are obtained statistically through the estimation of a demand function for cigarettes. A basic demand function usually includes the price of the cigarette, personal disposable income, and a time trend to reflect the change in consumer tastes and preferences. Several price elasticities have been estimated from Chinese provincial (Sichuan and Fujie) data, ranging from –0.40 to –0.91.[4–6] This chapter has used national aggregate per capita time series data from the Chinese statistical year book[3] to estimate the price and income elasticities of the demand for cigarettes.

Two equations are used to provide these estimates: one without the lagged dependent variable (last period of cigarette consumption) which can provide an overall price elasticity, and one which includes the lagged dependent variable, which can provide both short run and long run price elasticity. The estimated demand equations are as follows:

$$\text{Ln } Q_t = 3.80 - 0.525 P_t - 0.002 I_t + 0.102 T_t$$
$$(6.323) \quad (1.003) \quad (13.172)$$

$$R^2 = 0.962 \quad DW = 2.17 \tag{1}$$

$$\ln Q_t = 1.677 - 0.331 P_t + 0.007 I_t + 0.556 \ln Q_{t-1} + 0.047 T_t$$
$$(2.399) \quad (0.443) \quad (2.261) \quad (1.594)$$

$$R^2 = 0.976 \quad h = 1.25 \tag{2}$$

where

$\ln Q_t$ = logarithm of annual aggregate cigarette sales in packs per capita, year t (1980–1996)
P_t = cigarette price per pack (yuan) in 1980 price, year t,
I_t = income per capita (yuan) in 1980 price, year t,

---

[4] Mao Z and Jiang JL, "Determinants of the Demand for Cigarettes, a Cross-Sectional Study," *Chinese Health Industry Management* (1997): 227–229.
[5] Mao Z, Jiang JL and Gong ZP, "Demand for Cigarette and Pricing Policy: A Time-Series Analysis (in Chinese)," *Chinese Health Economics*, 16 (1997): 50–52.
[6] Mao Z, Hsieh CR, Hu TW, *et al.*, *The Demand for Cigarettes in China*, (Chengdu, Sichuan: West China Medical Sciences University, 2000).

T_t time trend from 1980 = 1,..., 1996 = 17,
R^2 = adjusted coefficient of determination with degrees of freedom,

DW = Durbin Watson statistics for testing autocorrelation, h = h statistics for testing autocorrelation in lagged dependent variable equation.

Values in parentheses are t-values.

There is no autocorrelation in the first equation. The second equation has autocorrelation but is corrected by the Cochran–Orcutt method, with h statistics showing that there is no autocorrelation. Since these two equations are expressed in semi-log, the price elasticities can be calculated by the product of the price coefficient and the sample mean price of 1.03 yuan, during the period 1980–1996. Thus, the overall price elasticity derived from Eq. (1) is −0.54, while the short run price elasticity of −0.35 and −0.66 for long run price elasticity is derived from Eq. (2). All these estimated price elasticities are significant at the 1 percent level. These estimated national price elasticities are within the range of previous provincial estimates. With this estimated price elasticity one can address the issue of the impact of cigarette tax on cigarette consumption and government tax revenue.

To illustrate the possible impact of an increase in cigarette sales and additional resultant tax revenue, 1997 data on price and sales figures were used. The average nominal retail price per pack was 4.00 yuan.[3] For simplicity, we use yuan as a currency benchmark. The sales of cigarettes were 33.67 million cases or 84.175 billion packs. The effective tax rate (expressed in retail price) is 38 percent. For simplicity, we assume it is at 40 percent, or 1.60 yuan. If the Chinese government increases tax from 1.60 yuan to 2.00 yuan per pack, or a 25 percent tax increase, the new retail price would be 4.4 yuan/pack, a 10 percent increase in retail price. Using the above estimated price elasticity, −0.54, cigarette consumption can be reduced by −5.4 percent, the equivalent of 4.545 billion packs. The new cigarette consumption becomes 79.63 billion packs. Comparing the new tax revenue of 159.26 billion yuan (79.63 × 2 yuan), and the previous tax revenue of 134.68 billion yuan (84.175 × 1.60 yuan), the additional tax gain would be 24.58 billion yuan. Similarly, if the price elasticity is set at −0.64, cigarette consumption will be reduced by 5.387 billion packs, but the revenue will still increase by 22.89 billion yuan. In summary, when the percentage decrease in quantity consumed is offset by the increase in prices (through the increase in tax), the increase in tax will lead to a reduction in cigarette consumption and an increase in tax revenue. In the long run, given the price elasticity is higher, −0.66, than in the short run, −0.35, it is expected that cigarette consumption will further decrease. This is a concern for the Chinese government. However, international experience shows that it will take time for smokers to adjust to the tax increase.

STATUS OF CHINESE TOBACCO ECONOMY AND HEALTH COSTS

To study the negative impact of tobacco tax on a tobacco economy, it is important to describe the status of the tobacco economy in both the agricultural and industrial sectors.

In 1997, China used 2.161 million hectares for tobacco growing[3] and produced 39.08 million metric tons of tobacco leaves, with an average productivity of 1.81 metric tons per hectare. It has been estimated that about 5.6 million agricultural households are involved in tobacco production,[7] although most of those households produce other agricultural crops as well. Their income does not rely entirely on tobacco. The tobacco leaf price was set by the government at an average of 3.962 yuan per metric ton, or 242 yuan per 50 kg, in 1997. The total value of tobacco leaf production was 22.9 billion yuan in 1997.

The tobacco manufacturing industry is a monopoly in China and is administered within the Ministry of Economics and Trade. China's tobacco industry produced 33.67 million cases (2,500 packs per case) at a value of 129.6 billion yuan. Cigarettes are a much value added

---

[7] Nie HP, "How to Deal with WTO — Issues of China Tobacco Leaf (in Chinese)," *China Tobacco* 183, no. 7 (2000): 21–22.

product. The average profit of the cigarette manufacturing industry is 10.3 percent[8] of the total revenue. It has been estimated that it takes 0.041 metric tons of tobacco leaves to produce one case of cigarettes.[9] The industry employs about 500,000 people in the manufacturing sector and an additional 3.5 million are engaged in retail cigarette sales.[10] However, only a few retailers are engaged solely in cigarette sales, as cigarettes represent only one commodity in the retail merchandise sector.

One negative aspect of cigarette smoking is its impact on healthcare costs. Cigarette smoking is harmful to one's health, causing premature death through smoking related illnesses such as lung cancer and cardiovascular disease. Smoking is also responsible for substantial healthcare costs and lost productivity as a result of illness and premature death.

A recent study by Jiang and Jin,[11] using the 1998 mortality study of one million deaths in China,[12] estimated that 514,100 premature deaths occurred in 1998 from smoking related illness. Of these premature deaths, 210,000 were caused by cancer, 190,300 deaths involved the respiratory system, and 113,700 involved the circulatory system. The number of person–years lost as a result of cigarette smoking was estimated at 1.146 million, using age 60, the year of retirement in China, as a reference of productive age.

The study used 1998 national health services survey data to estimate the direct medical costs attributable to smoking. It was

---

[8] Hong Kong City University, *China Markets Yearbook, Cigarettes*, (Hong Kong: Hong Kong City University, 1999), 224.
[9] Wang S and Li B, "1999–2000: Analysis and Estimate of the Situation of China's Tobacco Sector (in Chinese and English)," *Sino-World Tobacco* 47 (2000): 6–11.
[10] Zhu J, "How to Coordinate the Conflict Between Tobacco Control and Tobacco Production in China," *Periscope* 46 (1996): 12–13.
[11] Jiang Y and Jin S, "Social Economic Burden Attributed to Smoking in China," 1998, Paper presented at the National Conference on Policy Development of Tobacco Control in China in the 21st Century, Beijing, May 29–31, 2000.
[12] Liu BQ, Peto R, Chen ZM, *et al.*, "Emerging Tobacco Hazards in China: I. Retrospective Proportional Mortality Study of One Million Deaths," BMJ 317 (1998): 1411–1422.

estimated that 347 million outpatient visits and 1.52 million inpatient admissions were attributable to smoking related illnesses. These services were valued at 17.1 billion yuan for outpatient visits and 5.8 billion yuan for inpatient services. Therefore, total direct medical costs attributable to smoking was 22.9 billion yuan. As the overall total cost of medical services in China during 1998 was 377.6 billion yuan,[13] smoking accounted for 6 percent of China's healthcare expenditure.

EFFECT OF CIGARETTE TAX ON THE ECONOMY

An increase in cigarette taxes will reduce cigarette consumption. Therefore, it will have a negative effect on the cigarette industry and tobacco farmers. It is important to estimate these negative impacts so that government policymakers can be better informed when it comes to making decisions concerning cigarette tax.

When an additional tax is levied on cigarettes, the immediate impact is a reduction in sales, which will lead to a reduction in revenue as well as employment in the cigarette industry. Overall, the cigarette manufacturing industry employs about 500,000 people. The value of cigarette production was 129.60 billion yuan.[3]

If we use the example of a 25 percent tax increase on a 40 percent tax base, as shown previously, the reduction in sales would be 4.545 billion packs (estimated at a price elasticity of −0.54). With a net price of 2.4 yuan/pack (excluding tax, 4.4 yuan −2 yuan), the industry would lose revenue amounting to 10.91 billion yuan. The average profit of the cigarette manufacturing industry is 10.3 percent[8] of the total revenue. Thus, the loss of profit would be 1.12 billion yuan.

If we consider employment to be a linear function of production volume, with a 5.4 percent loss of sales in the cigarette industry, employment rates would drop by the same percentage, which is about 27,000 employees. This probably represents the maximum number of job losses, calculated at the average linear production

---

[13] Ministry of Health, *Research on National Health Services — an Analysis Report of the National Health Service Survey in 1993*, (Beijing: Ministry of Health, 1994), 8.

relationship. In most cases, the attrition rate would be lower because of early retirement and job transfers. If one were to estimate the value of the loss of earnings from 27,000 workers, assuming an annual income of 7,200 yuan,[3] the total loss of income would be 194.4 million yuan.

The China Tobacco National Company is already in the process of eliminating inefficient factories and consolidating production. The increase in tax and reduction in cigarette consumption may provide further impetus to improve the efficiency of cigarette production. The effect of the reduction in cigarette consumption could lead the cigarette manufacturing industry to diversify into other products. Furthermore, the amount of money smokers save from cigarette consumption could also be spent on other food or household goods. Therefore, the net effect on employment could be smaller than estimated.

The Chinese tobacco farmers have been overproducing tobacco in recent years, according to the government purchase programme.[9] In 1997, farmers produced 39.08 metric tons on 2.161 million hectares of land, with an average productivity of 1.81 metric tons per hectare. It takes 0.041 metric tons of tobacco leaves to produce one case of cigarettes (2,500 packs).[9] Thus, the reduction of 4.545 billion packs (or 1.82 million cases) as a result of the 25 percent tax increase would lead to a reduction in the demand for tobacco leaf by 0.0746 million metric tons. The average government purchase price for tobacco leaf was 484 yuan per 100 kg; thus tobacco farmers would lose 361.1 million yuan. The average productivity per hectare was 1.808 metric tons; therefore, farmers could reduce the area of land they use to grow tobacco by 41,261 hectares. This does not necessarily mean that this land would be left unfarmed. It could be used to grow other cash crops, such as tea or sunflowers. Although the return from these crops may not be as high as that from tobacco, by growing alternative crops the actual amount of revenue lost to tobacco farmers would be much less than the estimated 361.1 million yuan.

The reduction in sales of tobacco leaves at the farm level implies a loss of local government tax revenue. As mentioned earlier, local governments encourage farmers to sell tobacco leaves in order to collect their local revenue. The local tax rate was 30 percent before 1999 (20 percent since 1999). Since tobacco farmers would lose 361.1 million yuan, the local government could lose 108.3 million yuan.

Considering the loss of revenue for the cigarette industry and income for tobacco farmers, the government may grant subsidies to the cigarette industry and tobacco farmers in order for them to transfer to other manufacturing industries as well as provide production opportunities. Needless to say, there are costs associated with this transition, as well as uncertainty over income and employment. Further studies or pilot experiments are required to examine these negative economic impacts on the tobacco industry and tobacco farmers.

HEALTH BENEFITS OF ADDITIONAL CIGARETTE TAX

It has been estimated that the price elasticity of the demand for cigarettes can be divided into two parts: the elasticity of participation (or quitting), and the conditional elasticity of quantity demanded among smokers. The ratios vary from one third quit smoking to two thirds reduce consumption among smokers, or half the elasticity will reduce cigarette consumption.[14]

With a 25 percent tax rate increase (40 cents) at the 4 yuan retail price (with a 40 percent tax base), a new retail price would increase by 10 percent to 4.40 yuan. Using the price elasticity of −0.54 as an example, with 320 million smokers in China and a 10 percent increase in price due to tax, 1.8 percent (5.76 million) to 2.7 percent (8.64 million) smokers in China would quit smoking. Using estimated epidemiological analysis reported by the World Bank,[15] 1.44–2.16 million lives could be saved by a price increase of 10 percent, or a tax increase of 25 percent.

---

[14] Warner KE, Chaloupka FJ, Cook PJ, *et al.*, "Criteria for Determining an Optimal Cigarette Tax: the Economist's Perspective," *Tobacco Control* 4 (1995): 380–386.

[15] World Bank, *Curbing the epidemic: Government and the Economics of Tobacco Control* (Washington DC: World Bank, 1999), 23.

Recent work by Jiang and Jin[11] estimated that the total direct medical cost attributable to smokers was 22.9 billion yuan or 72 yuan per smoker (22.9 billion/320 million smokers). With 5.76 million to 8.64 million smokers quitting, it implies that medical cost savings could be 415 million yuan to 622 million yuan.

A cigarette tax increase in China could, therefore, reduce cigarette consumption, generate more government tax revenue, save lives, reduce medical care costs, and increase productivity.

CONCLUSIONS AND RECOMMENDATIONS

Many countries around the world have taken the initiative to control cigarette consumption because of its impact on public health and healthcare costs. China is in a unique position because its relatively high smoking prevalence provides a large tax base; therefore, the imposition of a cigarette tax increase will have a significant effect in generating additional central government revenue and reducing cigarette consumption.

As an illustration of the impact of an increase in tobacco tax, a 25 percent tax increase would reduce cigarette consumption by 4.54 billion packs, resulting in additional tax revenue of 24.58 billion yuan. Statistical analysis indicates that between 5.76 million and 8.64 million smokers would quit smoking, resulting in 1.44 million to 2.16 million lives saved. The savings of medical care costs would be 415 million to 672 million yuan, not to mention the gains that would be made in productivity due to avoidance of premature death. These monetary benefits would offset the industry revenue loss of 10.91 billion yuan (including a profit margin of 1.12 billion yuan), the 27,000 lost jobs (with a loss of 194.4 million yuan in earnings) in the cigarette industry, the loss of tobacco income by 361.1 million yuan (caused by a surplus of 0.0746 million metric tons of tobacco leaves), and the loss of local government revenue of 108.3 million yuan. In essence, the overall monetary benefit far exceeds the negative impact on the cigarette industry and tobacco farmers. In financial terms alone, not counting the number of lives saved and medical care cost savings, the gain of the central government tax revenue

(24.58 billion yuan) twice exceeds the loss of tobacco farmers' earnings, tobacco industry workers' earnings, and loss of industry and local government revenue (11.74 billion yuan.)

China is a major country in terms of tobacco consumption and production. Raising cigarette taxes for the government is both a public health issue and an economic issue. This chapter has addressed both of these aspects. There is an issue concerning the impact of increased cigarette tax among different sectors of the economy and in the tobacco growing regions of the country. A short term solution could be cross subsidy from additional tobacco taxation to tobacco farmers and the cigarette manufacturing industry, which may result in transition to other products in the long term.

This chapter is limited only to domestic cigarette production and consumption. Issues of cigarette smuggling in China and the pending impact of China's entry into the World Trade Organization (WTO) are not addressed. China's entry into the WTO has already led the government to consider further the implications of increased cigarette taxes on domestic and foreign cigarette production in the country. The findings of this chapter have clearly indicated that increasing additional tax on cigarettes would be beneficial to the Chinese government from both the financial and public health perspective.

ACKNOWLEDGMENTS

The World Bank and the Research for International Tobacco Control at the International Development Research Centre, Ottawa, Canada provided support of this study. The authors are grateful to three anonymous reviewers of the journal "tobacco Control" who provided most detailed suggestions. An earlier version of this paper was presented at the 11th World Conference on Tobacco or Health in Chicago, 20 September 2000. The authors alone are responsible for the content of this chapter.

Chapter 13

Cigarette Taxation in China: Lessons From International Experiences*

Teh-wei Hu

INTRODUCTION

Cigarette smoking is harmful to health, causing premature death through smoking-related illnesses such as lung cancer and cardiovascular diseases. Smoking is also responsible for substantial healthcare costs and lost productivity due to illness and premature death.

China, currently, has a relatively high prevalence rate of cigarette smoking. More than 300 million individuals in China are smokers, and approximately 30 percent of the world's smokers live in China.[1] Previous research has estimated that each ton of

---

*This revised chapter originally appeared as Hu TW, "Cigarette Taxation in China: Lessons From International Experiences," *Tobacco Control* 6 (1997): 136–140. Copyright © 1997 by BMJ (British Medical Journal). All rights reserved. Reprinted with permission from *Tobacco Control* and BMJ (British Medical Journal).

[1] Chapman S, "Chinese Smokers Pass the 300 Million Mark," *Tobacco International* 7 (1993): 3–5.

tobacco consumed results in approximately one death.[2] It has been predicted that 50 million Chinese children alive today will die prematurely as a result of tobacco use.[3]

According to the 1992 national household expenditure survey, urban per capita expenditures in China on cigarettes 54.28 Chinese yuan (US$9.05) were higher than healthcare and medical expenditures 41.51 yuan (US$6.92) and alcohol and soft-drink expenditures 45.92 yuan (US$7.95).[4] This survey also showed that on average, per capita annual cigarette consumption was 33.03 packs, ranging from 24.32 packs for the low-income group to 33.58 for the middle-income group and 45.09 for the high-income group.[4]

Given the size of the smoking population in China, it is not surprising that China is the largest cigarette-producing country.[4] It produced 32.85 million cases or 82.125 billion packs (one case consists of 2,500 packs) of cigarettes and used 1.85 million hectares for tobacco production during 1992, which represents a 93 percent increase in production and a 25 percent increase in tobacco growing area since 1981. Per capita consumption of cigarettes reached a peak in 1990 of 1,437.8 cigarettes, and then declined slightly to 1,417.3 in 1991 and 1,400.4 in 1992. From 1981 to 1992, per capita consumption increased by 62.8 percent.

In recent years, China has made major progress in tobacco control by banning all cigarette advertising, increasing import duties on cigarettes, and banning cigarette smoking in some public places. Still, China is a major world consumer of cigarettes. A recent study indicated that 895,600 individuals died of smoking-related illnesses in 1989.[5] Medical care expenditures due to smoking were estimated at 6.9 billion yuan (US$1.15 billion) in 1989, while the value of lost

---

[2] Barnum H, "The Economic Burden of the Global Trade in Tobacco," *Tobacco Control* 3 (1994): 358–361.

[3] Novotny T and Peto R, "Estimates of Future Adverse Health Effects of Smoking in China," *Public Health Reports* 103 (1988): 552–553.

[4] State Statistic Bureau, *1993 Statistical Yearbook in China* (China Statistical Publishing, 1993), 220, Table 6.6.

[5] Jin SG, Lu BY, Yan DY, Fu ZY, Jiang Y and Li W, "An Evaluation of Smoking Induced Health Costs in China (1988–1989)," *Biomedical and Environment Sciences* 8 (1995): 342–349.

productivity or premature death was about 20.13 billion yuan (US$3.35 billion) in the same year. The value of these resources could be used for many other productive services in society.

Government agencies and health policymakers around the world have used a variety of policy alternatives to control tobacco smoking.[6] These policies include a ban on cigarette advertising, the prohibition of cigarette advertising, the prohibition of cigarette smoking in public places, anti-smoking media campaigns, the prohibition of cigarettes sale to minors or in vending machines, health education in schools, and taxation on cigarette products. The objectives of some of those tobacco control instruments in reducing tobacco consumption are obvious, while others are less certain. It is universally recognized that taxation on the sale of cigarettes has been very effective in accomplishing its aims. Despite variations in cigarette taxes, it is generally agreed that a tobacco tax is a reliable source of government revenue, a convenient and effective method of collecting revenue, and, most importantly, a deterrent to cigarette consumption.

The government of China relies on revenue from the tobacco tax as a major financial resource. The question is whether sufficient opportunity exists for raising existing tax on cigarettes in China to control cigarette smoking, while still being financially beneficial to the government. The purpose of this chapter is to draw upon the experiences of foreign countries in implementing tobacco taxation, to provide lessons the Chinese government can use when considering the feasibility of raising the tax on cigarettes.

RATIONALES FOR CIGARETTE TAXATION AND INTERNATIONAL EXPERIENCES

A fundamental principle of economics indicates that increased cigarette prices will reduce cigarette consumption. The retail price of cigarettes consists of the prices of the raw materials, labor costs, and taxes. In general, cigarettes are taxed at various levels of government, encompassing federal, state, and local areas. The most common

---

[6] Warner K, "Tobacco Taxation as a Health Policy in the Third World," *American Journal of Public Health* 80 (1990): 529–530.

form of cigarette tax is based on units of quantity of sales (an excise tax) whereas some governments apply a cigarette tax based on a fixed percentage of the price (an *ad valorem* tax).

In China, cigarette taxes are collected by the central government at the level of the manufacturer, according to the number of cigarettes produced. Once these cigarettes leave the factory, no additional tax is added. Therefore, it is called a product tax. Because it is imposed according to quantity produced, it can also be considered an excise tax. All cigarette factories are owned and operated by the government. Thus, tax collection administration is very efficient.

Excise taxes are easier to collect and do not change over time, while an *ad valorem* tax changes as the price of cigarette changes, and may add more administrative costs in collecting tax revenues. Regardless of the form of cigarette taxes, an excise tax is a component of the retail price, thus reducing cigarette consumption. The reduction of the cigarette consumption could result from either a reduction in the number of cigarettes consumed by smokers, or a reduction in the number of smokers.

RATIONALES FOR CIGARETTE TAXATION

Two rationales are used to justify a tax on cigarettes.[7] The first rationale is simply to consider the cigarette tax as an efficient instrument with low administrative costs for collecting revenue for government spending. In the case of the United States, an increase in the federal cigarette tax was used to finance the Civil War in 1864, and the Korean War in 1951. Thus, before 1960, taxes on cigarettes were enacted and raised to generate revenue rather than to discourage consumption. Similarly, in Finland, a major increase in cigarette price (a 60 percent increase in a seven-month period during 1975/1976) was intended mainly to increase state revenue.[8]

---

[7] Zimring F and Nelson W, "Cigarette Taxes as Cigarette Policy," *Tobacco Control* 4, Suppl 1 (1995): 525–533.

[8] Pekurinen M and Valtonen H, "Price, Policy, and Consumption on Tobacco: The Finnish Experience," *Social Science and Medicine* 25 (1987): 875–881.

The second rationale for imposing a cigarette tax is to consider taxes as "user fees." It is argued that the tax covers the external costs of smoking and will discourage smokers from using cigarettes, thus leading to a reduction in tobacco-related healthcare costs by reducing the morbidity and mortality associated with cigarette smoking. This second rationale, with its anti-smoking objective for raising cigarette taxes, came into use after the release of the US Surgeon General's 1964 report on smoking and health. Since 1980, countries such as Finland, Denmark, Egypt, Canada, Nepal, Iceland, Peru, Australia, and New Zealand have raised cigarette taxes as a means to reduce cigarette consumption.

Given the rationale of raising the cigarette tax to control tobacco use, many countries and states have used part of the revenue from such taxes to support anti-smoking activities, such as health education, medical research on tobacco-related diseases, and anti-smoking media campaigns — for example, in Australia and New Zealand. In Victoria, Australia, a 5 percent tax was levied on the sale of tobacco products in 1987 to finance health promotion.[9] Other countries, such as Egypt and Nepal (personal communication with Ministry of Health, Yur Raj Sharma, 1995), have used the additional tax revenues for health-related activities, such as paying for low-income maternal and child healthcare or subsidizing medical expenditures for low-income families.[10]

In November 1988, voters in California (USA) approved the California Tobacco Tax and Health Promotion Act (Proposition 99). This ballot initiative increased the state excise tax on cigarettes from 10 cents per pack to 35 cents per pack, beginning in January 1989. It explicitly specified how the new tax revenue was to be used, including health education programs for the prevention and reduction of cigarette use, indigent health care, research, parks, recreation,

---

[9] Galbally R, "Using the Money Generated by Increased Tobacco Taxation," in *Tobacco and Health. Proceedings of the Ninth World Conference on Tobacco and Health,* ed. Slama K (New York: Plenum Press, 1995), 139–142.

[10] Reich M, *School Children's Health Insurance in Egypt. Harvard School of Public Health Teaching Case* (Cambridge, Massachusetts: Harvard University, 1994).

environmental programmes, and other activities.[11] Following a model program funded by tobacco tax revenues in the state of Minnesota,[12] Proposition 99 was the first state legislation in the United States that sought to deter cigarette consumption both by increasing the state excise tax and waging an anti-smoking campaign.

Studies show that six months after the tax increase in California, cigarette sales had declined by about one pack per adult, or 10.9 percent. One year after the tax increase, the decline per capita had remained at a rate of three-quarters of a pack per adult per month, or a 9.5 percent reduction throughout the next three years.[13]

The cigarette tax increase led to a reduction in cigarette sales. Did the state's total revenues from cigarette sales decline? The answer is no. Based on the results of an estimated price elasticity of demand of −0.40, it can be shown that a 10 percent increase in price reduces the quantity demanded by 4 percent.[14] Thus, the percentage increase in price is higher than the percentage decreased in quantity by six percentage points. In other words, the value of loss in sales is more than offset by the value of gains due to the increased price. Therefore, tax revenues have increased. The actual California state cigarette tax revenue increased 200 percent in 1989, despite a 14 percent reduction in total cigarette sales. Cigarette sales continued to decline each year, while the revenue continued to be much higher than the pre-tax (1988) period. The state cigarette tax revenue in 1993 was still 170 percent higher than in 1988.

This is a very important finding for policymakers in tobacco control and policymakers in tax revenue departments. As long as the price elasticity of the demand for cigarettes is less than −1, the

---

[11] Bal DG, Kizer KW, Felten PF, Mozar HN and Niemeyer D, "Reducing Tobacco Consumption in California. Development of a Statewide Anti-Tobacco Use Campaign", *JAMA* 264 (1990): 1570–1574.

[12] Harty KC, "Animals and Butts: Minnesota's Media Campaign Against Tobacco," *Tobacco Control* 2 (1993): 271–274.

[13] Hu TW, Keeler T, Sung H and Barnett P, "The Impact of California Anti-Smoking Legislation on Cigarette Sales, Consumption, and Prices," *Tobacco Control* 4, Suppl 1 (1995): 534–538.

[14] Sung H, Hu TW and Keller T, "Cigarette Taxation and Demand: an Empirical Model," *Contemporary Economic Policy* 7 (1994): 91–100.

increase in taxes will result in a net gain in total tax revenues. The less elastic the demand, the less effective the tax will be in reducing cigarette consumption, but the more effective the tax will be in generating additional tax revenues. To plan for the desired level of reduction in cigarette consumption and the desired amount of increase in tax revenues, it is important to know the magnitude of the price elasticity of the demand for cigarettes.

California's anti-smoking legislation, Proposition 99, is a major success for the voters of California. Besides Minnesota and California, similar tax-funded initiatives in tobacco control have been implemented in the states of Masschussetts,[15] Michigan, and Arizona.

CIGARETTE TAXES AND RETAIL PRICES AROUND THE WORLD

A cigarette tax is a major component of the retail price of cigarettes. It would be useful to know what proportion of the retail price is represented by cigarette taxes around the world. The Chinese government could use this information as a point of reference for their policy on cigarette taxes.

Most cigarette taxes are excise taxes, which means that the proportion of the retail price allocated to the tax may decline as a retail price increases. In other words, the real value of the excise tax will decline as inflation occurs over time. Some states in the United States and other foreign countries impose other sales tax fees on the cigarette product in addition to the excise tax. Therefore, it is more meaningful to compare the total taxes as a percentage of retail price. To make all prices comparable, it is useful to convert prices to US dollars per pack of cigarettes.

Based on data from December 1993 for 24 selected countries, the average retail price of cigarettes ranged from US$0.63 per pack in Spain to US$4.55 in Norway.[16] The retail price of cigarettes in

---

[15] Koh HK, "An Analysis of the Successful 1992 Massachusetts Tobacco Tax Initiative," *Tobacco Control* 5 (1996): 220–225.
[16] Lynch B and Bonnie R, eds. *Growing up Tobacco Free* (Washington, DC: Institute of Medicine, National Academy Press, 1994), 184.

many Scandinavian countries (Norway, Denmark, Sweden, Finland), Western European countries (United Kingdom and Eire), and Canada exceeded US$3.00 per pack. The United States price averaged US$1.80 per pack. Portugal, Argentina, Taiwan, Spain, and South Korea averaged less than US$1.50 per pack.

The amount of tax imposed on cigarettes in these 24 countries ranged from US$0.42 per pack in Spain to US$3.48 in Denmark, with an average of US$1.66 per pack. As a percentage of retail price, taxes in Denmark and the United Kingdom were the highest — 85 percent and 77 percent, respectively. The percentage in 12 of the 24 countries exceeded 70 percent.[16] Those countries with cigarette prices less than $1.50 per pack had high tax rates as well: 81 percent for Portugal, 70 percent for Argentina, 70 percent for Spain, and 60 percent for South Korea (with the exception of Taiwan, 47 percent).

According to official data reported by the General Taxation Bureau, Ministry of Finance, the cigarette product tax rates for China ranged from 35 percent to 60 percent in 1988. However, these tax rates are calculated from the producer's point of view. According to the 1993 China statistical yearbook, sales revenues were 68.89 billion yuan (US$11.48 billion) in 1990 and 76.75 billion yuan (US$12.79 billion) in 1991.[4] The government revenue from the cigarette tax was 27 billion yuan (US$4.5 billion) in 1990 and 29 billion yuan (US$4.8 billion) in 1991. The reported retail price per pack was 1.33 yuan (US$0.22 per pack) in 1992. Thus, the effective retail tax rate was 39.2 percent in 1990 and 37.78 percent in 1991. In other words, out of every 10 yuan (US$1.66) spent by consumers on cigarettes, consumers paid between 3.8 yuan (US$0.63) and 3.9 yuan (US$0.65) in taxes. Thus, in terms of tax rates at the retail level, in China, rates are not as high as in many other countries.

INTERNATIONAL EXPERIENCES WITH ENACTMENT OF A TOBACCO TAX

During the past decade, several countries have made major efforts to use tobacco tax legislation as an effective policy instrument to control tobacco use. The countries include Thailand, Poland, Brazil, South Africa, and Taiwan (China).

The US Section 301 Trade Act forced several Asian countries, including Thailand, to open their markets to US cigarette products. Fearing the harmful effects of this US legislation on the population's health, medical and health professionals in the Thai Heart and Lung Association and the Thai Cancer Association organized a united front to carry out an anti-smoking campaign in Thailand and to show the negative impact of smoking on health. They also invited world-renowned tobacco control experts to visit Thailand to provide evidence-based research findings about the harmful health effects of tobacco vis-a-vis lung cancer and heart disease. In addition, they convinced the national legislators as well as Buddhist leaders to support the tobacco control agenda. While the tobacco industry in Thailand was a national monopoly and actively took actions against this anti-smoking campaign, the Thai Parliament was able to enact legislation that increased the tobacco tax in 1992. Under this tax legislation, a portion of the additional tobacco tax revenue was allocated for tobacco control activities (including research) and for health care insurance coverage. The Thai smoking prevalence rate decreased from 26.3 percent in 1992 to 20.5 percent in 1999. Simultaneously, the Thai government increased its tobacco tax revenue to about US$1 billion during the seven-year period.

Poland had one of the highest male smoking prevalence rates of any country — between 65 percent and 75 percent in the early 1990s. By 1998, however, the prevalence rate had been reduced to 39 percent. Beginning in the early 1990s, the Polish Medical Association provided a series of reports on the negative health impact of smoking and its negative impact on economic burden. While the Polish government did not support those research findings, researchers published these findings in academic journals and media outlets. They established a health promotion and tobacco control association, which carried out numerous tobacco control campaigns. Against the tobacco industry's opposition, in 1991 the Polish Parliament initiated its first tobacco control law. After five years of persistent efforts, in 1995 the Polish Parliament enacted tobacco control tax laws.

Like China, Brazil is not only a tobacco consuming country, but also a major tobacco farming country. Tobacco farming has been an important component of Brazil's national economy. Therefore, tobacco control efforts faced very strong opposition from both the tobacco industry as well as the tobacco farm sector. During the mid-1980s, the Brazilian Ministry of Health established a tobacco control office and invited famous entertainers, movie stars, and well-known statesmen as spokespersons. The tobacco control office invited economists to study the impact of increasing the tobacco tax on the tobacco industry, tobacco farming, government revenue, and tobacco consumption. The findings of these studies showed that increasing the tax on tobacco has a rather limited impact on the tobacco industry, and researchers suggested that the Brazilian government provide financial resources and technologies to assist tobacco farmers to transfer to other plant crops. With these research findings and collaboration between the government and the private sector, the government passed tobacco control laws in 1995 and 1999. To reduce possible cigarette smuggling activities that might result from the tobacco tax increase, the Brazilian government increased its enforcement officers against illegal cigarette trafficking. Since 1999, Brazil has reduced its smoking prevalence rate and at the same time increased revenue from the tobacco tax.

Before 1993, South Africa had no tobacco control policy. However, by 1999, South Africa had become one of the most progressive countries in the world in tobacco control. It not only implemented policies prohibiting smoking in public places and all media promotion of smoking, but it also increased the tobacco tax. These achievements started after Cape Town Medical School professors published papers on the harm of smoking. The Minister of Health invited private organizations to join the tobacco control activities. It took five years, but by 1998 the new government and parliament had enacted tobacco control legislation. With rigorous implementation, cigarette consumption decreased, and government revenue increased. Between 1994 and 1995, the cigarette tax increased 25 percent. While consumption of cigarettes decreased, the revenue from cigarette consumption increased 14 percent between 1994 and 1995. A three-year follow-up analysis indicated that despite the industry's concerns, smuggling had not become a threat nor had the livelihood of tobacco farmers been seriously compromised.

Taiwan's situation was similar to that of Thailand because in 1987, the US section 301 Trade Act forced Taiwan to open their market to US cigarette products. Within one year, the foreign cigarette market share increased from 2 percent to 22 percent. A private nongovernmental organization initiated a tobacco control campaign by inviting celebrities and important statesmen to endorse various tobacco control messages through the media. Academic researchers testified at legislative committees about the harmfulness of smoking and the international experiences of earmarking tobacco tax revenues for health care financing and health promotion funding. Although tobacco products were produced in Taiwan under a government monopoly (Taiwan Tobacco Wine Monopoly Bureau, TTWMB), strong competition from foreign cigarette brands resulted in a 44 percent the foreign cigarette market share increase by 1999. Thus, TTWMB no longer was strongly opposed to tobacco control. By 2002, with Taiwan's entrance into WTO, legislators passed the Health and Welfare Tax Privatization TTWMB Law. This was an earmarked tax law which specified that additional tobacco tax revenue will be used for the following four categories:

(1) 70 percent for national health insurance,
(2) 10 percent for anti-smoking promotion,
(3) 10 percent for health promotion and disease control, and
(4) 10 percent for welfare subsidies.

As a result of the 2002 tobacco tax law in Taiwan, tax revenue was increased to NT$7 billion the following year and cigarette consumption was reduced by 1.86 billion packs (a 22 percent increase in price and a 6.6 percent reduction in consumption). A second increase in the tobacco tax was enacted in 2005 to further reinforce the earmarked tobacco control programs.

The above international experiences with tobacco control provide us with the following lessons:

(1) Success in tobacco control requires collaboration among private health promotion organizations, well-known public figures, and government agencies.
(2) Successful tobacco control legislation requires scholarly research on the health and economic burdens of smoking, media communication/publicity, together with the collaboration of key government offices. Success is not likely without all of these elements.
(3) Successful tobacco control requires not only passage of legislation, but also strict enforcement to make sure the public complies with the legislation.
(4) Among the many tobacco control policy instruments, increasing the tax on tobacco is the most effective option. If a portion of the additional tax revenue is used for tobacco control programs, tobacco control becomes even more effective.

Government Revenue and Price Elasticities

The optimum amount of tax levied on cigarettes could be based on the economic burden of smoking to society, depending upon whether the purpose of the taxation is to control tobacco use, or, based on price elasticity, to maximize revenue. Cost estimates of the economic burden of cigarette smoking in the United States range from US$0.50 per pack to US$5.00 per pack depending on the assumptions of the value of life and the extent of the negative impact of cigarette use — for example, smoking-related low birth weight — included in the calculation.[17,18] No consensus exists in the

---

[17] Manning W, Keeler E, Newhouse J, Sloss E and Wasserman J, "The Taxes of Sin: Do Smokers and Drinkers Pay Their Way?," *JAMA* 261 (1989): 1604–1609.

[18] Hay JW, "The Harm They Do to Others: A Primer on the External Costs of Drug Abuse," in *Searching For Alternatives: Drug-Control Policy in the United States* eds. Krauss MB and Lazear EP (Stanford: Hoover Institution, Sept 1995).

American research community as to which cost figure should be used as a basis for cigarette taxes.[19]

On the other hand, if the purpose of a cigarette tax is to control tobacco smoking and at the same time maximize revenue, then the magnitude of price elasticity of demand for cigarettes will be an important reference point. For instance, in President Clinton's Health Security Act of 1993, the White House proposed an increase of 75 cents per pack in the federal excise tax as one source of revenue to finance the health insurance program. Based on 1992 taxes and cigarette smoking data, it was estimated that a 75-cent per pack increase in the federal cigarette excise tax would have prevented 900,000 premature deaths.[20]

According to a 1990 World Bank report, revenue from tobacco products, alcoholic beverages, and gasoline accounted for approximately 27 percent of China's total product tax revenues in 1986. Cigarette tax revenue alone reached the peak percentage of 14.84 percent of total government revenue in 1983, and then declined to 6.70 percent in 1986. In recent years, cigarette taxes have contributed about 9.5 percent of total government revenues. For instance, in 1992, the total government tax revenue was 329.7 billion yuan (US$54.9 billion); the cigarette tax revenue that same year was 31.0 billion yuan (US$5.2 billion). Thus, cigarette taxes raised 9.4 percent of total government revenues. Clearly this tax represents a major source of government revenue.

To illustrate the possible revenue impact of an increased excise tax on cigarette sales, 1992 data on price and sales figures are used. According to the PRC (People's Republic of China) yearbook, the retail price per case of cigarettes was 3,320 yuan (US$533), and 32.65 million cases were sold.[4] A recent study estimated that the price elasticity of the demand for cigarettes in Sichuan province in

---

[19] Warner K, Chaloupka FJ, Cook PJ, et al., "Criteria for Determining an Optimal Cigarette Tax: the Economist's Perspective," *Tobacco Control* 4 (11995): 380–386.
[20] Congressional Budget Office, *Federal Taxation of Tobacco, Alcoholic Beverages, and Motor Fuels* (Washington, DC: US Government Printing Office, 1990).

China, ranges from −0.65 to −0.80, which is somewhat higher (that is, more price sensitive) than in many other developed countries, but not as high as estimates from Papua New Guinea.[4,7,21] The Papua New Guinea estimates were for excise tax elasticity (−0.50 to −0.71), and the price elasticity would be as high as −1.0 or −1.42. In this illustration, we assume −0.65 (the lower end of the Sichuan estimate) to be the price elasticity for the Chinese population.[22]

Given this information, if the Chinese government cigarette industry imposed a 10 percent increase in price, from 3,320 yuan (US$533) per case to 3,652 yuan (US$608), a 6.5 percent reduction in sales would occur, from 32.65 million cases to 30.53 million cases. However, the total revenue would increase from 108.41 billion yuan (US$18.07 billion) to 111.5 billion yuan (US$18.58 billion), a 3.10 billion yuan (US$516.7 million) increase, or an increase of 2.9 percent. Thus, given the inelastic demand for cigarettes, the total revenue will increase when the price is increased. Assuming the effective tax rate in 1992 was 37.78 percent, the effective tax rate would have to rise to 43.43 percent to achieve a 10 percent increase in price, an increase of 15 percent in the effective tax rate. Given these assumptions, total tax revenues would rise by 18.2 percent, while total sales revenues would rise by 2.9 percent.

OPTIONS FOR ADDITIONAL CIGARETTE TAXES IN CHINA

Given the negative health consequences of cigarette smoking, it is certainly justifiable to consider imposing additional tax on cigarettes. Furthermore, additional financial resources are needed to facilitate healthcare reform in China to expand the coverage of healthcare services for the poor, especially for the uninsured in the low-income

---

[21] Chapman S and Richardson J, "Tobacco Excise and Declining Consumption: The Case of Papua New Guinea," *American Journal of Public Health* 80 (1990): 537–540.

[22] Mao Z, *Demand for Cigarette and Pricing Policy: A Time-Series Analysis*. [In Chinese.] Working paper, School of Public Health, West China Vicinity of Medical Sciences, Sichuan, China (1996).

urban and rural population.[23] A number of countries, including the United States (California), Nepal, and Egypt, have been using tobacco tax revenues to pay for healthcare services or health insurance premiums. Finally, a serious need exists in China for a health promotion campaign and its financial support, which may include an anti-smoking media campaign or school health education programs. A small portion of the additional cigarette tax revenues could be used to fund health promotion and disease prevention activities.

As noted above, China currently imposes a product tax on cigarettes. These taxes are incurred and paid directly by the producer; but leeway exists, however, for the consumer to pay an additional tax on cigarettes at the retail level in the form of a sales tax or an excise tax. Currently, cigarette taxes account for less than 40 percent of the retail price in China, not as high as many other countries in the world, where taxes comprise more than 60 percent of retail prices.

Several factors determine how much tax should be imposed. One major factor relates to the objective of reducing cigarette consumption. US data suggests that a third of the reduction in cigarette consumption following tax increases is the result of current smokers quitting, and two-thirds is due to smokers reducing their individual cigarette consumption. The other factors relate to: (1) consumers' ability to bear the additional financial burden; (b) the amount of revenue the government needs to achieve a given objective; (c) the magnitude of the potential negative impact on the cigarette industry; and (d) smuggling.

In California, before Proposition 99 was implemented, the legislature had the intention of reducing the tobacco consumption in California by 75 percent by the year 2000. Canada, recognizing that its high tax rate caused major smuggling between Canada and the United States, subsequently lowered its tax rate. In Egypt, the tax rate was increased from five to 10 piasters per pack to produce enough revenue to provide health insurance for school children. Therefore, the Ministry of Health, the Ministry of Finance, and other

---

[23] World Bank, *Health Finance Study: Health-Care Financing Reform, 1996–2001.* (World Bank, Washington, DC, Sept 1995).

interested parties in China need to collaborate in developing China's tax increase agenda.

Several concerns have been expressed relative to an increase in cigarette taxes. The first two have immediate impacts: an increase in smuggling to avoid the additional tax burden, and the shifting from cigarette consumption to cigarette substitutes (such as pipe or cigar smoking). These two responses will weaken the effect of an additional cigarette tax. Many countries, such as Canada, have experienced the problem of cross-border smuggling. Smuggling in China is already a major problem, especially between Hong Kong and China. The Chinese government has not been able to effectively control the cigarette smuggling problem. The substitution effect could be minimized if the tax covers not only cigarettes, but also other tobacco products.

One long-term negative consequence of an increased cigarette tax is the reduction of the economic wellbeing of tobacco farmers and workers in the tobacco industry, who will face lost income and unemployment. In this case, the government should develop a long-range gradual plan to convert tobacco farm production into other agricultural production, and to convert tobacco factories into non-tobacco factories by providing loans, the money for which can come from the cigarette tax. There will certainly be disproportionate losses to particular geographical areas. A similar policy debate is occurring in the United States.[24,25] Brazil has encouraged tobacco farmers to transfer into other cash crop activities. Additional innovative policy alternatives in this area should be considered. Perhaps the World Bank can take further initiative, by not only refraining from lending for the purposes of tobacco production, but also by providing loans for converting tobacco production to production of alternative crops (H Barnum, unpublished paper, 1993).

---

[24] Price Waterhouse, *The Economic Impact of the Tobacco Industry in the U.S. Economy* (New York: Price Waterhouse, 1992).

[25] Chase Econometrics, *The Impact of the Tobacco Industry in the United States Economy in 1983* (Bala Cynwyd, Pennsylvania: Chase Econometrics, 1995).

CONCLUSIONS

Many countries around the world have taken the initiative to control cigarette use because of its impact on public health and healthcare costs. China is in a unique position because its relatively high smoking prevalence provides a large tax base; therefore, the imposition of a cigarette tax increase will have a significant effect in generating revenue and reducing cigarette consumption. When combining tax revenue from both producers and consumers, the total revenue for the state will increase, not decrease.

- The healthcare sector is currently facing limited financing sources, given the current state and local tax structure. Therefore, the option for raising additional revenues from an increased cigarette tax is a golden opportunity for China to finance healthcare reform and activities in health promotion and disease prevention.
- This review of international experiences with cigarette taxation and the current status of Chinese cigarette consumption leads to the following recommendations. Tobacco tax policies in China should be linked to the objective of reducing tobacco use. Government policymakers should consider using tobacco tax as an intervention in accomplishing the goals of health promotion and disease promotion. Researchers have shown that tobacco taxation is an effective means of reducing cigarette consumption. Using a portion of cigarette tax revenue for anti-smoking activities would further achieve the goals of tobacco control.

China is a major country both in terms of the size of its population and the wide geographic differences in the production of tobacco and the manufacture of cigarettes. Raising cigarette taxes could be a major political and economic issue. One option for the central government is to carry out small-scale experiments in certain areas, like many other social and health insurance experiences being implemented in various local areas, to examine the potential impact of additional cigarette taxation on cigarette consumption, government revenue, possible allocation of additional tax revenue to health promotion and healthcare financing, and the Chinese cigarette manufacturing industry and tobacco farm sector.

ACKNOWLEDGMENTS

An earlier version of this chapter was prepared for the Human Development Department of the World Bank. The author is grateful for comments and suggestions provided by Professor Michael Grossman of the City University of New York, Dr. William McGreevey of the World Bank, Professor Kenneth Warner of the University of Michigan, and three anonymous referees. Preparation of this chapter was partially supported by the Pacific Rim Research Program, University of California. The interpretation and views expressed in the chapter remain the responsibility of the author and do not necessarily represent the views of the World Bank or the University of California. The exchange rate for the yuan to the US dollar was 6:1 at the time of the figures quoted in this paper.

Chapter 14

Earmarked Tobacco Taxes: The US Experience*

Teh-wei Hu, Xiao-peng Xu and Theodore Keeler

An earmarked tax designates its revenue for spending on specific government or public services.[1] In other words, earmarking calls for a simultaneous choice both on the level of taxation and expenditures on an item-by-item basis. Although the literature on earmarked taxation is sparse, the actual practice of earmarking revenue for a variety of government services is quite common. In fact, in the United States, at least one-third of all federal, state and

---

*This chapter originally appeared as Hu TW, Xu XP, Keeler T, "Earmarked Tobacco Taxes: Lessons Learned," in *The Economics of Tobacco Control: Towards an Optimal Policy Mix*, ed. Iraj Abedian, Rowena wan der Merwe, Nick Wilkins, Prabhat Jha (South Africa: Applied Fiscal Research Center, University of Cape Town, 1998) 102–118. Copyright © by University of Cape Town. All rights reserved. Reprinted with permission from the University of Cape Town, South Africa.
[1] Buchanan J, "The Economics of Earmarked Taxes," *Journal of Political Economy* (October 1963).

local government expenditures are earmarked taxes.[2] Justification is often based on the benefit principle. Under this logic, for example, gasoline or automobile tax proceeds are used for highway financing, and property tax is used by local governments for residential services, including local public school education. Social security taxes, used for employee retirement income, are another example of earmarked taxation. Clearly, earmarked taxes are not new in government tax financing.

Taxation of tobacco products is similarly not a new phenomenon. The tobacco tax has been almost universal internationally for many decades, and has always been an important part of central or local government revenue. However, earmarking part of tobacco tax revenue for particular expenditures is relatively recent. The usual rationales used to justify a tax on cigarettes are (1) to consider the cigarette tax an efficient instrument with low administrative costs for collecting revenue for government spending; e.g., tobacco tax was used for increasing state revenue in the United States during the Korean War in 1951, and in Finland during 1975–1976, and (2) to impose the cigarette tax as "user's fees" or "sin tax". It is argued that the tax covers external costs of smoking and discourages smokers from using cigarettes, thus leading to a reduction in tobacco-related health care costs by reducing the morbidity and mortality associated with cigarette smoking. This second rationale, with its anti-smoking objective for raising cigarette taxes, was initiated after the release of the US Surgeon General's report in 1964 on smoking and health. Since 1980, countries such as Australia, Canada, and New Zealand have all raised cigarette taxes as a means of reducing cigarette consumption. Raising the cigarette tax to control tobacco use and using part of revenue from such taxes to support anti-smoking-related activities and for health-related expenditures, such as health promotion or health insurance, was widely utilized in the late 1980s and early 1990s. In a sense, tobacco tax has become a form of earmarked tax in many instances.

---

[2] McMahon W and Sprenkle CM, "A Theory of Earmarking," *National Tax Journal* 23 (1970): 255–261.

One justification for using an earmarked tax *is* to ease the pressure on general revenue finance for particular public goods or services when users or beneficiaries of these sources can be easily identified. Therefore, earmarked tax can be considered a replacement for direct charges for services.

However, public finance experts have argued that earmarking may not be a good tax budgeting procedure, since it introduces rigidities and does not permit proper allocation of general revenue among competing uses. On the other hand, one may argue that the use of a tobacco tax for health promotion ,and disease prevention may be appropriate, in line with the benefit taxation principle, which asserts that inducing better health behavior and health status contribute to better expenditure decisions. In essence, depending on how the tobacco tax revenue is used, earmarking *may* thus be all arbitrary fiscal policy leading to budgetary rigidity, or it may be a useful device for a form of benefit taxation.[3]

During the past decade, earmarking tobacco tax for health causes has been a popular fiscal instrument as well as a public health policy in several developed countries, particularly in the United States. The policy formulation, and the impact of earmarked tobacco tax on consumption, government revenue, the tobacco industry, and the economy in general, are valuable for other countries to examine. This information is especially useful because some less-developed countries (LDCs) are also tobacco-producing countries, which have economic stakes in maintaining the well-being of tobacco farmers and the tobacco industry.[4,5] It is important to examine the economic implications and the total social welfare loss or gain of earmarked tobacco taxes, so that more informed tobacco control policy-making can be considered for the future.

---

[3] Musgrave R and Musgrave P, *Public Finance in Theory and Practice* (New York: McGraw-Hill, 1996).

[4] Warner KE, "Tobacco Taxation as Health Policy in the Third World," *American Journal of Public Health* 80, no. 5 (1990): 529–531.

[5] Warner KE and Fulton GA, "The Economic Implications of Tobacco Product Sales in a Non-Tobacco State," *Journal of the American Medical Association* 271 (1994): 771–776.

The purpose of this chapter is to review international experiences with earmarked tobacco taxes, to analyze the economic implications of earmarked tobacco taxes, to draw lessons learned from these tax experiences, and to provide options and further recommendations for the international community. The following section will provide policy content, and the direct and indirect impact of earmarked tobacco taxes in the United States, Canada, Finland, and Australia. Thereafter, the chapter will present theoretical and some tentative quantitative estimates of total social welfare loss or gain from different sectors of the economy (using the United States and China as examples). Finally, options and recommendations are presented.

UNITED STATES EXPERIENCES OF EARMARKED TOBACCO TAXES

Tobacco taxes in the United States are collected at the federal and state levels of government. The amount of tobacco tax on each pack varies considerably among the 50 states, ranging from a low of 2.5 cents in Virginia to 81.5 cents In the state of Washington as of December 1995.[6] Several states have used tobacco tax for government expenditures. Although California is not the state with the highest tobacco tax (it ranked only 18th in 1995), in 1988 it became the first state in the United States to legislate additional tobacco tax to deter cigarette consumption and to further earmark the revenue to be used for anti-smoking health education programs, indigent health care, research, environmental programs, and tobacco health-related research, among other uses.[7] The California Tobacco Tax and Health Promotion Act, Proposition 99, was passed in 1988 by a popular vote of 58 percent to 42 percent, designed to increase tax from 10 cents a pack to 35 cents per pack. The goal of the Act was to achieve a 75 percent reduction in smoking among adults in California by the year 2000 (to 6.5 percent of

---

[6] Fishman *et al.*, *State Tobacco Control Highlights* 1996 (Centers for Disease Control, Atlanta, GA: US Department of Health and Human Services, 1996).

[7] Bal D, "Reducing Tobacco Consumption in California — Development of a State-Wide Anti-Tobacco Use Campaign," *Journal of the American Medical Association* 264 (1990): 1570–1574.

the population, from 26 percent in the pre-initiative period). The Act created the Tobacco Product Surtax Fund, composed of six accounts, which allocates 20 percent of funds to health education and media campaigns, 35 percent for indigent hospital services, 10 percent for indigent physician services, 5 percent for research, and 5 per cent for environment, with the remaining 25 percent to be placed in an unallocated account. The justifications for the additional taxation on tobacco and for the earmarking of its revenue are:

- smoking is harmful to health, and has increased costs of health care among smokers, thereby placing a burden on nonsmokers (who are taxpayers and pay insurance premiums);
- smoking will also expose nonsmokers to its pollutants; and
- resources are required to initiate tobacco control programs, other than taxes, to discourage youth and adult smoking.

The basic philosophy of the earmarked tobacco tax is that population-based tobacco control programs through the media, schools, worksites, and public areas will both reduce smoking prevalence and protect nonsmokers. Needless to say, the legislation and implementation of Proposition 99 required numerous and complex negotiations between public health organizations, politicians, and the tobacco industry.[8] Between 1989 and 1995, about US$1.5 billion in revenue has been appropriated for these earmarked accounts.

The direct impact of California tobacco tax increases on cigarette consumption was studied by a number of econometric analyses.[9-11] They have all shown a significant reduction in *per capita* cigarette

---

[8] Novotny T and Siegel M, "California's Tobacco Control Saga," *Health Affairs*, 15 (1996): 58–72.

[9] Flewelling R *et al.*, "First Year Impact of the 1989 California Cigarette Tax Increase on Cigarette Consumption," *American Journal of Public Health* 82 (1992): 867–869.

[10] Glantz S *et al.*, "Changes in Cigarette Consumption, Prices and Tobacco Industry Reviews Associated with California's Proposition 99," *Tobacco Control*, 2 (1993): 311–314.

[11] Hu TW, Bai J, Keeler T, Barnett P and Sung H, "The Impact of 1989 California Major Anti-Smoking Legislation on Cigarette Consumption," *Journal of Public Health Policy* 15 (1994): 26–36.

consumption in California, directly associated with the implementation of Proposition 99. For instance, it was reported that six months after the tax increase, cigarette sales had declined by about one pack per adult per month, or 11 percent.[11] One year after the tax increase, the decline per capita had remained at a rate of 3/4 pack per adult per month, or about a 10 percent reduction throughout the next three years. From January 1989 through December 1992, Proposition 99 reduced cigarette consumption by 1.3 billion packs of cigarettes, attributable to tax increase alone.[12] Other studies confirmed these findings.[10,13]

Although there was a significant reduction in cigarette sales due to the tax increase, the state of California experienced an impressive increase in revenue. This was because the percentage increase in tax, reflected by the increase in retail price, is higher than the percentage decrease in quantity. The estimated price elasticity of demand for cigarettes in California during this period was about −0.40.[14,15] It was shown that a 10 percent increase in price reduced the quantity demanded by 4 percent. Thus, the percentage increase in price is higher than the percentage decrease in quantity by 6 percent. In other words, the value of lost sales is more than offset by the value of gain due to the increased price. Therefore, tax revenue will increase. The actual California state cigarette tax revenue increased 200 percent in 1989, (US$764 million in 1989 versus US$254 million in 1988), despite a 14 percent reduction in total cigarette sales (2,538 million packs in 1988 versus 2,184 million packs in 1989). Cigarette sales continued to decline each year, while revenues continued to be

---

[12] Hu TW, Sung H and Keeler T, "Tobacco Taxes and the Anti-Smoking Media Campaign: The California Experience," *American Journal of Public Health* 85, no. 9 (1995).

[13] Pierce, J *et al.*, *Tobacco Use in California: An Evaluation of the Tobacco Control Programs*, 1989–1993 (La Jolla, CA: University of California at San Diego, 1994).

[14] Keeler T, Hu TW, Barnett P and Manning W, "Taxation, Regulation and Addiction: A Demand Function for Cigarettes Based on Time-Series Evidence," *Journal of Heath Economics*, 12 (1993): 1–18.

[15] Sung H, Hu TW and Keeler T, "Cigarette Taxation and Demand: An Empirical Model," *Contemporary Economic Policy*, 7(1994): 91–100.

Table 1: California Cigarette Sales, Tax Revenue, and Tax Rates: 1989–1993

Year	Sales (Millions of Packs)	Tax Revenue (US$ Million)	Tax Rate (US$)
1987	2,563	258.25	0.10
1988	2,538	253.85	0.10
1989	2,184	764.42	0.35
1990	2,205	771.70	0.35
1991	2,054	719.09	0.35
1992	2,019	706.70	0.35
1993	1,970	689.64	0.35

Source: California Tax Equalization Board.

much higher than the pre-tax (1988) period. The state cigarette tax revenue in 1993 was still 170 percent (US$690 million) higher than that in 1988, as shown in Table 1.

This is a very important finding for policy-makers in tobacco control and tax revenue departments. As long as the price elasticity of the demand for cigarettes is less elastic than a value of −1, the increase in taxes will result in a net gain in total tax revenues. The less elastic the demand, the less effective the tax will be in reducing cigarette consumption, but the more the gain in tax revenues. To plan for the desired level of reduction in cigarette consumption and the desired amount of increase of tax revenues, it is important to know the magnitude of the price elasticity of demand for cigarettes.

On the other hand, the direct effect of additional cigarette tax on the tobacco industry was obviously negative. It was estimated[10] that from 1989 to June 1993, Proposition 99 reduced cigarette consumption by 802 million packs, resulting in a loss of US$ 1.1 billion in pre-tax sales and approximately US$286 million in profit for the tobacco industry.

As noted, one unique feature of California's Proposition 99 is its earmarking of revenue from cigarette taxes on tobacco control activities, tobacco-related disease research, and expenditures for indigent health care services. For instance, US$125 million a year has been allocated for health education. Because of the extra tax revenues, the California Department of Health Services spent US$26 million on a state-wide media campaign designed to change tobacco-related attitudes and behaviors of certain target groups, including adult smokers, pregnant women, children, and ethnic minorities.

Time-series regression analysis, based on cigarette sales data in California during 1989–1992, indicates that both the 25 cents per pack state tax and the antismoking media campaign were statistically significant in reducing cigarette consumption.[12] The estimated results show that cigarette sales decreased by 819 million packs from the third quarter of 1990 through the fourth quarter of 1992 as a result of an additional 25 cents state tax increase, while the antismoking media campaign reduced the cigarette sales by 232 million packs during the same period. In other words, both taxation and anti-smoking media campaigns are effective ways of reducing cigarette consumption. The strength of these effects. however, is influenced by the magnitude of the taxes and the amount of media campaign expenditure. It is perhaps easy to overstate the magnitude of the effects of taxes versus media campaigns, given that they represent two different ways of reducing cigarette consumption. Taxation provides an economic disincentive, whereas the media campaign educates the public, by directing its focus on the psychological basis underlying the demand for cigarette consumption.

The implementation of Proposition 99 in California indicates that raising taxes and using part of the tax revenue for an anti-smoking campaign is an effective approach to reducing cigarette consumption. The tax is an economically effective and revenue-producing method of reducing cigarette consumption. At the same time, a tax increase may not deter some segments of the population from smoking. A media campaign, financed by the earmarked tobacco tax revenue, may reach those segments of the population. Thus, additional tobacco tax and earmarking part of its revenue for media and other anti-smoking educational campaigns provide appealing policy instruments for tobacco control policy-makers.

There are other impacts of Proposition 99, such as the reduction of and decreased exposure to environmental tobacco smoke for nonsmokers. The California Department of Health Services reported in 1994 that children's protection from exposure to environmental tobacco smoke increased 6.2 percent (from 75.2 percent to 80.4 percent protected at home in 1993), because the number of children living in smoke-free homes increased. In addition, 22.8 percent fewer adults were exposed to environmental tobacco smoke at workplaces in California.[13]

Other earmarked tax revenue has been spent on classroom teaching, which reached over two-thirds of Californian schoolchildren. Over half of all students in California (more than 2.9 million) have also participated in anti tobacco assemblies and community programs involving teens teaching teens through sports, theater, and music activities. Public school health education, teachers' training, and new methods of delivering tobacco use prevention programs have been utilized. The actual quantitative impact of these on cigarette consumption has been difficult to document. However, public opinion indicated that 95 percent of Californians approved the tobacco education that Proposition 99 initiated.[16]

Some argue that the cigarette tax is a "sin tax"[17] because smoking causes economic burdens to society, through the increased use of medical services. Between 1989 and 1994, the California Department of Health Services received US$660 million for hospital services and physician services to cover medically indigent patient costs.

California's anti-smoking legislation, Proposition 99, is a major success for voters of California. Several other states in the United States, including Massachusetts, Oregon, and Arizona, have implemented similar legislation by earmarking revenue for specific health education and medical uses. Michigan earmarked its tobacco tax for local public education. This chapter will briefly summarize the experiences of Massachusetts, Arizona, and Oregon.

Voters in Massachusetts approved a ballot petition in November 1992 to increase cigarette tax on each pack from 26 cents to 51 cents

---

[16] Tobacco Education Oversight Committee, *Toward a Tobacco-Free California: Exploring a New Frontier*, 1993–1995 (Sacramento, CA: TEOC, 1993).

[17] Manning W, Keeler E, Newhouse J, Sloss E and Wasserman J, "The Taxes of Sin: Do Smokers and Drinkers Pay Their Way?," *Journal of the American Medical Association*, 261 (1989): 1604–1609.

(i.e., a 25-cent increase), beginning January 1, 1993. The petition requested that the legislature spend the proceeds on tobacco control and health education. After one year, in early 1994, the state began funding local boards of health, and youth programs to promote policies to reduce public expenses to environmental tobacco smoke and to restrict youth access to cigarettes. Efforts were also made to support health education programs, primary care providers, and other services to help smokers quit. Through June 1996, the Massachusetts Tobacco Control Program (MTCP) expenditures totaled US$ 116 million, including US$43 million for the mass-media campaign.

The impact of the increase of tobacco tax, its earmarked expenditures, and the anti-smoking media campaign in Massachusetts indicates that in the 3 years after the implementation of the petition in 1993, the smoking prevalence rate declined to 21.3 percent, down from 23.5 percent during 1990–1992.[18] The number of packs of cigarettes sold per adult was also reduced from 117 packs in 1992 to 94 packs in 1996, a decline of 19.7 percent. These are gross estimates; possible cross-border purchases due to lower taxes in neighboring states (New Hampshire) and the overaJi declining national trend are not accounted for in these reduced figures.

By comparing the number of packs of cigarettes purchased per adult in Massachusetts, California and the 48 remaining states (and the District of Columbia), the Centers for Disease Control (CDC) (1996) reported that from' 1992 through 1996 per capita consumption declined 19.7 percent in Massachusetts and 15.8 percent in California, but only 6.1 percent for the rest of the nation. The CDC concluded that the significant declines in cigarette consumption in Massachusetts and California suggest that a tax increase combined with earmarked expenditures for an anti-smoking campaign can be more effective in reducing per capita consumption than a tax increase alone, as shown in Table 2.

---

[18] Centers for Disease Control, "Cigarette Smoking Before and After an Excise Tax Increase and An Anti-Smoking Campaign — Massachusetts: 1990–1996," *Morbidity and Mortality Weekly Report* 45 (1996): 966–970.

Table 2: Number of Packs of Cigarettes Purchased Per Adult[a] by Year, Selected US Sites, 1990–1996[b]

Year	Massachusetts	California	Other States and District of Columbia
1990	125	100	139
1991	120	92	134
1992	117	89	131
1993	102	88	125
1994	101	73	127
1995	98	76	125
1996[c]	94	75	123

Source: Centers for Disease Control (1996). (See Footnote 18).
[a] 18 years of age or older; [b] Based on reports of tax receipts for wholesale cigarette deliveries; [c] Estimated as twice the cumulative values for January–June.

A national study,[19] based on 1992, 1993 and 1994 youth survey data, further confirmed that those states that have earmarked a portion of their tobacco tax revenue for anti-smoking education, in the media or in schools, have experienced a negative and statistically significant impact on both the probability that a youth will smoke and on the average daily cigarette consumption among young smokers.

Voters in the state of Arizona approved the Tobacco Tax and Health Care Act in the 1994 general election. The Act increased cigarette tax from 18 cents per pack to 58 cents per pack. Additional revenues were earmarked for establishing a Health Education Account, 23 percent of the increased tax revenue. In addition, the Act allocated 70 percent of the revenue for health care for the medically needy, medically indigent, and low-income children, and 5 percent for research on prevention and treatment of tobacco-related disease and addiction. The remaining, 2 percent was used for an adjustment account for appropriate uses in the case of future decline in tobacco tax revenue.

---

[19] Chaloupka F and Grossman M, *Price, Tobacco Control Policies and Youth Smoking*. Working paper no. 5140, Cambridge, Mass: National Bureau of Economic Research (1996).

The Health Care Act formally became law in July 1995. The administration of funding was carried out by the Arizona Department of Health Services, and the media campaign was implemented in January 1996. Survey evaluation was initiated in April 1996. No published findings have yet been available.

Following California, Massachusetts, and Arizona, in late 1995, a state-wide coalition of health care and tobacco use prevention interests in Oregon began a citizen petition to increase the tax on each pack of cigarettes from 38 cents to 68 cents, and to increase the tax on non-cigarette tobacco products from 35 percent to 65 percent of wholesale prices, beginning February 1, 1997. The initiative authorized 10 percent of the new tobacco tax revenue for use in developing and implementing statewide tobacco use prevention and education programs, and the remaining 90 percent for use in expanding insurance coverage under the Oregon Health Plan for medically underserved persons. Both Arizona and Oregon have only recently initiated additional tobacco tax and used its earmarked revenue for tobacco control. They are in an early stage of impact evaluation.

Besides these four states, Michigan passed an initiative in 1994 .to raise taxes — an additional 25 cents per pack — to add to property tax funding of schools. Two states, Montana in 1990 and Colorado in 1992, have tried to use citizen initiatives to raise cigarette tax and earmark the revenue for tobacco control activities, but failed to gain voter approval.

In summary, there are four major states in the United States that have used voter initiatives to support additional tobacco taxes and earmark portions of the new tax revenue for health education, tobacco prevention, and health care services, as shown in Table 3. Although there are variations of percentages of allocation, the largest portion has been allocated for health care, at least 50 percent or more. Health education and media campaigns have been identified as a common earmarked item. The issue of economic efficiency and welfare loss or gain to the society of this type of earmarked tobacco will be analyzed in the following section.

Table 3: Earmarked Tobacco Tax in Four US States.

	California[a]	Massachusetts[b]	Arizona[c]	Oregon[d]
Year enacted	1988	1992	1994	1995
Amount of tax increase (US$)	0.25 (to 0.35)	0.25 (to 0.51)	0.40 (to 0.58)	0.30 (to 0.68)
Earmarked allocation				
Health education/ media campaign	20%	65%	23%	10%
Indigent health care	50%	33%	70%	90%
Research	5%	2%	5%	—
Environment	5%	—	—	—
Unallocated	20%	—	2%	—

Source: [a] Bal (1990) (See Footnote 7); [b] Centers for Diseases Control (1996) (see Footnote 18); [c] Centers for Diseases Control, "Tobacco Tax Initiative — Oregan; 1996," *Morbidity and mortality, Weekly Report* 46 (1997): 246–248; [d] Arizona Department of Health Services, Center for Prevention and Health Promotion.

ECONOMIC EFFECTS OF EARMARKED TOBACCO TAX: THEORY AND IMPLICATIONS

The basic criteria used to evaluate taxation are (1) efficiency and (2) equity. Efficiency in taxation means that tax revenue should be maximized with minimum alteration of consumers' choices among various goods or services. The less responsive the consumer is to changes in the price of a given commodity (i.e., the demand is inelastic), the more effective taxes are in collecting revenue. Less response to changes in price means less negative change to consumers' satisfaction, if the tax has been shifted to an increase in price. Since demand for cigarettes is regarded as relatively inelastic, with estimates of price elasticity of demand of −0.4 to −0.5 in many industrialized economies, taxes on cigarettes should be efficient. A study in the United Kingdom[20] indicates that a 1 percent increase

---

[20] Jones A and Posnett J, "The Revenue and Welfare Effects of Cigarette Taxes," *Applied Economics,* 20 (1988): 1223–1232.

in the tax rate generates about a 0.9 percent increase in revenue. The example of California also illustrates that cigarette tax is a powerful tool in generating revenue.

Equity in taxation means that there should be an equal tax burden among taxpayers. There are two main principles to evaluate equity: (1) taxes should be based on individual benefit received from services provided by the government, and (2) taxes should be based on an individual's ability to pay. These two principles are not necessarily always consistent or contradictory to each other, depending on the type of taxation. For instance, some excise taxes are collected on the basis of the benefit principle, while income taxes are assessed on the ability-to-pay principle. Proponents of tobacco control groups have cited the benefit principle, indicating that smokers should pay for the burdens (negative benefits) that smoking brings about, such as pollution, social costs (e.g., fire hazard), and additional medical costs, which are imposed on others through insurance premiums or added government expenditures. The concept of users' fees or "sin tax" is based on the benefit principle. In other words, one of the goals of cigarette taxation is to raise the retail price of cigarettes to a level that fully reflects the social costs generated by their consumption.[17,21] In terms of this objective, an economically efficient price for cigarettes is one where the net benefit of cigarette smoking is at least larger than the price of the cigarettes, where part of the cigarette's price reflects social costs of consumption. Thus, the amount of tax on cigarettes should be set such that total tax revenue extracted from smokers would be equal to total social cost generated by smokers.

While additional cigarette taxation based on both efficiency and equity (the benefit principle) seems quite convincing, the use of the tobacco tax instrument alone may not be able to bring about tobacco control. The inelastic demand for cigarettes may result in revenue maximization, but it is inconsistent with the goal of public health, which is minimizing cigarette consumption. For instance,

---

[21] Elleman-Jensen P, "The Social Costs of Smoking Revisited," *British Journal of Addiction* 86 (1991): 957–966.

a 10 percent increase in price can result in 4 percent of tobacco consumption reduction. The anticipated health gain in reducing smoking will be limited with tax increases through price increases. That is, consumers may not respond to price change alone. Also, youth may have less understanding of the negative impact of smoking on their health. Therefore, the earmarking of a collected cigarette tax for spending on media or other educational anti-smoking campaigns is fully justified, because education makes up for the shortfalls of price effects under the efficiency arguments. In addition, earmarked revenues for research on tobacco-related disease and medical care costs, especially for those incurred by indigent people, are justified under the benefit principle.

The justification for earmarking tobacco tax revenues for health promotion, disease prevention, and medical care services on the grounds of efficiency and equity do not convince all fiscal specialists,[22] smokers, and the tobacco industry. On efficiency grounds, there is always a loss of consumer surplus (a reduction of utility or satisfaction) due to price (tax) increase and lesser consumption, a loss of producers' surplus (a reduction of revenue), and dead-weight loss (excess burden) to the society. On equity and efficiency grounds, although there is a high correlation between smoking and increased medical costs,[23] it is also necessary to consider intergenerational transfer between current young or adult smokers, and patient costs incurred by those who smoked years ago, as well as the possible medical costs and social security cost savings due to tobacco-related early death. There is much debate about these issues, but there is not yet conclusive agreement.[24]

---

[22] Wagner R (ed.), *Charging the Government: User Charges and Earmarked Taxes in Principle and Practice* (London: Routledge, 1991).

[23] Bartlett J, Miller L, Rice D and Max W, Office on Smoking and Health, Centers for Disease Control, "Medical Care Expenditures Attributable to Smoking — United States, 1993," *Morbidity and Mortality Weekly Report,* 43 (1994): 469–472.

[24] Warner KE, Chaloupka F, Cook P, Manning W, Newhouse J, Novotny T, Schelling T and Townsend J, "Criteria for Determining an Optimal Cigarette Tax: The Economist's Perspective," *Tobacco Control* 4 (1995): 385–386.

To evaluate economic implications of an earmarked tobacco tax, it is necessary first to estimate the welfare effect of the increase of tobacco tax for consumers and producers, and the net loss (excess burden) to society, and then to consider the magnitude and type of tax revenue transfer affected. One should examine the distributional impact of tobacco tax, and the possible options of using earmarked tax to compensate losers as a result of increased tobacco tax.

The economic and welfare effects of a tobacco tax increase depend on both the response of market price to a change in the tax rate, the response of demand to the change in market price, and the response of supply to the change in market price. The simplest assumption of tax incidence on retail price is that price changes by the full amount of the tax. In fact, most of US studies show that after each tax increase the retail price rose by an amount greater than or equal to the amount of tax. Two studies in the United Kingdom[20,25] have shown the welfare effects of cigarette taxes. To illustrate the estimation and magnitude of the economic and welfare effects of a tobacco tax increase, the cases of the United States and China will be presented in this section.

United States

From 1993, the United States Federal government taxed cigarettes at a rate of 24 cents per pack. In addition to that, as of mid-1996, state governments in the United States taxed cigarettes at an average rate of 31.7 cents per pack, so that the average total tax per pack in the United States at that time was 55.7 cents; this yielded revenues of US$7.3 billion to various US governments.[26] Obviously, the effects of US cigarette taxation, at various government levels, are quite substantial, but it is clear that consumption of cigarettes could be further reduced by an increase in the tax. To provide insight into the potential

---

[25] Townsend J, "Cigarette Tax, Economic Welfare and Social Class Patterns of Smoking," *Applied Economics,* 19 (1987): 355–365.
[26] Tobacco Institute, *The Tax Burden on Tobacco* (Washington, DC: Tobacco Institute, 1997).

effects of an increase in cigarette taxation on consumption and economic welfare, this chapter presents calculations simulating the effects of a further 1 cent increase in the US Federal cigarette tax.

These calculations are based on the earlier work of Barnett *et al.*[27] but they extend that work in some important ways. Before describing those extensions, the discussion will summarize the methods on which the work by Barnett *et al.*[27] is based. That earlier research takes account of several important facts crucial to the US cigarette industry. Firstly, it is an oligopoly, so the model is based on Cournot-type behavior with conjectural variations. The relevant model assumes that the firms are profit-maximizing oligopolists, who, at the same time, take account of their interdependence in setting prices. Secondly, it takes account of the fact that cigarette manufacturers are able to set wholesale prices to maximize profits, and that they can, as a result, respond to the Federal tax, and to an average state tax, but they cannot set retail prices. The cigarette distribution and retail sales businesses are likely to be much more competitive in nature. Thirdly, the model is based on separate estimates of marginal costs for manufacturing, distribution, and retailing of cigarettes. Knowledge of each of these costs, as well as the knowledge of taxes at the Federal and State levels, is necessary to get a full picture of how taxes are passed on as prices.

The details of the model, cost function estimates, and other underlying assumptions of this analysis are set forth by Barnett *et al.*[27] Further modifications of this model are set forth below; results are shown in Table 4.

The first change that has been made is that the price elasticity has been adjusted downward from −0.709, as it was estimated by Barnett *et al.*,[27] to −0.5. This is because the recent consensus of estimates of the price elasticity of demand for cigarettes in the United States is much closer to −0.5 than to −0.7, as has been established above.

The second change made from the study of Barnett *et al.*,[27] is that allowance has been made for different weightings of consumer

---

[27] Barnett P, Keeler T and Hu TW, "Oligopoly Structure and the Incidence of Cigarette Excise Taxes," *Journal of Public Economics*, 57 (1995): 457–470.

Table 4: Simulation of a One cent Increase in US Federal Cigarette Tax

λ (Consumer surplus weight)	1	0	−0.25	−0.5	−1
Mean change in qty (million packs/year)	−226	−226	−226	−226	−226
Mean change in price (real 1990 cents/pack):					
Retail price paid by consumers	1.106	1.106	1.106	1.106	−1.106
Price received by retailers	0.016	0.016	0.016	0.016	0.016
Wholesale price	−0.134	−0.314	−0.314	−0.314	−0.314
Change in consumer surplus (λCS)	−394	0	99	197	394
Change in producer surplus	−101	−101	−101	−101	−101
Total change in welfare	−495	−101	−2	96	293
Consumer's share	0.8	0	−49.5	2.1	1.3
Producer's share	0.2	1	50.5	−1.1	−0.3
Dead-weight loss	222	−171	−270	−368	−565
Government revenue	272	272	272	272	272
Total change in gain	495	101	2	−96	−293
Dead-weight loss as percentage of lost welfare	0.45	−1.7	−1.08	3.84	1.93

The table is based on Barnett et al.[27] with two modifications: (1) price elasticity is adjusted down from −0.709 in the above study to −0.5; (2) a more general from of social welfare functions is used, namely, PS + λCS, where PS and CS are the producer and consumer surplus, respectively, and λ is the relative weight that the government assigns to the consumer welfare. In Barnett et al.[27] λ = 1.

and producer surplus in the social welfare function. In doing welfare analysis of taxation, one often calculates the "dead-weight" or welfare loss from a tax under the assumption that everyone's welfare (i.e., a dollar that either the consumer or producer is willing to pay) is weighted the same, regardless of the person or whether he or she is a consumer or producer. However, in the case of goods that are thought by most in society to be "vices", such as tobacco or alcohol, the society may choose to attach a welfare weight to such consumption less than that for consumption of other goods. Indeed, the welfare weight attached to such "vices" could be zero or even negative.

Therefore, the calculations shown as Barnett et al.[27] have been further revised to allow for welfare weights on consumer surplus in cigarette consumption. Specifically, weights have been allowed that are either less than 1 (allowing positive consumer surplus from the consumption, albeit less than from other goods) or less than 0 (allowing for negative weights in the social welfare function from consumption of cigarettes). The alternative levels of consumer welfare weight attached to cigarette consumption are shown in Table 4. Barnett et al.[27] assume that the welfare weight for consumers is 1 ($\lambda = 1$). A lower weight has been shown ($\lambda = 0$), and negative weights, from -0.25 to -1.

It can be seen from Table 4 that the welfare change from a one cent tax increase (based on 1990 prices and consumption figures) for the United States ranges from an additional dead-weight loss of US$222.5 million (with consumer surplus weighted at 1), to a dead-weight welfare gain of over US$500 million (with a welfare weight" of -1 for consumer surplus from cigarettes). Such a tax increase would; at the same time, increase government revenues by over US$270 million, again in 1990 prices.

Further, based on these calculations it can be shown that a one cent Federal tax increase in 1990 would reduce cigarette consumption in the United States by 226 million packs per year, with corresponding improvements in health. This assumes that none of the tax increase would be earmarked for anti-smoking media and school advertising. The analysis included in preceding parts of this chapter indicates clearly that earmarking a significant part of such a tax increase to anti-smoking activities could further reduce cigarette consumption.

China

The 1996 National Survey of Smoking in China indicates that 66.9 percent of adult males and 4.2 percent of adult females in China were current smokers. The overall prevalence rate was 37.6 percent.[28] This implies that more than 300 million individuals in China are smokers,

---

[28] State Statistical Bureau (China), *1993 Statistical Yearbook of China* (China Publishing Ltd, 1993).

and approximately 30 percent of the world's smokers live in China.[29] China produced 82 billion packs of cigarettes and used 1.85 million hectares for tobacco production in 1992, which represents a 93 percent increase in production and a 25 percent increase in tobacco growing since 1981.

A recent study indicated that 12 percent of male deaths and 3 percent of female deaths in 1987 were due tobacco-attributable diseases.[30] The economic loss in medical care expenditures due to smoking was estimated at 6.9 billion yuan in 1989, while the value of lost productivity or premature death was about 20.13 billion yuan in 1989. The value of these resources could be used for many other productive services in the society.[31]

China has made major progress in reducing cigarette consumption by banning all advertising, increasing import duties on cigarettes, and banning cigarette smoking in some public places. However, China has not used cigarette tax as a tobacco control instrument. Cigarette tax revenue in China was 31.0 billion yuan in 1992, representing 9.4 percent of total government revenue, and clearly a major source of revenue.[32] Although the Ministry of Health is interested in seeing an increase in tobacco tax, the Ministry of Agriculture and the state-controlled tobacco industry have opposed the tax increase due to the potential negative impact on tobacco farmers' employment. Several major tobacco-producing provinces, such as Yunan, Guizhou, and part of Sichuan, are relatively poor. The government and the population in these provinces have relied upon tobacco as their main source of income for some time. Furthermore. the Ministry of Finance is not quite sure about the long-run tax revenue impact of a tax increase on cigarettes. It is only

---

[29] Tobacco International, "Chinese Smokers Pass the 300 Million Mark," *Tobacco International* (1993): 7.

[30] Liu BQ, Peto R, Chen Z, *et al.*, "Tobacco Hazards in China: Proportional Mortality Study of 1,000,000 Deaths," *British Medical Journal* (1992, in press).

[31] Jin S, "Smoking-Induced Health-Related Economic Costs in China," *Journal Biomedical and Environmental Sciences* 8 (1995): 342–349.

[32] Hu TW, "Cigarette Taxation in China: Lessons From International Experiences," *Tobacco Control* 6 (1997):136–140.

in recent months that, in response to public health opinions, the government has tentatively agreed to raise a minimal amount of additional tobacco tax in a few metropolitan areas. such as Shanghai, Tianjin, etc., as experiment sites for tobacco control.

To illustrate the possible impact on revenue of an increased excise tax on cigarette sales in China, 1992 data on price and sales figures are used. China has sold 32.65 million cases' of cigarettes (one case contains 2,500 packs), with an average retail price of 3,320 yuan per case.[28] A recent study[33] estimated that the price elasticity of demand for cigarettes in Sichuan province in China ranges from −0.65 to −0.80, which is somewhat higher than many other developed countries. It is assumed that −0.65 is the price elasticity of demand for the Chinese population. Given this information, and assuming the Chinese state cigarette industry imposes a 10 percent increase in price from 3,320 yuan to 3,652 yuan, additional tax will result in a 6.5 percent reduction in sales, from 32.65 million cases to 30.53 million cases. However, the total revenue will increase from 108.41 billion yuan to 111.5 billion yuan, an increase of 2.9 percent. Thus, given the inelastic demand for cigarettes, the total revenue will increase when the price is increased. Assuming the effective tax rate in 1992 was 37.9 percent,[32] to achieve a 10 percent increase in price, the effective tax rate would have to rise to 43.43 percent, an increase of 15 percent of the effective tax rate, and an increase of 26.5 percent in the amount of tax. Given these assumptions, the total tax revenue would rise by 18.2 percent, while total sales revenues would rise by 2.9 percent.

Following the same approach used in estimating consumer and producer surplus, and the "dead-weight" or welfare loss from a tax in the United States, a simplified version is applied to the Chinese example. It is assumed that the price elasticity of the supply of cigarettes in China ranges from 1.0 to 1.5. The estimated demand elasticity is −0.65,[33] with the 1992 cigarette consumption being 81,625

---

[33] Mao Z, *Demand for Cigarettes and Pricing Policy: A Time-Series Analysis* (in Chinese), Working paper, School of Public Health, Sichuan, Chengdu: China West China University of Medical Sciences, 1996.

Table 5: Impact of a One cent Increase in Cigarette Excise Tax in China

$\varepsilon^0 = -0.65, \varepsilon^0 = 1\lambda$	1	0	−0.25	−0.5	−1
Reduction in consumer surplus (λCS) (millions of 1992 yuan)	494.0	0	−123.5	−247.0	−494.0
Reduction in producer surplus	321.1	321.1	321.1	321.1	321.1
Reduction in welfare	815.1	321.1	197.6	74.1	−172.9
Increase in government revenue	813.8	813.8	813.8	813.8	813.8
Net dead-weight loss	1.2	−492.7	−616.2	−739.7	−986.7
$\varepsilon^0 = -0.65, \varepsilon^0 = 1.5\lambda$	1	0	−0.25	−0.5	−1
Reduction in consumer surplus (λCS)	568.5	0	−142.1	−284.2	−568.5
Reduction in producer surplus	246.4	246.4	246.4	246.4	246.4
Reduction in welfare	814.9	246.4	104.3	−37.9	−322.1
Increase in government revenue	813.5	813.5	813.5	813.5	813.5
Net dead-weight loss	1.4	−567.1	−709.2	−851.4	−1135.6

million packs. A linear demand and supply function is used to estimate the impact of a one cent increase on consumer surplus, producer surplus, government revenue, and net welfare loss. Table 5 is a summary of these calculated results, allowing for different weightings of consumer surplus in the social welfare function, from traditional weighting ($\lambda = 1$) to the maximum negative weights (sin or vice behavior, $\lambda = -1$).

It can be seen from Table 5 that the welfare change from a one cent tax increase (based on 1992 prices and consumption figures) for China ranges from an additional dead-weight loss of 1.2 million yuan, with consumer surplus weight at one, to a dead-weight welfare gain of almost 1 billion yuan, with welfare weight of −1 for consumer surplus from cigarettes. Such a tax increase would, at the same time, increase government revenues by over 800 million yuan. Therefore, these results indicate that even if smoking is not considered a negative behaviour ($\lambda = 1$), the dead-weight loss due to tax increase is very small (1.2 to 1.4 million yuan) as compared to the gain in government revenue (813.5 million yuan). Furthermore, when a reduction in smoking is considered a societal gain, then the dead-weight loss becomes society gain with a magnitude ranging from 0.5 billion yuan to over I billion yuan.

If the tax is not earmarked, the increase in revenue could be appropriated as general government revenue. For example, one informal recommendation from the State Economic Council regarding the pending increase in cigarette tax among experimental sites is to subsidize deficit-ridden state enterprises. However, from the viewpoint of public health and the benefit principle of earmarked taxation, although there is no change of total dead-weight loss or gain, .some of the additional tax revenue could be allocated to:

- health promotion and disease prevention activities, such as anti-smoking media campaigns and community education;
- health care insurance premiums for rural and low-income households; and
- subsidies for tobacco farmers and tobacco industry for their loss of revenue for possible transition and technology transfers from tobacco production to other productions such as tea, coffee, horticulture, and other agricultural products.

The first two allocations will help to reduce consumer surplus and the third type of allocation will reduce producer surplus and further enhance the cause of tobacco control.

CONCLUSION: LESSONS LEARNED

Cigarette smoking is harmful both to the health of the smoker and the health of those who are exposed to secondary smoke, causing premature death through tobacco-related illness. Smoking has also increased health care costs and resulted in a loss of productivity due to early death and illness. Because, as has been shown, consumers are less sensitive to changes in the price of cigarettes compared to other goods, taxes could be a powerful tool to raise revenue. In other words, both from an efficiency and equity point of view, it is important to use cigarette tax as a fiscal instrument, not only for revenue purposes, but also for tobacco control. Further, it would be useful to designate the earmarked tax revenues for health education and antismoking media campaigns to complement the goal of tobacco control.

Questions remain about (1) what amount of tax should be levied on cigarettes, and (2) how that tax revenue should be used. To determine the appropriate amount of tax on cigarettes, one would not only need to examine the price and income elasticities of demand for cigarettes, but also the social consequences of taxation. Any tax increase would effect a loss of consumer surplus (the difference between the value of cigarettes to smokers and the amount that they pay for it), producer surplus (the loss in revenue to producers less the costs of production and distribution), and the net welfare costs (the loss in consumer surplus less the revenue generated from the tax). This chapter has shown examples from the United States and China concerning the possible impact of an increase in cigarette tax. Given the magnitude of the negative externalities associated with cigarette smoking, the appropriate magnitude of loss of consumer surplus may not be negative. That is, reducing smoking will improve the health of smokers and nonsmokers. Thus, depending on the relative weight assigned to consumer surplus versus producer surplus, it seems that raising cigarette tax in the United States and China would be especially appropriate, since the relative cigarette tax rate in these two countries is much lower than many other countries in the world. The increase in tax revenue is always smaller than the loss of consumer surplus. When the loss of consumer surplus is considered a positive gain, there is more reason to raise cigarette tax. The net welfare costs of the tax would also be offset by the positive gain of consumer surplus. Conceptually, the amount of tax on cigarettes should be set such that total tax revenue extracted from smokers would be equal to total social costs generated by smokers.

The question as to how cigarette tax revenue should be allocated is the subject of this chapter. Although an earmarked tax is not always an ideal tax-expenditure fiscal instrument (since it introduces rigidities and does not permit proper allocation criteria of general revenue among competing uses) evidence and experience have shown that the use of tobacco tax for health promotion and disease prevention may be quite appropriate, in line with the benefit taxation principle, consistent with the principle that inducing better health behavior and health status contribute to better expenditure decisions.

One area that previous studies have not discussed is the use of earmarked tobacco tax revenue to compensate producers' surplus loss. In other words, if a portion of the tax revenue can be allocated to tobacco farmers and tobacco manufacturing industries to transfer productivity to alternative cash crops and industries, the loss of producer surplus can be reduced. At the same time, the future economy can rely less upon tobacco products. This is especially true for developing countries where tobacco products are a major source of income and tax revenue.

Several lessons may be learned from the review of international experiences with cigarette taxation and the use of earmarked tax:

1. A tobacco tax is an effective and efficient instrument in raising government revenue, because there is a relatively price-inelastic demand for cigarettes.
2. Tobacco tax policy should be linked to tobacco use. Government policymakers should consider using tobacco tax as an intervention In accomplishing the goals of health promotion and disease prevention.
3. When earmarked tobacco taxes are used for anti-smoking campaigns and other health promotion or health education activities, tobacco control is further enhanced. These additional measures have been more effective than using a tax alone.
4. Although any tax increase will increase the welfare cost to society and reduce consumer and producer surplus, the reduction of external costs of smoking will offset the loss of consumer surplus and welfare costs to society. In addition, if a portion of the earmarked tax can be allocated for producers to transfer production

away from the tobacco sector, the loss of producers' surplus will also be minimized. The use of portions of earmarked tax revenue for health care and health insurance premiums will also reduce the magnitude of the loss of consumer surplus.

Tobacco tax is a major instrument of health policy as well as of fiscal policy. Each country varies in terms of its demand, production, and tax treatment of tobacco products. Many countries around the world have taken the initiative to control tobacco use, but may not have earmarked tax, or used tobacco tax specifically as a policy instrument. More information and study are needed to consider the feasibility of imposing additional taxes on tobacco and earmarking these revenues for various purposes. This is a critical time for researchers and policy-makers to contemplate this important issue.

ACKNOWLEDGMENTS

This work was supported by the US Department of Human Development, the World Bank's Research Support Board (Grant No. 681–95), and the Robert Wood Johnson Foundation's Addictive Substances Program. The opinions expressed are those of the authors, and not of the US Department of Human Development, the World Bank or its member countries, or the Robert Wood Johnson Foundation.

Section V

Policy Directions

Chapter 15

China at the Crossroads: The Economics of Tobacco and Health*

Teh-wei Hu, Zhengzhong Mao, Michael Ong, Elisa Tong, Ming Tao, Hesheng Jiang, Katherine Hammond, Kirk R Smith, Joy de Beyer and Ayda Yurekli

China consumes and produces more cigarettes than any other country. An estimated more than 4 million Chinese households rely on tobacco for their livelihood, either as tobacco farmers, cigarette industry employees, or cigarette retailers.[1] China's state-owned tobacco monopoly company produces over 1.7 trillion cigarettes annually, generating almost US$2 billion profit and taxes in 2003, 7.4 percent of central government total revenue.[1]

---

*This chapter originally appeared as Hu TW, Mao Z, Ong M, Tong E, Tao M, Jiang H, Hammond K, Smith K, de Beyer J, Yurekli A, *Tobacco Control* 15 (2006): 37–41. Copyright © 2006 by *British Medical Journal*. All rights reserved. Reprinted with permission from *Tobacco Control* and *British Medical Journal*.

[1] Liu T and Xiong B, *Tobacco Economy and Tobacco Control* (in Chinese) (Beijing: Economic Science Press, 2004).

China has over 350 million smokers and about 460 million passive smokers.[2,3] The negative health impact of smoking has contributed to about one million premature deaths.[4] If this pattern of smoking continues, premature deaths attributable to smoking can be expected to exceed two million deaths annually by 2020.[5] Therefore, the Chinese government has a policy conflict between the economic interests of the tobacco industry and the health concerns of its people.

In this chapter, tobacco farming in China first reviewed and then an analysis of the country's tobacco industry, is presented. The potential impact of a cigarette tax on government revenue is also analyzed and concluded with a discussion of opportunities and challenges related to tobacco control in China. These findings will provide policy-makers with an economic assessment of using a tobacco tax as one of their tobacco control options.

METHODS AND DATA SOURCES

Two separate surveys have been conducted by this project: 1,003 farm households in Sichuan and Guizhou provinces were interviewed during 2002, and 586 farm households were interviewed in Yunnan province in 2004. The survey instruments collected information about the cost of producing each crop and the revenue received from each crop so that economic returns could be compared by crop. Most farmers do not have accounting records. To help farmers recall their costs and revenues, the survey developed a resource-accounting framework that asked farmers specific questions about each type of input (seeds, fertilizer, land use, days worked, etc.), amount of inputs, and cost per unit of inputs. Costs included rent,

---

[2] Yang G, "The Epidemiologic Investigation of the Smoking Behavior Among Chinese Population in 2002," *Chinese Smoking and Health* 62 (2004): 7–18.

[3] Zhu J, "To Coordinate the Conflict Between Tobacco Control and Tobacco Production in China," *Periscope* 46 (1996): 12–13.

[4] Liu BQ, Peto R, Chen AM, *et al.*, "Emerging Tobacco Hazards in China: 1. Retrospective Proportional Morality Study of One Million Deaths," *British Medical Journal* 317 (1998): 411–422.

[5] Peto R and Lopez AD, "Future World Wide Health Effects of Current Smoking Patterns," *Critical Issues in Global Health*, Chapter 18 (2001), 155.

expenditures, hired labor (full-time or part-time expenditures), cost of curing tobacco, and market transportation costs. Detailed questions were asked about the quantity and type of crop that each household sold to the market (or government) and the average unit price it received. Based on these collected interview data, a cost accounting and revenue analysis was carried out to analyze the rate of return from each crop including grain, vegetable oil, bean, fruit, and tobacco leaf.

Aggregate national statistics reported by the Chinese National Tobacco Company and the Chinese National Development Research Center are used to describe and analyze the Chinese tobacco industry's structural profit and tax collected from cigarette sales, as well as the impact of China's membership in the World Trade Organization (WTO) on foreign cigarette products in the Chinese market.

Addressing the issues of the impact of taxation on cigarette consumption and on government revenue and tobacco leaf production requires an analysis of the relationship between price and consumption of cigarettes. This relationship is measured by price elasticity which is the percentage change in consumption in response to a percentage change in price.

Price elasticities are obtained statistically through the estimation of a demand function. A basic demand function usually includes the price of the item (cigarette), personal disposable income, and a time trend to reflect changes in consumer tastes and preferences.

To analyze the impact of additional tax on cigarettes, a statistical linear regression model was used to estimate the quantity and price relativity, with data from the 2000 national survey of smoking of 16,000 adult individuals.

In addition, about 3,400 urban and rural households from 36 townships/districts in southwest China were interviewed in 2002. These data were used to analyze differences in smoking behavior and smoking expenditures among low- and high-income households in China and the impact of smoking on the standards of living of low-income households in China.[6] Cross-tabulations and regression

---

[6] Hu TW, Mao Z, Liu Y et al., "Smoking, Standard of Living, and Poverty in China," *Tobacco Control* 14 (2005): 247–250.

analysis were used to examine the differences in major household expenditures, including food, housing, clothing, and education between households with smokers and those without smokers.

ANALYSES AND DISCUSSION

Tobacco Farming: Costs and Return

China is the largest grower of tobacco leaf in the world. In 2000, China produced 2.66 million tons of tobacco leaf, about one-third of the world's production.[7] To control the supply of tobacco leaf, a tobacco leaf production quota is determined by the State Tobacco Monopoly Administration (STMA). The Chinese Ministry of Agriculture does not have jurisdiction over the production, pricing, or marketing of tobacco leaf.

While the Chinese government is well aware of the negative health effects of smoking and is willing to consider tobacco control options, such as banning cigarette advertisements, teen smoking, and smoking in public places, the government has yet to use a tobacco tax to control tobacco smoking. The government is reluctant to use a tax because it fears that increasing the tobacco tax would reduce the livelihood of tobacco farmers and threaten the economic base of the cigarette industry. Recently, the government produced a publication documenting the importance of the tobacco economy in China and the negative health impact of cigarette smoking.[1] However, there has been no economic analysis of tobacco farming or the economic prospects of the Chinese cigarette industry in China.

The China National Tobacco Company (CNTC), a monopoly organization under the STMA, controls all Chinese tobacco leaf production and cigarette marketing. Therefore, any discussion of tobacco control in China requires a good understanding of the impact of tobacco leaf production on the country's overall agricultural economy and on government revenue, as well as the government's role in tobacco production.

---

[7] Mackay J and Eriksen M, *The Tobacco Atlas* (Geneva: World Health Organization, 2002), 94–95.

The contribution of tobacco leaf to the Chinese agricultural provincial economy is about 1–2 percent, except in the Yunnan, Guizhou, and Sichuan provinces.[8] Yunnan alone collected 62 percent of all tax revenue from tobacco leaf production in 2003. Nationally, the overall contribution of tobacco leaf to the Chinese agricultural economy is less than 1 percent. However, tobacco leaf is also a major source of local government tax revenue. In 2005, China removed all tax on agricultural products, except for tobacco leaf. Keeping a tax on tobacco leaf does not mean that the government discourages its production since leaf production is set by a government quota; rather, the tax is mainly for local government revenue. Also, tobacco leaf is the main input allowing the cigarette industry to generate high profit and tax revenue. Therefore, the Chinese government has played an important role in the production of tobacco leaf.

In spite of the alleged importance of tobacco leaf production to farmers, very little empirical research exists on farmers' costs and return for producing tobacco leaf. This project has carried out two surveys on the economic return on tobacco leaf production compared to other crops planted by tobacco farmers.[9,10]

Table 1 provides a summary of total costs and revenue for each crop by farm size from 1003 farming households in Sichuan and Guizhou provinces. Results indicate that citrus is a specialty crop with high market value in these two provinces. Fruits produced the highest revenue, followed by tobacco. While tobacco was the second highest revenue producer, its revenue was equal to only about two-thirds of fruit revenue for small farms, half of fruit revenue for medium farms, and one-third of fruit revenue for large farms. However, comparing the ratio between revenue and costs of each crop, grain production and tobacco had lower returns than vegetable oil, beans, or fruit. These ratios imply that for every yuan

---

[8] China National Statistics Bureau, *China Statistical Yearbook* (Beijing: China Statistics Press, 2000, 2004).

[9] Hu TW, Mao Z and Yurekli A, "Tobacco Farmers in China: Their Economic Status and Alternative Options," Report submitted to World Bank (2002).

[10] Jiang H, Mao Z and Hu TW, "An Analysis of Costs and Revenue of Tobacco Leaf Production," *Rural Economy* (in Chinese) 6 (2004): 46–48.

Table 1: Total Costs and Revenue by Major Crops by Size of Form, in Sichuan and Guizhou Counties, 2002

	Small (<0.5 hectare) (7.5 mou) (n = 302)	Medium (0.5–1.0 hectare) (7.5–1.5 mou) (n = 361)	Large (>1.0 hectare) (>15 mou) (n = 340)	Total Sample (n = 1003)
Total cost (yuan)				
Grain	372	628	926	652
Tobacco	900	1,244	1,963	1,113
Beans	43	28	95	44
Vegetable oil	55	79	173	122
Fruit	666	2,196	4,510	2,937
Total revenue (yuan)				
Grain	913	1,455	2,436	1,624
Tobacco	2,218	3,216	5,509	3,741
Beans	131	165	277	189
Vegetable oil	170	319	637	452
Fruit	3,146	7,487	16,859	10,763
Revenue minus cost				
Grain	541	827	1,510	972
Tobacco	1,228	1,882	3,546	2,328
Beans	88	137	182	145
Vegetable oil	115	240	464	330
Fruit	2,480	5,291	12,349	7,826
Revenue/cost ratio				
Grain	2.5	2.3	2.6	2.5
Tobacco	2.4	2.6	2.8	2.6
Beans	3	5.9	2.9	4.3
Vegetable oil	3.1	4	3.7	3.7
Fruit	4.7	3.4	3.7	3.7

[a] 1 mou = hectare/15.

farmers spent, they received on average 3.7 yuan (US$0.45) for fruit. Small farmers benefited even more, receiving 4.7 yuan (US$0.57) per yuan spent for fruit. On the other hand, for every yuan farmers spent on tobacco production, they received only 2.4–2.8 yuan (US$0.29–0.34), a smaller return than that from other crops, such as beans or vegetable oil. Obviously, some farmers do not plant fruit for a variety of reasons: different land endowments, climates, marketing, assurance of government purchase of tobacco leaf, and government tobacco quotas assigned to some farmers.

Similarly, results of the 2004 survey in Yunnan province indicated that tobacco leaf had the lowest revenue-to-cost ratio per mou (a standard unit of land measurement in China, equivalent to 1/15 of a hectare), 0.99.[10] The highest revenue-to-cost ratio was for mulberry and silkworm, 4.00; followed by fruit, 2.00; rice and wheat, 1.99; and vegetable oil, 1.70.

The finding that tobacco may not always produce the best economic return is not unique to China.[11] A study from India indicated the following revenue-to-cost ratios: 4.01 for safflower, 1.33 for mustard, and 1.2 for flue-cured tobacco leaf.[12] Tobacco farming is often labor-intensive and requires equipment to cure the leaf, which reduces the net return to land. Therefore, alternative crops sometimes yield greater revenue-to-cost ratios than tobacco leaf.

As indicated by STMA, the relatively low return from tobacco leaf production could be due to an oversupply of tobacco leaf on the market, which could be reflected by the government's relatively low purchase price.[13] The government does not have a price subsidy policy for tobacco leaf. In fact, the overall farm product price index in China did not increase during the last decade although the general consumer price index increased over the same time period.[14] If production of tobacco leaf does not provide a better economic return than other crops, why do farmers continue to plant

---

[11] Kweyuh PHM, "Does Tobacco Growing Pay? The Case of Kenya," in *The Economics of Tobacco Control: Towards an Optimal Policy Mix,* eds. Abedian I, van der Merwe R, Wilkins N and Jha P (1998), 245–250.

[12] Chari MS, Kameswara, Rao BV, "Role of Tobacco in the National Economy: Past and Present," in *Control of Tobacco-Related Cancers and Other Diseases: International Symposium 1990,* eds. Gupta PC, Hammer JE and Murti PR (Bombay: Oxford University Press, 1992).

[13] Chen Y, "From monopoly to consolidation," *China International Business,* Beijing, China, 2002, 26–28.

[14] China National Statistics Bureau, *China Agricultural Yearbook 1990–2002,* (Beijing: China Statistics Press, 2003).

it? One reason is that local government collects local tax revenues from tobacco leaf by assigning a quota to farmers to produce tobacco leaf for revenue. Second, the ongoing agreement with STMA assures farmers of revenue from tobacco leaf without having to worry about storage or marketing problems. Under the agreement, STMA provides technical assistance and guaranteed purchase. Third, the soil and weather in China are ideal for tobacco plantations. Finally, some farmers may not be aware of the alternative crop options.

This is a prime time for the Chinese government to encourage less profitable tobacco farmers to produce other crops. The Chinese Ministry of Agriculture should collaborate with the STMA to provide technical assistance and economic incentives to aid the transition from tobacco leaf production to other crops. The survey results of this study indicate that tobacco leaf production is not a way for farmers to escape poverty or become wealthier.

Cigarette Industry: Monopoly and WTO

CNTC, a government-run monopoly company, is the world's largest tobacco company, producing 1,722 billion cigarettes in 2002 and generating 140 billion yuan (US$17 billion), or about 7.4 percent of government revenue.[1] Since CNTC is a government-owned monopoly company, its contribution to the central government includes both profit and tax revenue. As shown in Table 2, while the nominal amount of tax and profit revenue from tobacco has been increasing over time, the percentage of total government revenue has decreased from a high of 11.2 percent in 1996 to 7.38 percent in 2003; the lowest share was 7.02 percent in 2001. The decline in the relative tax/profit contribution to the central government is due to recent rapid Chinese economic development in the automobile, petroleum, textile, and high tech industries.

The government levies two taxes on tobacco producers: a producer value-added tax, about 17 percent of the producer price, and a consumption tax, an additional 50 percent of the wholesale price. From the producers' point of view, the tax paid to the government is 67 percent of the producer price, but the effective tax rate is 38 percent if the amount of tax paid by the producer is compared to the

Table 2: Tobacco Tax and Profit Contribution to Chinese Central Government Revenue.

Year	Tax and Profit Contribution (in billion yuan)	Total Government Revenue (in billion yuan)	Percentage of Total Revenue
1996	83	74.08	11.2
1997	90	865.1	10.4
1998	95	987.6	9.62
1999	99	1,144.40	8.64
2000	105	1,339.50	7.84
2001	115	1,638.60	7.02
2002	140	1,893.60	7.41
2003	160	2,168.10	7.38

Source: Liu T and Xiang B *Tobacco Economy and Tobacco Control* (in Chinese) (Beijing, China Economic Science press, 2004), 169.
8.2 yuan = US$1.

retail price of cigarettes.[15] To promote their own local product, provincial tobacco companies sometimes set trade barriers for out-of-province cigarettes. The most profitable companies are in Yunnan, Shanghai, and Henan provinces, where companies have invested in cigarette manufacturing. However, unprofitable companies still exist because the local government is willing to subsidize them for the sake of employment and tax revenue.

The government's concern over the employment of tobacco industry workers and farmers has been a barrier to enacting tobacco control. CNTC employs more than half a million people, about 0.4 percent of total employment in the economy. Approximately half a million individuals are employed in the tobacco manufacturing industry (excluding farmers), which translates to 0.51 percent of total employment in the manufacturing industry.

China entered the WTO in 2001. As a member, China had to agree to (1) reduce the tobacco leaf import tariff, (2) reduce the cigarette tariff, (3) eliminate the export rebate for flue-cured tobacco

---

[15] Hu TW and Mao Z, "Effects of Cigarette Tax on Cigarette Consumption and the Chinese Economy," *Tobacco Control* 11 (2002): 105–108.

leaf and cigarettes, and (4) eliminate the export bounty, a reward for exporting cigarettes. All these agreements have made foreign cigarettes more competitive in the Chinese market and China's tobacco leaf less competitive in the world market.

Even with the WTO removing China's long-standing restrictions on tobacco imports and the numerous domestic companies within the state monopoly, the largest Chinese tobacco company cannot yet directly compete with the transnational tobacco companies. From 1995–2000, total official cigarette imports and exports comprised only 0.8 percent of the domestic market. By early 2000, foreign imported products represented about 3 percent of the Chinese market. CNTC anticipates that before the end of the decade, foreign products may reach 8–10 percent of the Chinese tobacco market.[16]

The WTO's import tariff reductions on tobacco leaf and cigarettes are increasing the competitiveness of foreign tobacco products. The tariff on tobacco leaf has gradually been reduced from 64 percent in 1999 to 25 percent in 2003 to 10 percent in 2004.[16] This tariff reduction has made foreign tobacco leaf as competitive as Chinese domestic tobacco leaf, and China's tobacco farmers already face a tobacco leaf surplus. The tariff on cigarette products dropped from 49 percent in 2001 to 25 percent in 2003. China's cigarette imports have increased by 37 percent, from 68.51 million packs in 2002 to 93.92 million packs in 2003. Before 2003, foreign brands, such as Marlboro or 555, cost about 20 yuan (US$2.50) per pack. The current market price is now 12 yuan (US$1.50) per pack, similar to popular domestic brands, such as "Hong-Ta-Shan", which costs about 10 yuan. As the Chinese economy is growing and personal incomes are rising, the demand for foreign brands is increasing, particularly among urban young adult male and female smokers. Special retail permits for foreign tobacco products used to be issued by CNTC to control foreign cigarette retail sales. Since 2003, with the elimination of this special retail permit under the WTO agreement,

---

[16] Tao M, "Impact of WTO on China Tobacco Import and Export," *Research on Productivity* (in Chinese) 10 (2004): 129–131.

any retailer with a CNTC general retail permit to sell domestic cigarettes can sell foreign cigarettes.

Facing these economic challenges, CNTC has tried to reduce the number of domestic cigarette brands and close inefficient and small cigarette factories. The number of brands dropped drastically from 1,049 brands in 2001 to 423 in December 2004. The number of regional companies decreased from 185 in 2001 to 57 in December 2004. Whereas provincial governments previously could have a local regional monopoly, CNTC has forced regional companies to compete against each other. Through mergers and integration, CNTC hopes to achieve economic efficiency in cigarette production, pricing, and marketing. In spite of China's entry into the WTO, the central government has not permitted foreign companies to either establish factories or have joint ventures with local cigarette companies.

Product improvement has been a priority in anticipation of competing with foreign brands. Chinese cigarettes used to have a high tar content, but beginning in July 2004, China prohibited the sale of cigarettes with more than 15 mg. Manufacturers are now required to use new technology to reduce the tar content to meet the international standard of 11.2 mg. Other "quality improvements" include importing tobacco leaves, for example, from Zimbabwe with its high quality leaf, and changing the packaging of cigarette products, the paper quality, and printing.

As China's economy changes, tobacco control efforts may benefit from the decline in the tobacco industry's relative contribution to employment or government tax revenue. The industrial manufacturing sector (for example, textiles, electronics, and automobile products) is developing rapidly. The value of Chinese cigarette production increased from 8 billion yuan (about US$1 billion) in 1981 to 130 billion yuan (US$15.8 billion) in 1997 to 169 billion yuan (US$20.6 billion) in 2002; however, its relative share of the total value of national industrial production fell from 1.57 percent in 1980 to 1.14 percent by 1997 to less than 1 percent in 2002. With these reductions in the government's dependence on the tobacco economy and tobacco tax revenue, along with the reduction in demand for domestic cigarette leaf, the importance of the tobacco sector in China is declining.

Understanding these changing economic priorities and the tobacco industry situation within China can help identify new solutions for tobacco control. The impact of additional tobacco taxes will have smaller negative effects on China's tobacco industry as the number of regional tobacco companies is reduced. Instead, the central government could remove its special tobacco leaf tax, as demand for domestic cigarette leaf is reduced, and instead impose an additional cigarette product tax. The central government and local governments could share the revenue income, resolving the concern over replacing lost government revenue. At the same time, this strategy would free tobacco farmers to plant any product they desire and help resolve the domestic tobacco leaf surplus problem resulting from increased imports of higher quality foreign leaf.

Cigarette Consumption and Taxation

Using data from the 1990s, several price elasticities were estimated from Chinese aggregate data and cross-sectional household data; they ranged from −0.35 short-run elasticity to −0.66 long-run elasticity. Using national time series data from 1990–2002 on per capita cigarette consumption and cigarette price, the estimated price elasticity is −0.144.[17] Using the 2000 survey of 16,000 individuals, price elasticity was found to be −0.154.[18] Both of these more recent price elasticities are lower than using 1990s data. The household consumption survey reveals that each household on average spent 25–125 yuan per month on cigarettes — 5–7 percent of household expenditures. With a price elasticity of −0.15 and a 10 percent price increase, cigarette consumption would be reduced by 1.5 percent, equivalent to 1.02 packs per capita or a total of 1,017 million packs.

The reduction in consumption of 1,017 million packs would result in a reduction in use of 16,900 metric tons of tobacco leaf,

---

[17] Mao Z, Hu TW and Yang GH, "Price Elasticities and Impact of Tobacco Tax Among Various Income Groups (in Chinese)," *Chinese Journal of Evidence-Based Medicine* 5 (2005): 291–295.

[18] Mao Z, Hu TW, Yang GH, "New Estimate of the Demand for Cigarettes in China" (in Chinese), *Chinese Journal of Health Economics* 24, no. 5 (2004): 45–47.

according to the cigarette/tobacco leaf production technical ratio.[19] This reduction of 16,900 metric tons is very insignificant compared to national production of 2.66 million metric tons, especially given the surplus of tobacco leaf in China.

Cross-sectional data can be used to compare income groups. The data show that lower income groups are more responsive to price. The price elasticity for the poor was −0.59, for low income, −0.23, for middle–high income, −0.02, and the high-income group had a positive price elasticity of 0.25. The 2005 study showed that a tax increase of 10 percent would increase the net tax revenue by 30 billion yuan (US$3.6 billion).[17] Since the low-income group has a higher price elasticity (in absolute value) and will cut their consumption more when prices increase, a tax increase on cigarettes is not regressive for low-income smokers.

The 3,400 urban and rural household surveys showed that lower income households with smokers paid less per pack and smoked fewer cigarettes than higher income households with smokers.[6] Poor urban households spent an average of 6.6 percent of their total expenditures on cigarettes; poor rural households spent 11.3 percent of their total expenditures on cigarettes.

As noted, China currently levies a fixed 67 percent tax at the producer level, equivalent to a 38 percent tax at the retail level, a relatively low rate compared to cigarette tax rates around the world, the median of which is about 60 percent.[7] Analysis of these survey data suggests that raising cigarette tax rates in China would reduce consumption more among low-income households than among high-income households, increasing available household funds for other major household items, such as food, housing, clothing, and education.[20] Furthermore, an *ad valorem* (a percentage of the price) tax instead of a specific (a fixed amount per pack) tax would lower the financial burden of a higher cigarette tax on low-income

---

[19] Wang S and Li B, "Analysis and Estimate of the Situation of China's Tobacco Sector" (in Chinese and English), *Sino-World Tobacco 2000* 47 (1997–2000): 6–11.

[20] Wang H, Sindlar J and Busch S, "The Impact of Tobacco Expenditure on Household Consumption Patterns in China," *Social Sciences Medicine* 62 (2006): 1414–1426.

households (who tend to smoke cheaper cigarettes), and in this respect would be "pro-poor".

CONCLUSION

Tobacco control in China is facing an economic and public health crossroads. China is the world's largest tobacco consumer and producer and has a state-owned tobacco monopoly. However, tobacco leaf's contribution to the agricultural economy is declining. The cigarette industry's contribution to government tax revenue is also declining. As a result of China's entry into the WTO in 2001, transnational tobacco companies are expected to gain increased market access and compete with China's tobacco monopoly. China recently ratified the World Health Organization's Framework Convention on Tobacco Control (FCTC). The FCTC will bring new incentives for the Chinese government to implement tobacco control provisions: price and non-price options. The Chinese government's competing priorities between its tobacco industry interests and protecting its population's health may be shifting toward better public health. It is hoped that levying an additional tax as a tobacco control policy will be a message to Chinese smokers.

Despite the challenges discussed, numerous opportunities exist to implement measures to reduce tobacco demand. China's experience in planning and implementing tobacco control activities in seven major cities under the World Bank "Health VII Project" could be drawn on to develop and enforce effective local tobacco control regulations, train for and expand FCTC surveillance programs nationally and locally, and help mobilize private sector organizations. Secondhand smoking should receive emphasis as a crucial component of tobacco control; a first step toward realizing this goal can be achieved through smoke-free workplace programs for health professionals. Spreading knowledge is the next step toward reducing tobacco demand in China.

A Chinese government official statement issued upon their ratification of the FCTC (Chinese National Development and Reform

Commission, State Council announced on October 11, 2005), indicated that the government will first implement non-price tobacco control options, such as banning smoking in public places, refusing to sell cigarettes to minors, and banning smoking advertisements. Many potential future projects could be conducted to monitor these programs' influence and effects — for example, examining second-hand smoke exposure in public places, surveying smoke-free regulation enforcement and government official smoking behavior, and evaluating the effects of FCTC-related activities.

Tobacco control in China is crucial to global efforts to reduce the burden of tobacco-related illnesses. China has not only the largest number of active and passive smokers in the world, but also the largest amount of tobacco production. Hence, reductions in Chinese tobacco use will significantly decrease the global burden of tobacco-related illnesses and deaths. In addition, studies of tobacco control in China will be of great importance to other developing countries because China shares many of the social and economic challenges facing other developing nations.

ACKNOWLEDGMENTS

This study is funded by the Fogarty International Center, National Institutes of Health, Bethesda, Maryland, USA, grant No. R01TW05938. The authors are grateful for the comments and suggestions provided by Dr Judith Mackay, Dr Ruth Malone, and two anonymous referees of the journal, *Tobacco Control*.

Index

Ad valorem Tax   149, 150, 152, 170, 171, 262
Ad valorem cigarette excise tax   156
Adults' demand for cigarettes   134
Adverse health effects   25, 106, 120, 260
Aggregated time-series data   132, 134, 136
Arizona   265, 285, 287–289
Average expenditure   110–112

Behavioral Risk Factor Survey   50
2002 Behavior Risk Factors Survey   15, 16
Beijing Tobacco Company   224
Beijing's Outdoor Advertising Regulations   38
Brand of cigarettes   139
Brazil   2, 193, 205, 267, 268, 274
Breast cancer   101, 103
British American Tobacco Company (BAT)   8, 192, 206, 218, 220, 221, 231, 237–240
Bronchitis   123
Burden of disease (See "Disease burden")   v, 5, 41, 83, 85, 87, 88, 91–95, 100–103, 106

California   ix–xi, xvii–xx, 60, 95, 108, 137, 263–265, 273, 276, 280–290
California Tobacco Tax and Health Promotion Act   263, 280

Cancer   5, 15, 25, 29, 41, 44, 48, 51, 54, 69–71, 76, 85–90, 92–101, 103, 107, 114–118, 120, 159, 174, 204, 253, 259, 267, 311
Capacity building   2, 47
Cardiovascular disease   89, 107, 114–118, 159, 211, 253, 259
China Association of Smoking and Health   4, 130
China Health and Nutrition Survey   134
China National Tobacco Company (CNTC)   7, 8, 42, 43, 190–195, 199, 200, 207, 213–216, 219–223, 226, 228, 229, 232–234, 239, 249, 308, 312–315
China Statistical Yearbook   115, 118, 119, 125, 190, 196, 212, 249, 266, 309
China's National Bureau of Statistics   122
Chinese Academies of Preventive Medicine and Medical Sciences   36
Chinese Association on Smoking and Health   36
Chinese Association on Tobacco Control   36, 130
Chinese Center for Disease Control and Prevention   36, 60, 61, 139
China's National Development and Reform Commission   46

322 Index

Chinese National Development Research Center 307
Cigarette consumption ix, xiv, 1, 6, 8, 40, 42, 54, 76, 80, 105, 118, 131–136, 138, 143, 146, 149–154, 156, 160, 161, 163, 165, 166, 168–170, 177, 178, 190, 217, 247–257, 260–266, 268, 269, 273–275, 278, 280–287, 290, 295–297, 307, 313, 316
Cigarette expenditures 6, 131, 155, 160, 164–167
Cigarette price elasticities 133
Cigarette price per pack 250
Cigarette retail price 142, 143, 151
Cigarette tax xiv, 4, 6, 8, 9, 54, 80, 131–135, 149–154, 156, 157, 160, 169, 171, 190, 209, 217, 242, 245, 247–249, 251, 254, 256–259, 261–266, 268, 271–275, 278, 281–283, 285, 287–294, 296, 299–301, 306, 313, 317
Cigarettes smoked per month 138
Conditional cigarette demand equation 137
Consolidation 8, 204, 223, 226, 311
Consumer surplus 291, 294, 295, 298–302
COPD 89, 90
Counterfeiting 237, 241
Crop substitution 7, 28, 208
Cross-sectional 27, 101, 133, 135, 136, 139, 140, 250, 316, 317
Current smokers 16, 18, 22–24, 31, 57, 61, 64–66, 68–71, 74, 77, 105, 109, 113, 120, 129, 137–139, 141–143, 146, 150, 151, 154, 155, 176, 247, 273, 295

Disability Adjusted Life Years (DALY) 3, 5, 87, 88, 90–92, 95–99, 103

Days lost from work 109, 112, 123
Dead-weight loss 291, 294, 295, 298, 299
Demand for cigarettes xiv, 4, 6, 55, 127, 129, 133, 134, 136–138, 154, 155, 169, 250, 256, 264, 265, 271, 272, 282–284, 289, 290, 293, 297, 300, 301, 316
Developing countries x, 3, 80, 133, 149, 160, 161, 163, 173, 174, 185, 208, 301, 319
Direct costs 5, 41, 110, 120–122, 185
Disease burden 41, 83, 85, 87, 88, 91, 93–95, 101–103
Disease-specific medical costs 106
Disproportionate burden of cigarette tax 132
Disproportionate Tax Burden 135, 152, 154, 157
Diversification 28, 223, 230, 235
Domestic brands 160, 222, 236, 314

Earmarked tax 9, 269, 277–279, 285, 291, 292, 299–302
Earmarked tobacco tax 277, 279–281, 284, 289, 292, 301
Economic burden of smoking, economic costs of smoking 3, 41, 105–108, 118, 119, 121–124, 129, 130, 156, 157, 160, 270
Economic losses 6, 118
Effectiveness of cigarette taxation 132
Efficiency 223, 230, 255, 288–291, 300, 315
Elasticity of participation (or quitting) 256
Elasticity of quantity demanded 256
Employment-population ratio 112
Environmental tobacco smoke 25, 94, 95, 100, 123, 211, 284–286
Epidemiological approach 123
Equity 176, 232, 289–291, 300

Ever-smokers   22–24, 105, 113, 122, 129
Ever-smoking rates   17, 31, 105, 113, 129
Excess expenditures   124
Excise tax   131, 133, 136, 139, 154, 156, 262–265, 271–273, 286, 290, 293, 297, 298
Exports   205, 216, 221, 222, 229, 232, 236, 239, 240, 314

Food and Agriculture Organization   209
Former smokers   23, 61, 64, 65, 74, 75, 109, 113, 120, 176, 179, 180
Framework Convention on Tobacco Control (FCTC)   v, vi, x, 3, 4, 9, 28, 34, 43–48, 52, 53, 80, 130, 132, 190, 174, 207, 243, 244, 318, 319

Gallagher Tobacco Company   231
General Agreement on Tariffs and Trade (GATT)   219
Global Youth Tobacco Survey   19
Golden Deer   231
Government revenue   1, 8, 35, 42, 54, 131, 135, 148–150, 157, 190, 191, 207, 242, 243, 248, 249, 257, 258, 261, 266, 268, 270, 271, 276, 278, 279, 294–296, 298, 299, 301, 306–309, 312, 313, 316
Gross Domestic Product (GDP)   113, 122
Guangdong China Tobacco Industrial Company   234, 235
Guangdong Tobacco Company   234, 235
Guangxi   134, 228
Guizhou   131, 134, 161, 197–201, 203, 207, 228, 233, 249, 296, 306, 309, 310

Health care utilization rate   110
Health consequence   5, 57, 76, 101, 106, 120, 175, 190, 272
Health costs   vi, 85, 106, 174, 252, 260
Health regulations in public places   39
Health care utilization   110, 123, 124, 176, 184
Heavy smoker   16, 64
Henan   42, 88, 134, 193, 198–200, 214, 217, 313
Hong-Ta Shan Group or Corporation   220, 224, 225
Hospital stays   110
Household expenditures   127, 163, 166, 167, 168, 169, 308, 316
Hubei   134, 214, 218
Human capital approach   112
Hunan   38, 134, 214, 224, 225, 228

International Classification of Diseases, 9th revision (ICD-9)   107
Import tariff   205, 206, 219, 221, 236, 313, 314
Imperial Tobacco Company   231
Imports   205, 221, 222, 236–240, 314, 316
Impoverishment   181, 182, 185
Income elasticities   250, 300
Income groups   6, 132, 135, 137, 140, 141, 143, 146, 148, 152, 155, 156, 163, 165, 170, 178, 181–183, 316, 317
Indirect morbidity costs   5, 41, 107, 111, 116, 119, 120
Indirect mortality costs   5, 41, 107, 112, 119, 122
Inpatient hospitalizations   109–111, 114, 115, 120
Interim Measures on Tobacco Advertising   38
International experience   8, 52, 53, 80, 171, 249, 252, 259, 261, 263,

265–267, 269–271, 273, 275, 280, 296, 301
Ischemic heart disease   5, 62, 69, 71, 77, 78, 87–90

Japan Tobacco   212, 220, 231, 243, 244
Joint ventures   34, 192, 206, 222, 225, 229, 231, 239, 315

Kidney disease   123
Kunming Tobacco Company   224

Law on the Protection of Minors   37
Legislation on the Implementation of People's Republic of China Advertisement   38
Law of the Hunan Province   38
Life expectancy   109, 112, 113
Life tables   109, 112
Liver cirrhosis   122, 123
Logit model   137
Logistic model
Low birth weight   101, 123, 270
Lung cancer   5, 29, 41, 44, 48, 51, 69, 71, 85, 87–89, 92–100, 103, 120, 174, 253, 259, 267

Marlboro   15, 222, 232, 235, 238, 314
Massachusetts   179, 263, 265, 285–289
Medical expenditures   106, 123, 159, 160, 176, 178, 184, 185, 260, 263
Medical spending   7, 174, 175, 178–182, 184
Merger   8, 223–225, 315
Michigan   265, 276, 285, 288
Ministry of Agriculture   ix, 35, 192, 204, 208, 209, 213, 248, 296, 308, 312
Ministry of Finance   ix, 35, 243, 248, 266, 273, 296

Ministry of Health   ix–xi, 3, 4, 18, 27, 33, 35, 36, 39, 41, 43–45, 47, 48, 52, 108, 109, 131, 175, 185, 248, 254, 263, 268, 273, 296

National health expenditures   121
National Health Services Survey, 1998   5, 7, 108, 175–177, 181–185, 253
National Institute of Health Education   36
National No Tobacco Day   36
National personal health care expenditures   120
National Prevalence Survey   15, 17, 18, 23, 28, 40, 60, 83, 86, 122, 176, 211, 247
1996 National Prevalence Survey on Smoking Behavior   15
1996 National Smoking Prevalence Survey   4, 6, 33, 129, 135, 142
2002 National Smoking Prevalence Survey   4, 6, 33, 99, 129, 135, 139–142
National Smoking Prevalence Survey (NSPC)   4, 6, 33, 99, 129, 135, 139–143
National Survey of Smoking in China   295
National Tobacco Control Office   36, 52
Near-poor households   165, 166, 170
NHSS, National Health Services Survey   108–113, 122
Non-poor households   165, 166, 169–171
Non-smokers
Number of cigarettes smoked per day   17, 139

On the Hazards of Smoking and Tobacco Control Advocacy Notice   35

Out-of-pocket payment   111
Outpatient visits   109–111, 114, 115, 120, 254

Passive smoke exposure   16, 25
Passive smoker   27, 85, 123, 190, 306, 319
Passive smoking   vi, xiii, 5, 20, 25–27, 40, 41, 57, 62, 69–73, 77, 78, 83–86, 91–96, 98–105, 123, 129
People's Congress Standing Committee   130
People's Republic of China Advertisement Law   37, 38
People's Republic of China Tobacco Monopoly Law   37
Per capita cigarette consumption   134, 138, 143, 146, 316
Per capita cigarette sales   136
Philip Morris   14, 15, 110, 212, 215, 220, 221, 229, 231, 232, 238, 240, 244
Poland   267
Poor households   163, 165, 166, 169, 170, 171
Population attributable risk   107
Poverty   3, 6, 7, 124, 131, 159, 160, 163, 169, 173, 175, 177, 180–185, 205, 307, 312
Prevalence   xii, 4–6, 13, 15–23, 25–28, 31, 33, 34, 40, 41, 43, 44, 48, 50, 51, 57–60, 64, 69, 75–77, 83, 86, 89, 93, 99, 100, 101, 105–109, 113, 114, 122, 124, 129, 135, 138, 139, 141–143, 148–151, 160, 174, 176, 211, 244, 247, 257, 259, 267, 268, 275, 281, 286, 295
Prevalence rate of ever-smoker   122
Prevalence of current smokers   16, 18
Prevalence-based approach   107
Preventable illnesses (or diseases)   49, 124

Prevention of Juvenile Delinquency Act   38
Price   2, 6, 53, 54, 131–157, 160, 161, 164, 165, 169, 170, 177, 178, 191, 193, 194, 196–199, 201, 204–208, 213, 214, 216, 217, 221, 222, 227, 232, 233, 235, 236, 238–240, 248–252, 254–256, 261, 262, 264–266, 269–274, 281–283, 287–295, 297–301, 307, 311–314, 316–319
Price elasticities   6, 132, 133, 135, 137, 141, 146–148, 156, 170, 249–251, 270, 307, 316
Price elasticity of cigarette demand   132, 134
Price elasticity of smoking intensity   138, 146, 152
Price elasticity of smoking participation   138, 146, 150
Price responsiveness   132, 148, 157
Price responsiveness on cigarette consumption   132
Price unification   227
Procurement price   191, 193, 194, 197, 199, 204, 207
Producer surplus   294, 297–301
Productivity losses   106, 116, 124
Proposition   99 263–265, 273, 280–285
Protectionism   226, 234
Pulmonary heart disease   107
PVLE, present value of lifetime earnings   112, 113, 116, 121, 122, 125

Regressive   ix, 2, 132, 133, 156, 317
Regular smoker   16
Respiratory disease   29, 89, 101, 107, 114, 116
Rheumatic heart disease   107
RJ Reynolds International   231

RR, relative risk 88, 89, 92, 94, 95, 108, 121
Rural areas 5, 15, 19–22, 26, 29–31, 80, 113, 116, 118, 124, 141, 163, 165, 166, 175, 176, 178, 241

Secondhand smoke (SHS, also see "Passive smoking") v, 5, 20, 24–29, 31, 39–41, 57, 58, 62, 67, 69–73, 77, 78, 83–87, 89, 91–101–105, 123, 129, 319
Sensitivity analysis 121, 122
Shanghai Tobacco Company 224
Sichuan x, 133, 134, 161, 163, 198–201, 203, 228, 231, 250, 271, 272, 296, 297, 306, 309, 310
Simulation analysis 149, 152
Sin tax 278, 285, 290
Smoke-free Olympic Games 35
Smokers v, ix, 1, 2, 4, 6, 15–19, 22–24, 28, 31, 33, 34, 40, 41, 43, 44, 49, 50, 52, 57, 59, 61, 62, 64–81, 83, 85, 86, 88, 89, 93, 103, 104, 105, 107–109, 114, 116, 118, 120, 122–124, 129, 131, 132, 135, 137–143, 146, 149–152, 154–156, 160, 161, 163, 165, 169, 170, 173, 174, 176–180, 182–184, 189, 190, 206, 211, 222, 236, 238, 247, 252, 255–257, 259, 262, 263, 270, 273, 278, 281, 284–287, 290, 291, 295, 296, 300, 306, 308, 314, 317–319
Smokers' tax burden 135, 149, 152
Smoking v–vii, ix, xiii, xiv, 1–7, 9, 13, 15–31, 33–41, 43–52, 57–62, 64–67, 69–81, 83–125, 129–152, 154–157, 159–167, 169, 173–185, 190, 207, 211, 212, 218, 220, 243, 244, 247, 248, 253, 254, 256, 257, 259–261, 263–265, 267–275, 278, 280–282, 284–287, 290–292, 295, 296, 298–301, 306–308, 318, 319
"Smoking and Health" monitoring mechanism 48
Smoking and Health — 2006 Report 4, 41, 44, 48
Smoking attributable deaths 34, 112, 116
Smoking attributable diseases 41
Smoking expenditures, SAE 110, 114, 116
Smoking attributable fraction, SAF 107, 108, 110, 111, 114
Smoking attributable indirect morbidity cost 111
Smoking attributable risks 123, 124
Smoking behavior 3, 15, 21, 57–59, 61, 65, 69, 75–78, 80, 124, 136, 139, 161, 165, 211, 306, 307, 319
Smoking prevalence rate 41, 44, 57, 75, 106, 109, 114, 122, 124, 141–143, 148, 150, 267, 268, 286
Smoking-caused illnesses 106
Smoking-related diseases 107, 110, 111, 120, 122, 123, 174, 185
Smuggling ix, 135, 136, 237, 238, 240, 243, 258, 268, 269, 273, 274
South Africa 204, 267, 268, 277
Specific tax 170, 171
State Council ix, 35, 39, 45–47, 213, 319
State Tobacco Monopoly Administration (STMA) ix, 7, 14, 54, 190, 191, 213, 221, 308
Stroke 89, 90, 101, 102, 107

Taiwan 13, 14, 123, 174, 212, 218, 266, 267, 269
Tariff 8, 205, 206, 212, 219–222, 232, 233, 236–238, 313, 314

Tax revenue ix, 6–9, 14, 131, 132, 135, 149–151, 156, 157, 174, 198, 200, 207, 216, 217, 234, 241, 242, 248, 249, 251, 252, 255, 257, 262–265, 267, 269–273, 275, 276, 278, 279, 282–285, 287–292, 296, 297, 299–302, 309, 312, 313, 315, 317, 318
Thailand 14, 18, 212, 218, 267, 269
Tobacco consumption 1, 3, 14, 42, 105, 129, 160, 173, 174, 185, 232, 258, 261, 264, 268, 273, 280, 291
Tobacco control policies 1, 3, 7, 28, 30, 107, 130, 208, 287
Tobacco control programs ix, 4, 7, 8, 33, 36, 48, 52, 104, 124, 130, 157, 269, 270, 281, 282
Tobacco epidemic 6, 28, 79, 80, 104, 105, 121, 124, 129, 130
Tobacco excise taxes 131, 133
Tobacco farming ix, 204, 268, 306, 308, 311
Tobacco leaf production v, 7, 42, 189, 195, 197, 200, 205, 207, 208, 213, 217, 229, 232, 249, 252, 307–309, 311, 312, 317
Tobacco leaf tax 7, 208, 243, 316
Tobacco products vi, 16, 37, 38, 61, 131, 149, 161, 174, 217, 221, 222, 232, 235, 263, 269, 271, 274, 278, 288, 301, 302, 314
Tobacco tax vi, ix, 1, 2, 6, 8, 9, 35, 42, 53–55, 130–133, 135, 156, 161, 190, 199, 200, 204, 215, 216, 242, 243, 252, 257, 258, 261, 263–269, 273, 275, 277–282, 284–292, 296, 297, 301, 302, 306, 308, 313, 315, 316
Total cost 5, 201, 254, 309, 310
Total economic cost 118, 120–122, 124, 129

Total health care expenditure 110
Total indirect morbidity expenditure 111
Total price elasticity 138, 141, 146, 150, 154, 155
Transnational Tobacco Companies (TTCS) 8, 212, 213, 218–222, 229–231, 233, 235, 242–244, 314, 318
Trans-theoretical model 22
Tuberculosis 89, 90, 107
Two-part model 137, 143, 144, 146

US Surgeon General's Report 278
Unconditional cigarette demand 146
United States ix, 9, 28, 75, 81, 101, 104, 107, 120–123, 133, 174, 221, 222, 262, 264–266, 270, 273, 274, 277–280, 285, 288, 291–293, 295, 297, 300
Urban households 6, 162, 163, 165, 166, 168, 170, 317
User's tax 278

Welfare loss 279, 280, 288, 294, 297, 298
Western countries 22, 88, 120
WHO classification of smoking definitions 15
  Ever smoker 15, 22–24, 105, 113, 122, 129, 178, 180
  Current smoker 16, 18, 22–24, 31, 57, 61, 64–66, 68–71, 74, 77, 105, 109, 113, 120, 129, 137–139, 141–143, 146, 150, 151, 154, 155, 176, 247, 273, 295
  Regular smoker 16
  Heavy smoker 16, 64
  Passive smoker 27, 85, 123, 190, 306, 319
World Bank ix, x, 3, 35, 48–54, 58, 106, 136, 163, 171, 173, 181,

201, 209, 256, 258, 271, 273, 274, 276, 302, 309, 318
World Bank Health VII project 49, 318
10th World Conference on Tobacco or Health 49
World Health Organization (WHO) vi, vii, x, 3–5, 9, 15, 16, 19, 34, 36, 43, 44, 48, 49, 61, 75, 80, 85, 87, 88, 91, 92, 100, 103, 109, 130, 174, 189, 190, 207, 243, 308, 318
World No Tobacco Day 36, 49, 50

World Trade Organization (WTO) 8, 190, 191, 205–208, 211–213, 215, 217–219, 220, 221, 223, 226, 234, 236, 242–244, 252, 258, 269, 307, 312–315, 318

Years of potential life lost, YPLL 112, 117, 123, 129
Yunnan 42, 131, 175, 193, 197–201, 205, 207, 214, 215, 224, 226, 228, 306, 309, 311, 313

Zimbabwe 2, 193, 205, 233, 315